I0902374

POSTCARD HISTORY SERIES

Memphis

in Vintage Postcards

This book is dedicated to Chad Selden.

POSTCARD HISTORY SERIES

Memphis

in Vintage Postcards

Scott Faragher and Katherine Harrington

ARCADIA
PUBLISHING

ISBN 978-0-7385-0560-2

Published by Arcadia Publishing
Charleston, South Carolina

Printed in the United States of America

Library of Congress Catalog Card Number: 00-100375

For all general information contact Arcadia Publishing at:
Telephone 843-853-2070
Fax 843-853-0044
E-mail sales@arcadiapublishing.com
For customer service and orders:
Toll-Free 1-888-313-2665

Visit us on the Internet at www.arcadiapublishing.com

Contents

ACKNOWLEDGMENTS

First and foremost, thanks to Debra Gust and the folks at Curt Teich Postcard Archives. Curt Teich was a German immigrant who came to America in 1895 at the age of 18 and started the most significant company of its type. His Chicago-based company sent photographers throughout the nation, from one end to the other, photographing Americans and their lifestyles, culture, and architecture in the years between 1898 and 1978. The more than 360,000 images produced by his company provide the most complete photographic record of American life as it existed, and developed. The Archives were established in 1982 as part of the Lake County Museum in Wauconda, Illinois, and now house the largest public collection of postcards and related materials in America. Today, the Curt Teich Postcard Archives preserve and protect this valuable part of American history through reproduction, research services, and its exciting museum.

Thanks also to Henry Juszkiewicz and Gibson Guitars, and congratulations on the new 'Lucille' factory in Memphis. Just ask B.B. King. Gibson rules!

Last but not least, a word about Hunter Fans. This company invented the electric ceiling fan. They moved to Memphis in 1949 and produce a variety of quality lighting and electrical products, but most importantly, they still make the best fans in the world, just like they did when they started over a century ago.

Introduction

This postcard book examines Memphis as it entered into and progressed throughout the twentieth century. Memphis emerged quickly into the modern era, having survived the War Between the States, the horrors of Reconstruction, and frequent and severe battles with Yellow Fever. It would quickly become the largest city in Tennessee and, with the exception of New Orleans, the most important city on the entire Mississippi River.

As its population grew, so did its architecture and infrastructure. Public parks were layed out, churches, hospitals, and educational facilities were put into place, and Memphis became a major city. Construction boomed, and the city quickly outpaced Nashville, 215 miles east, and north. The golden era of the city, at least from an architectural standpoint, was prior to 1955. Skyscrapers began as early as 1895 with the D.T. Porter building and continued with other structures such as the Columbian Mutual Tower and the magnificent art deco Sears and Sterick Buildings. Large, palatial houses were built in the area now known as Midtown, and the city prospered.

Memphis, like other major cities, has suffered its share of growing pains, including loss of jobs, racial problems, white flight to the suburbs, and attendant loss of revenue. Today, however, Memphis retains its unique character, as it moves into the next century, blending of old and new, and remains Tennessee's most interesting and colorful city.

There has always been a rivalry of sorts between Memphis and Nashville, Tennessee's capital city. Memphians perhaps resent the fact that Nashville became the state capital and that Nashvillians were involved in the design and creation of Memphis. Nashvillians, on the other hand, have long envied Memphis' wealth, its economic and cultural importance, and its size. Memphis and Nashville are not in the least bit similar. And yet, while Nashville has come to be known internationally as "Music City," Memphis itself is certainly as qualified as Nashville to hold that title. The idea that any rock and roll hall of fame, of any kind, should exist anywhere in the world, other than Memphis, is an absurd blasphemy. Hopefully, Memphians will band together and start a "real Rock and Roll Hall of Fame," and place it on Mud Island, ending this obscene charade once and for all. Memphis is not only the birthplace of Rock and Roll, but it is the birthplace of the Blues. It has often been called "the Crossroads of American Music," an apt title indeed. Memphis is also the home of the best ribs in the world. While several chain restaurants around the country profess to have "the best ribs in America," that title has no merit at all, unless the award came from the annual Memphis competition.

Hopefully you will enjoy these postcard images, but ultimately, Memphis can only be experienced in person.

Selected Reading

Johnson, Eugene and Robert Russell. *Memphis, An Architectural Guide*. Knoxville, TN: University of Tennessee Press, 1991.

Plunkett, Kitty. *Pictorial History of Memphis*. Norfolk, VA: Donning Company, 1976.

Robert Sigafoos. *Cotton Row to Beale Street*. Memphis, TN: Memphis State University Press, 1980.

William Worley. *Beale Street, Crossroad's of America's Music*. Lenexa, Kansas: Addax Publishing Group, 1998.

One

GREETINGS

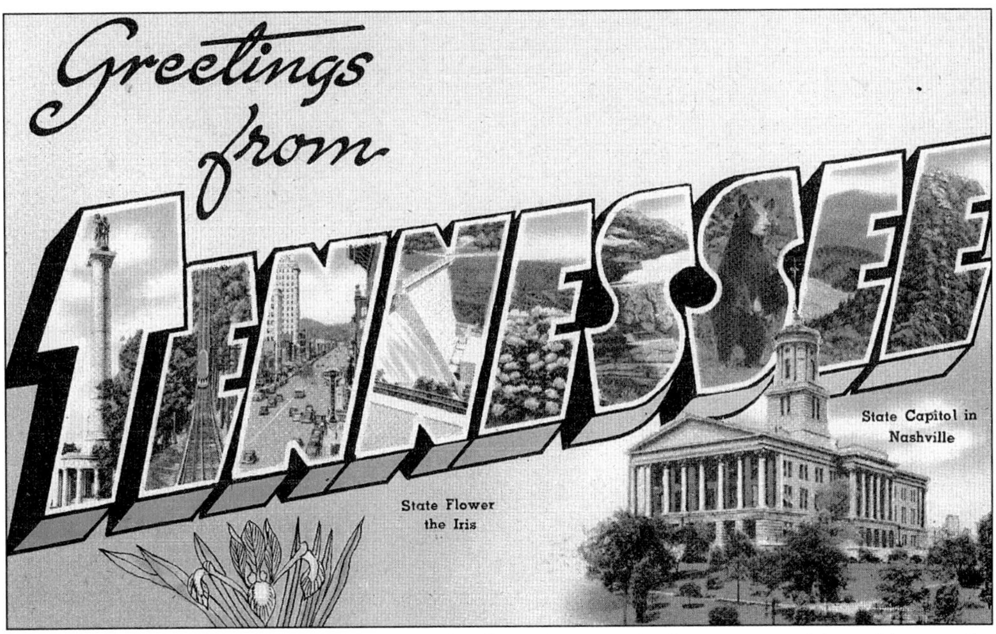

GREETINGS FROM TENNESSEE. While Nashville is the capital of Tennessee, Memphis was, for most of the twentieth century, the largest city in Tennessee. Its central location on the nation's main waterway and proximity to agricultural areas gave the city an early prosperity unequaled in any other Tennessee city. According to this postcard, the total 1940 population of the state was 2,915,841.

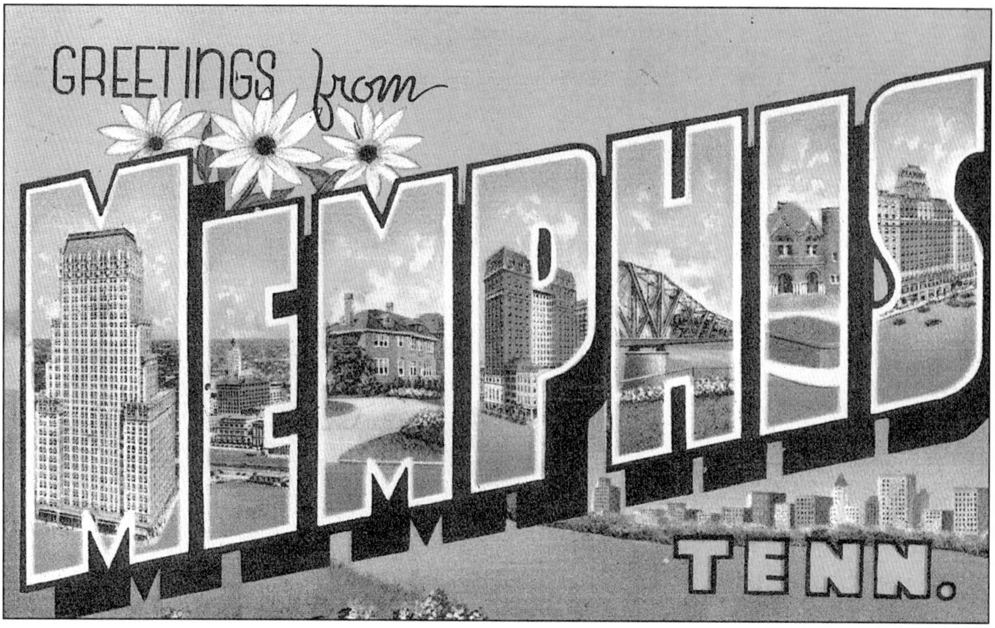

GREETINGS FROM MEMPHIS, TENNESSEE. This typical greeting from Memphis is similar in tone to greetings cards from all cities in that local points of interest and significant sites are pictured within the letters of the city's name. This one is from 1939. (Curt Teich Archives.)

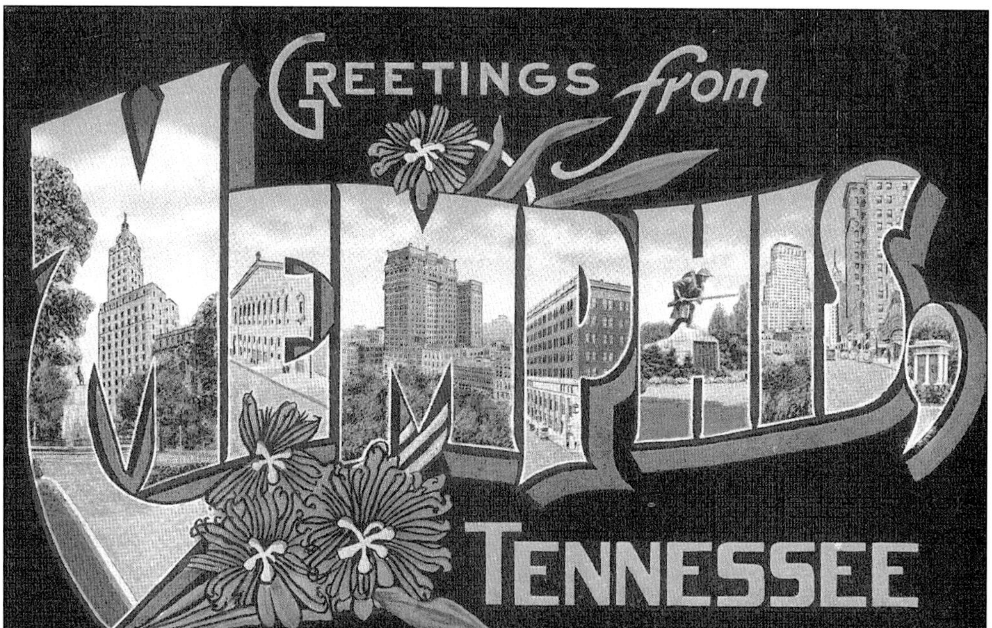

GREETINGS FROM MEMPHIS, TENNESSEE. Memphis is referred to as the "City of the Valley" on the reverse of this old postcard. Some of the sites contained within the letters of this postcard include the Columbian Mutual Tower, Ellis Auditorium, the Exchange Building, the Doughboy statue at Overton Park, and the Sterick Building.

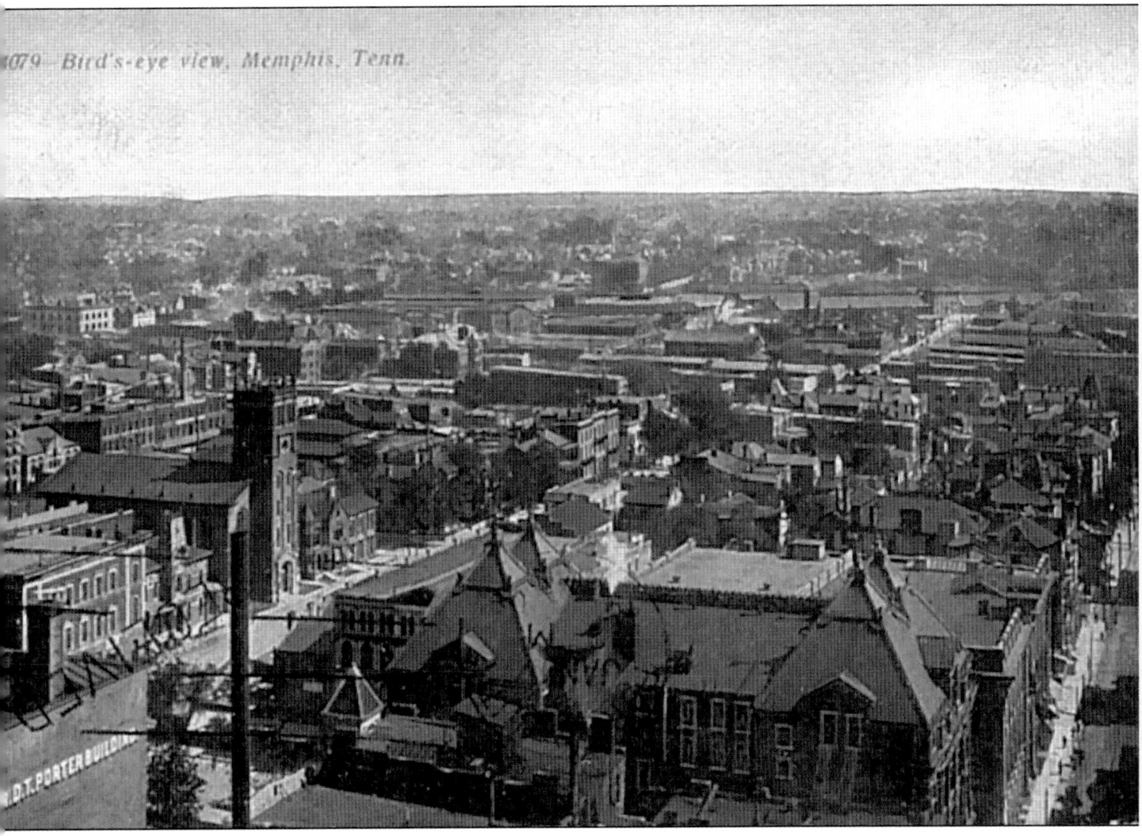

Bird's-Eye View. This 1909 bird's-eye view shows a downtown view of a Memphis that no longer exists. Photographs of this nature were usually taken from atop the tallest building in the city and often placed on postcards of the day. Note the letters indicating the Dr. D.T. Porter Building in the lower left corner of this image. The Porter Building was built in 1895 and is considered to be the city's first skyscraper.

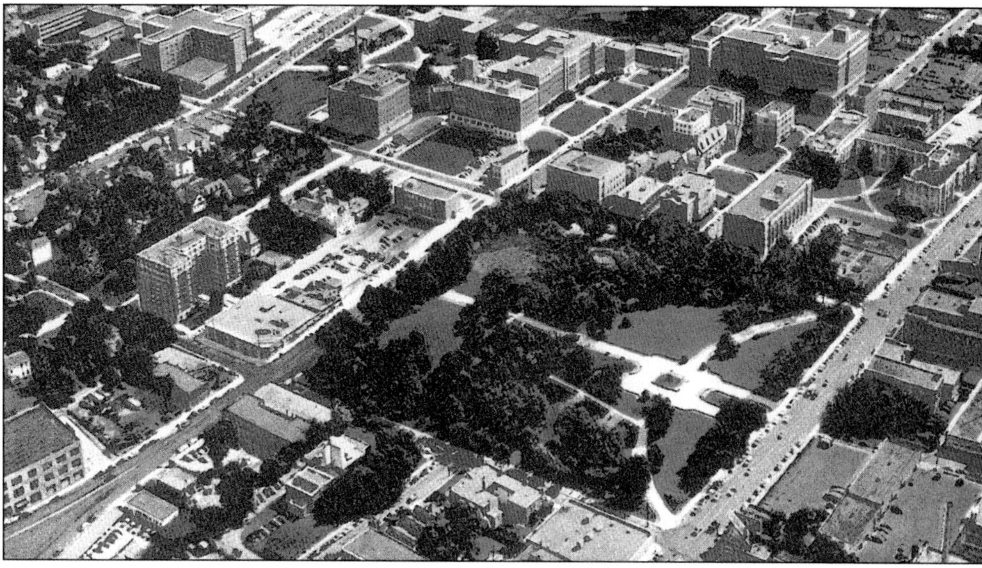

Aerial View of Memphis Hospital Center. At the time of this postcard, Memphis had 22 hospitals containing over 10,000 beds. The square in the center of the card is Confederate Park, with hospitals across the top of the picture.

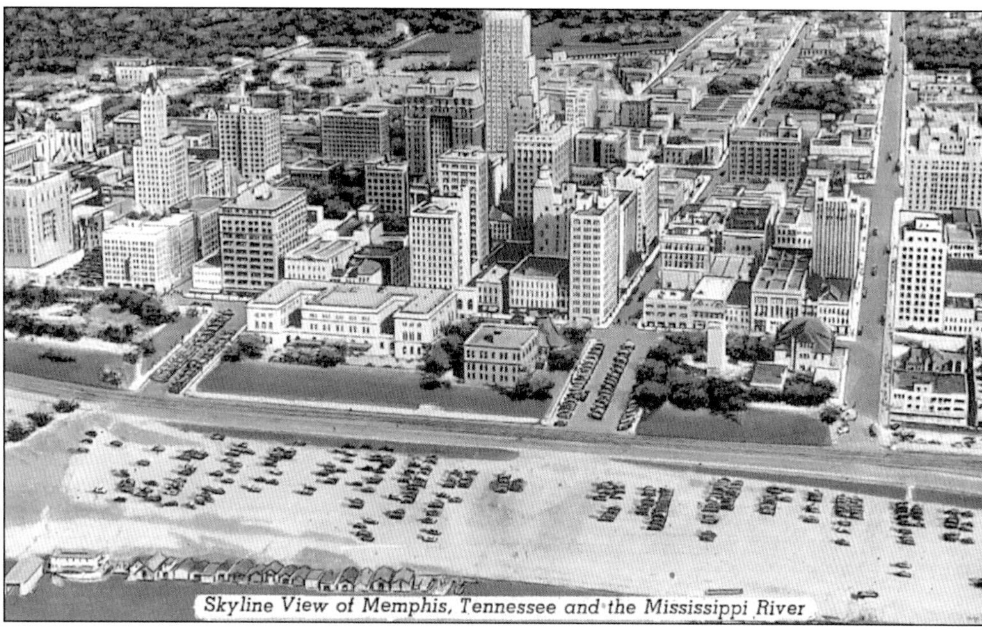

Skyline View of Memphis, Tennessee, and the Mississippi River. This postcard is undated, but it is usually possible to accurately estimate a city photograph's age by the visible architecture. We know by looking at the changes in the Customs House that this image was made after 1929. The 1930 Sterick Building, as well as the Columbian Mutual Tower, the Exchange Building, and other Memphis landmarks, are clearly visible. Regrettably, none of the buildings just mentioned were made after 1930. The Cossitt Library building is still standing in this picture. It was destroyed in 1958, so we can conclude that this picture was taken sometime after 1929 but before 1958.

Two

WATER AND BRIDGES

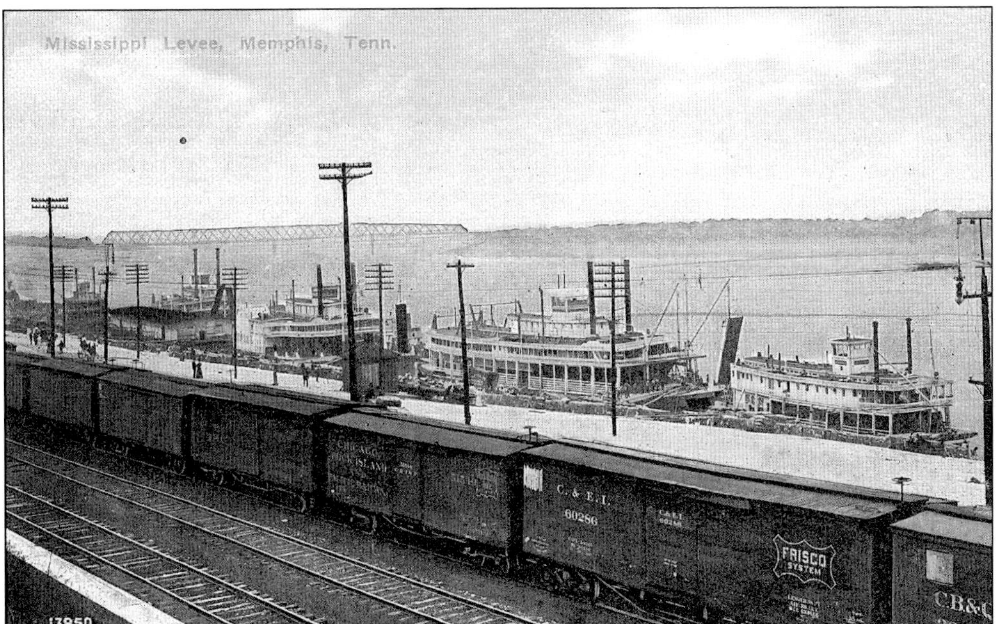

MISSISSIPPI LEVEE. This early postcard photo shows the juxtaposition of rail and river. Eventually, the railroad would supercede the riverboats as the principal means of transporting cotton and other goods.

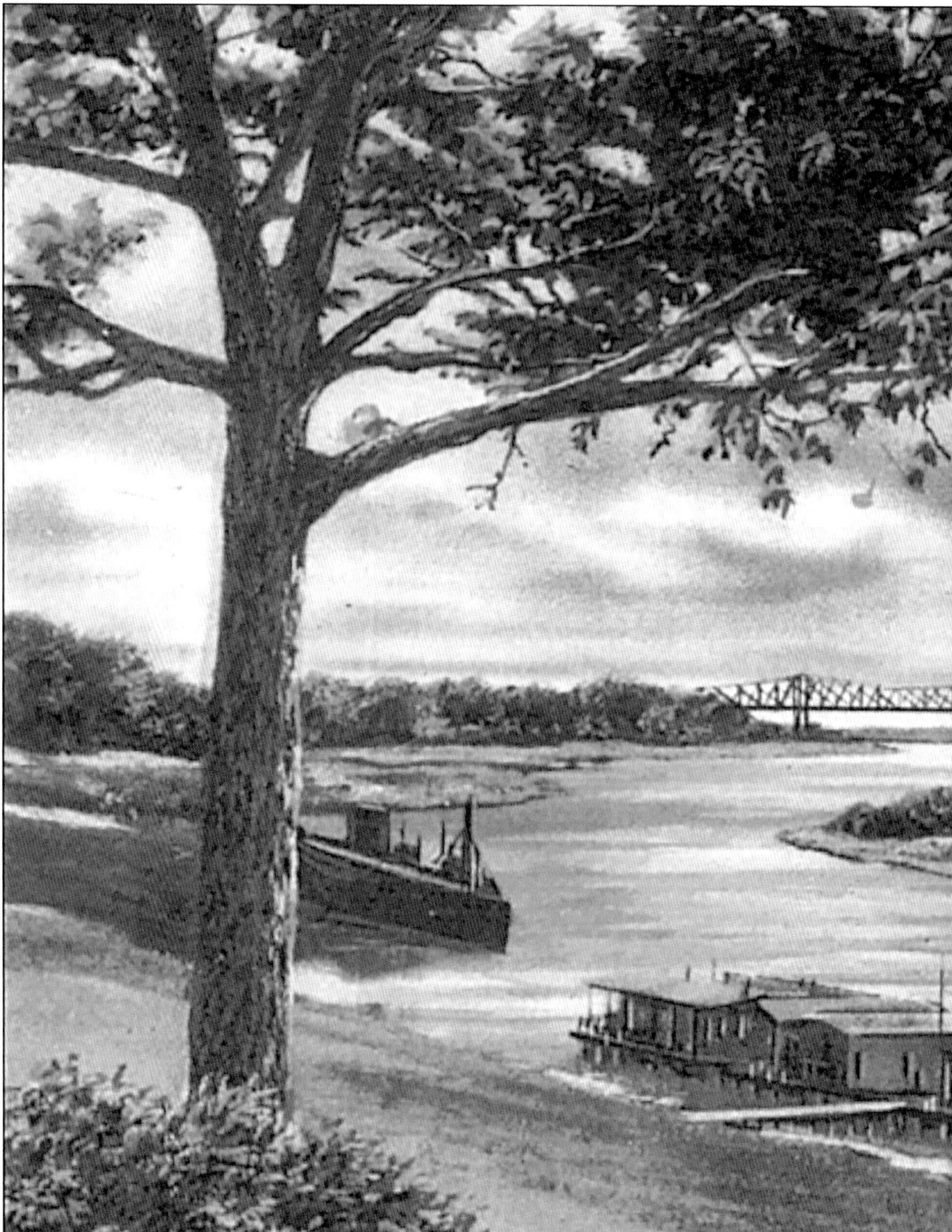

Sunset on the Mississippi River. The fishing shacks and boathouses seen lining the shore of the Mississippi River in this old postcard reflect a much slower and more tranquil time in an

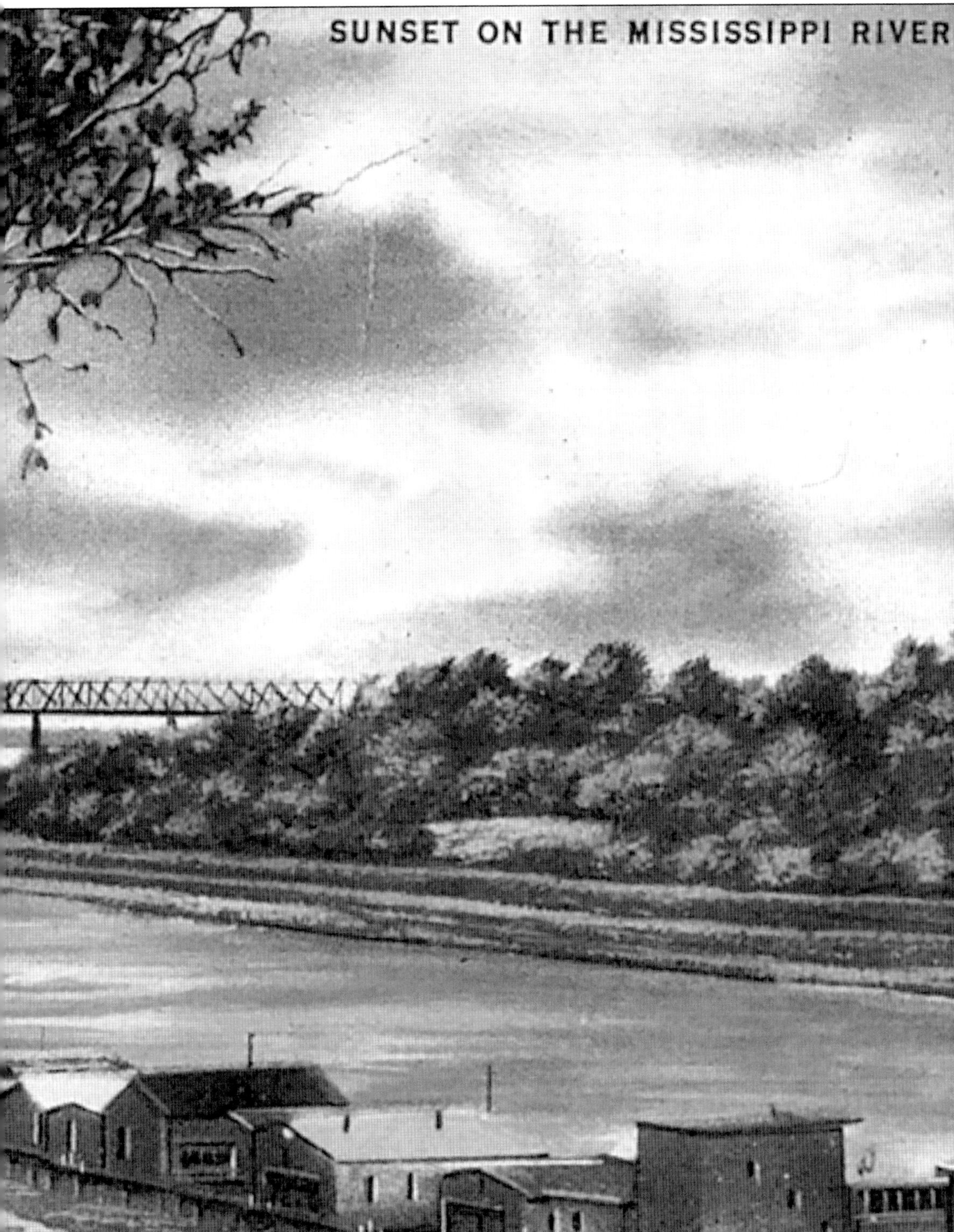

earlier Memphis, and yet, despite the rural setting, the bridge in the distance portends an end to this peaceful scene.

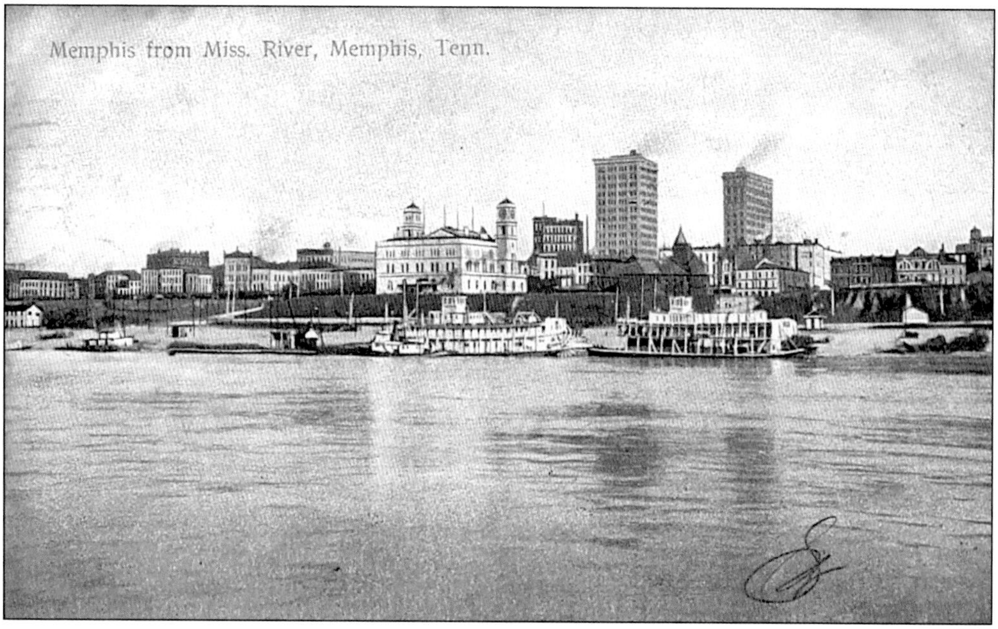

Memphis from Miss. River, Memphis, Tennessee. This 1908 postcard shows the waterfront and two of the city's first skyscrapers, including the Union Planters Bank Building and the Memphis Trust Company Building. By 1910, Memphis had survived the War between the States, the Carpetbaggers, and the Yellow Fever epidemics and was finally on the way to becoming one of the most successful business centers in the South.

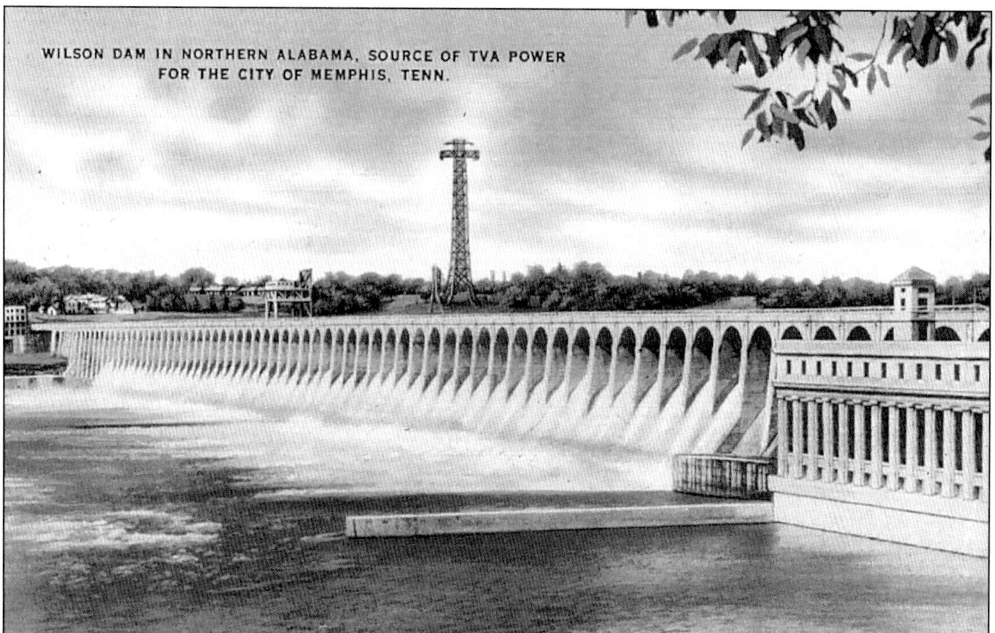

Wilson Dam. The Tennessee Valley Authority's Wilson Dam, located in Muscle Shoals, Alabama, 150 miles southeast of Memphis, provided most of the city's electricity at the time of this postcard.

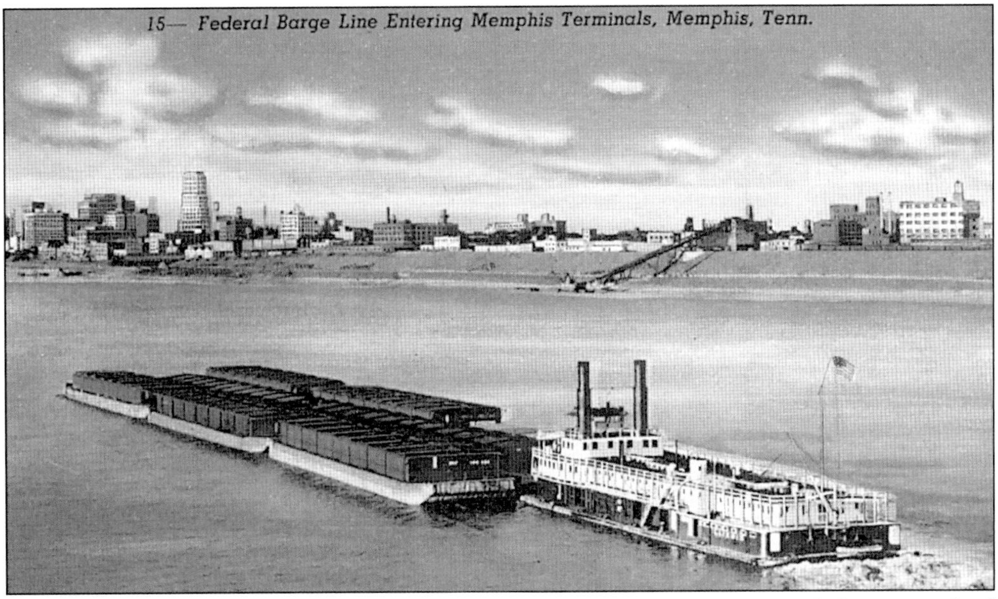

Federal Barge Line Entering Memphis Terminals. This 1942 postcard shows a Federal Barge Line boat bringing barge containers into Memphis. An almost identical postcard from the same period shows the same scene with New Orleans in the background. The boat pictured here pushing the barges looks like a modern-day (for the period) version of the old sternwheeler steamboats. It is flat bottomed, low to the water, and possesses the traditional side-by-side twin stacks. Instead of the rear paddlewheel, this boat boasts more efficient underwater propellers, or screws, as they are referred to in nautical jargon. (Curt Teich Archives.)

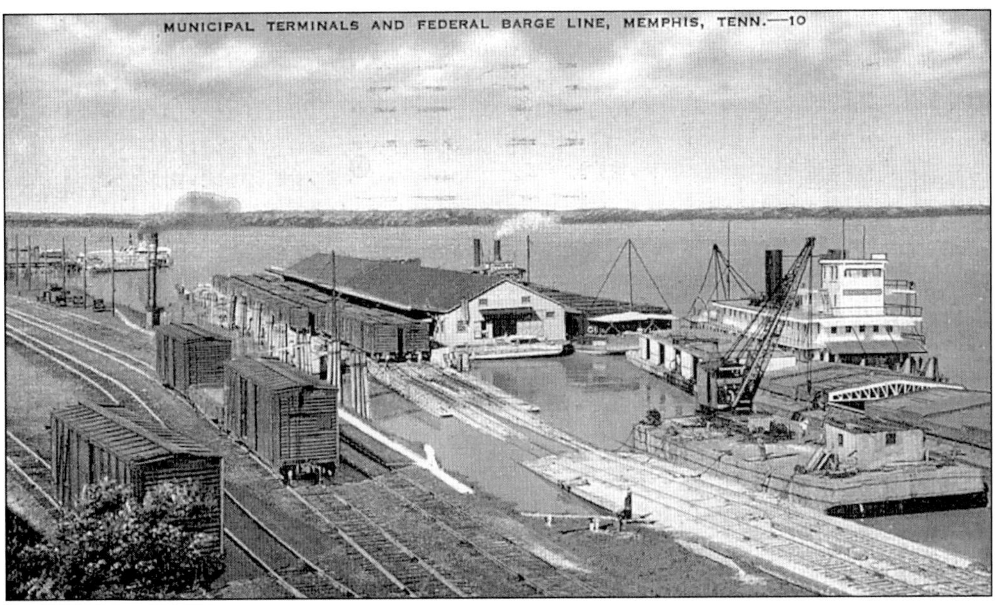

Municipal Terminals and Federal Barge Line. According to this 1942 postcard, "The Mississippi River, with its Federal Barge Line, affords Memphis an all water haul through the Panama Canal to the ports of the world. The River and all terminals co-ordinate rail and river transportation."

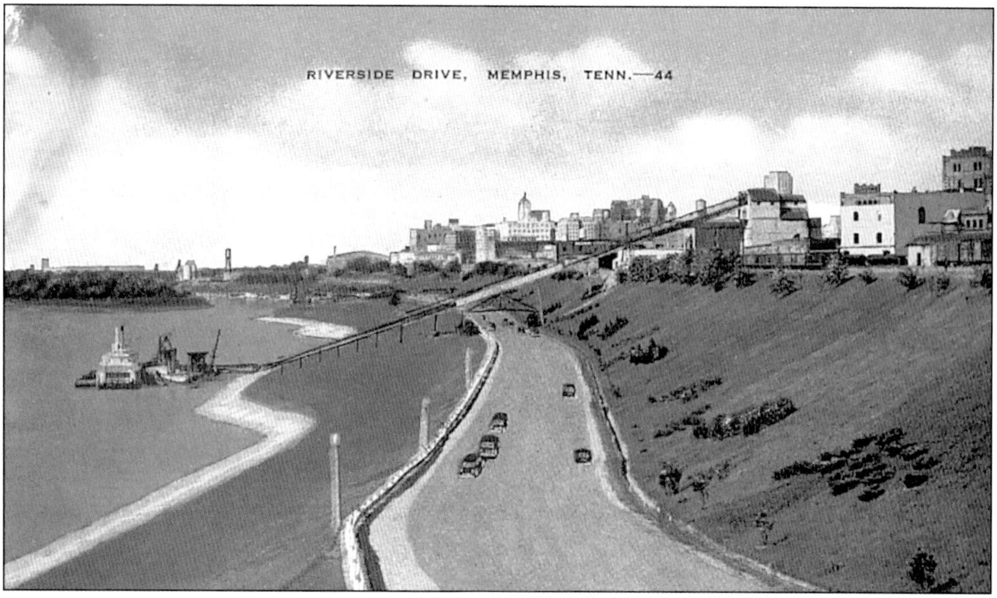

RIVERSIDE DRIVE. Riverside Drive runs North to South, parallel to the Mississippi River, and is fairly unchanged since this postcard photo from the 1940s. The city of Memphis, however, has changed considerably, and most of the buildings pictured here are long gone. The area to the far left center of this image is the location of Mud Island, a development of questionable utility. Be that as it may, its outdoor amphitheatre, on a hot summer night, is one of the best concert venues in America.

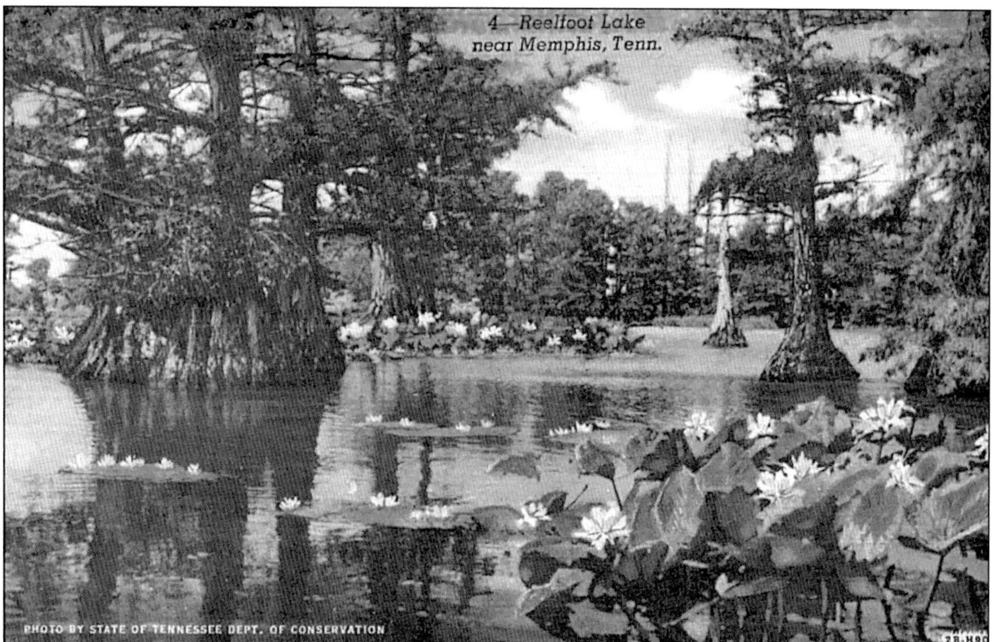

REELFOOT LAKE NEAR MEMPHIS. Reelfoot Lake was formed by a massive earthquake in the early 1800s. The scene here looks almost prehistoric. Note the large Cypress trees growing from the water. (Curt Teich Archives.)

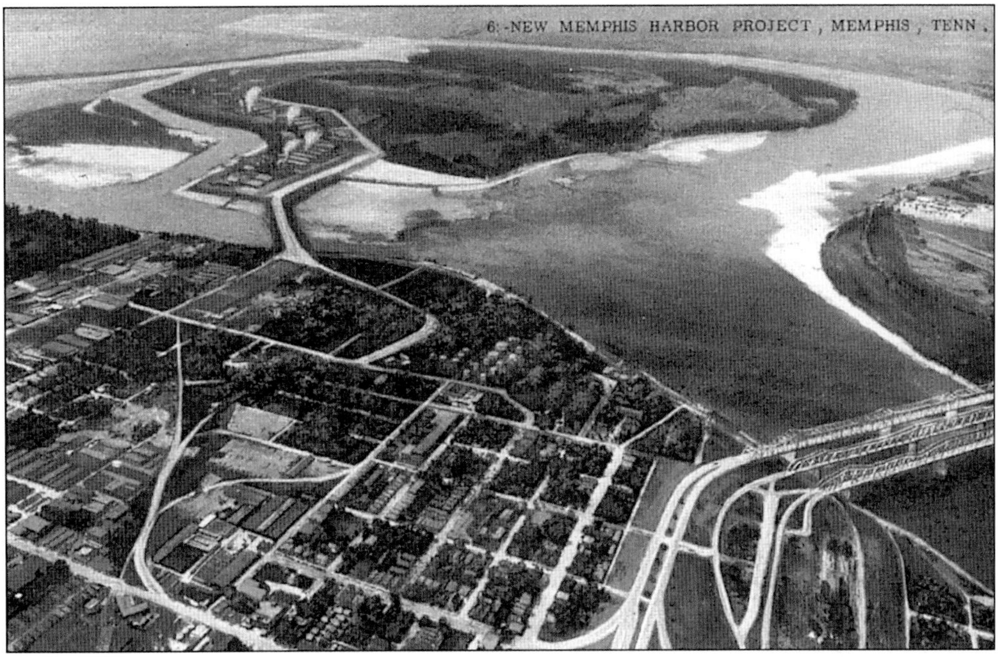

MEMPHIS HARBOR PROJECT. The Mississippi River shifts constantly, leaving sand and soil and then taking it away. This aerial view shows part of the Army Corps of Engineers project to control erosion along the banks of the Mississippi.

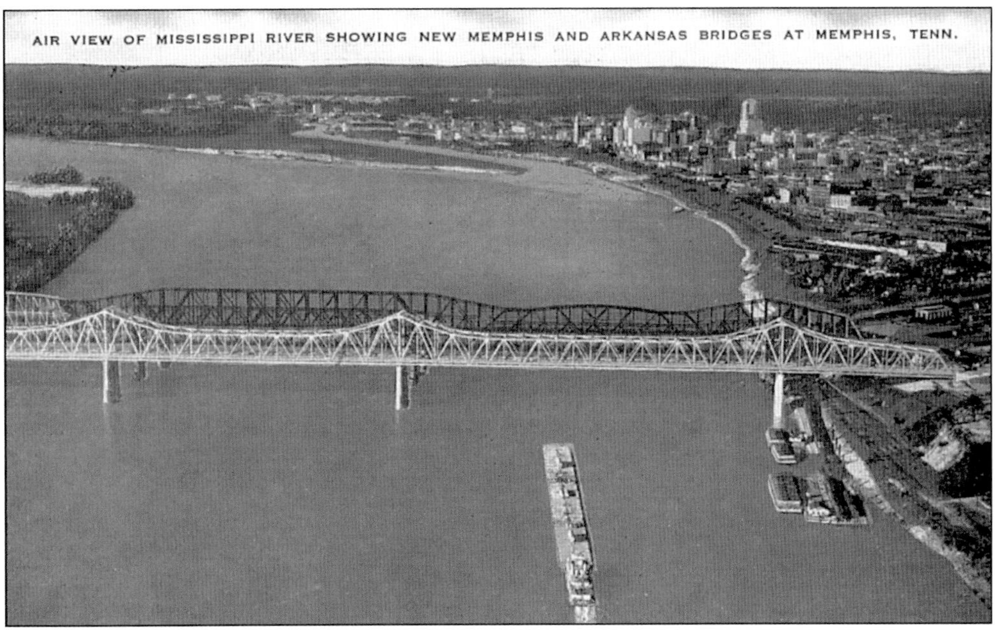

AIR VIEW OF MISSISSIPPI RIVER SHOWING NEW MEMPHIS AND ARKANSAS BRIDGES. From the first days of American westward expansion, Americans sought to cross the Mississippi River and gain access to the west. These bridges were the first to cross the river south of St. Louis. Immediately north of these bridges is Memphis itself. As a point of reference, the peninsula seen jutting toward the city, is the site of Mud Island.

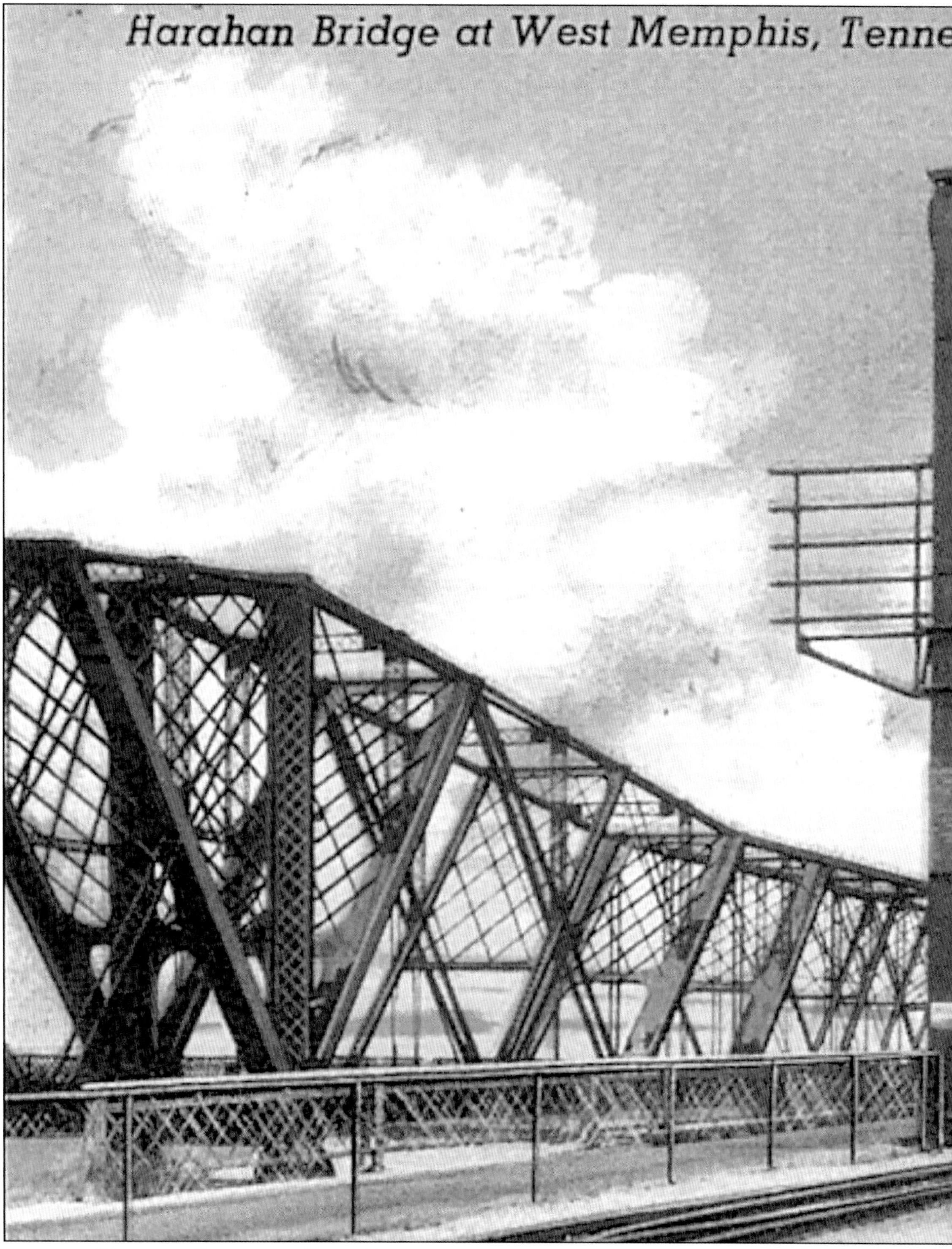

HARAHAN BRIDGE AT WEST MEMPHIS, TENNESSEE, CROSSING THE MISSISSIPPI RIVER. The Harahan Bridge (on the right), which connects Tennessee and Arkansas, opened in July 1916,

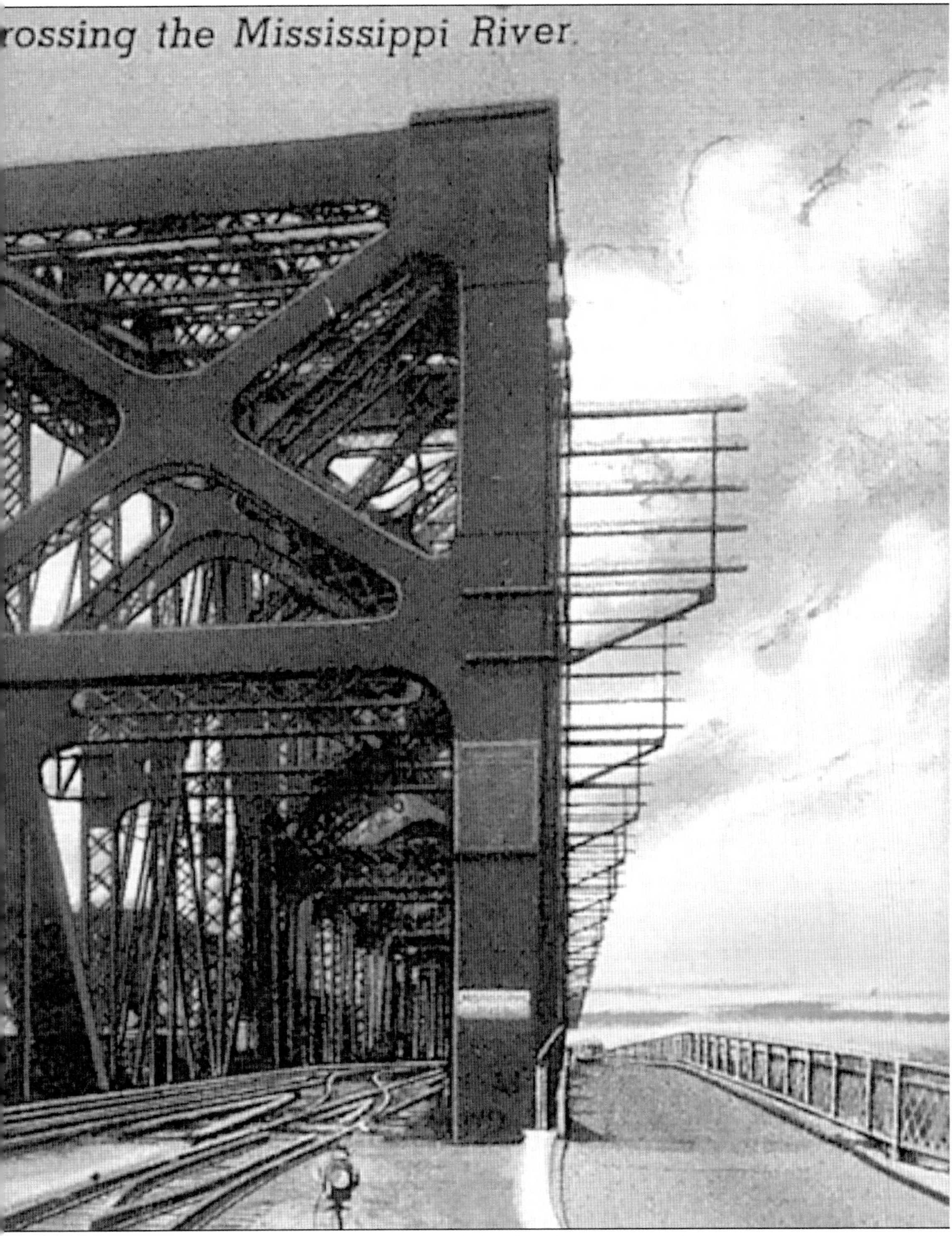

and was named for James Harahan, president of the Illinois Central Railroad. In addition to railroad tracks, the new bridge also offered lanes for automobile traffic.

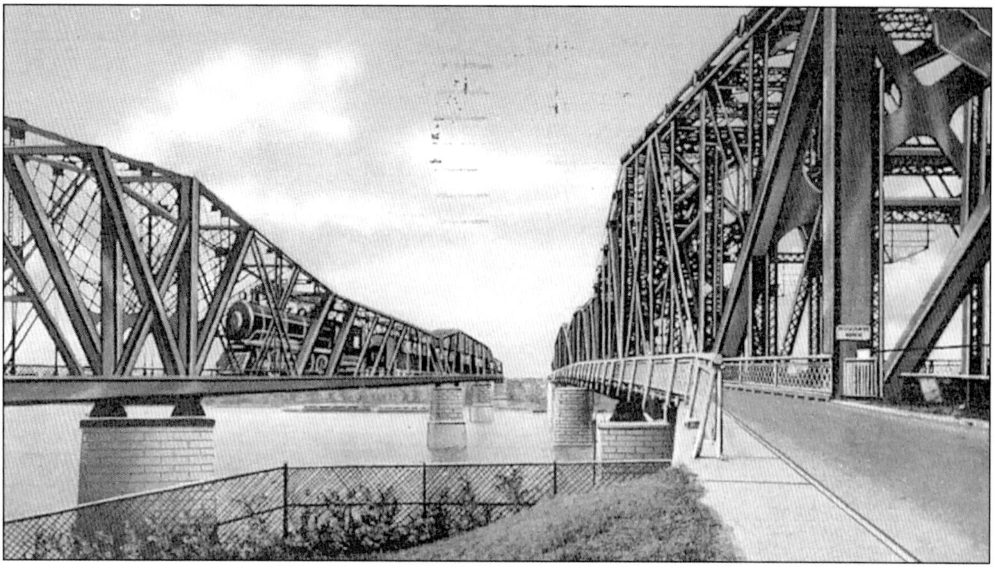

Memphis and Harahan Bridges, Memphis, Tennessee. The Memphis Bridge, at the left, was the first bridge built across the Mississippi River at Memphis. It was constructed as a railroad bridge by the Kansas City, Fort Scott, and Memphis Railroad and opened on May 12, 1892, to the applause of a gathered crowd of onlookers in excess of 50,000. It was subsequently sold to the Frisco Railroad in 1903 and became known as the Frisco Bridge. As a matter of consequence, the names of the bridges are often confused. They are sometimes called the Memphis or Arkansas Bridges, the old bridges, or the old railroad bridges. No matter what they may be called, Memphians always know what they are. (Curt Teich Archives.)

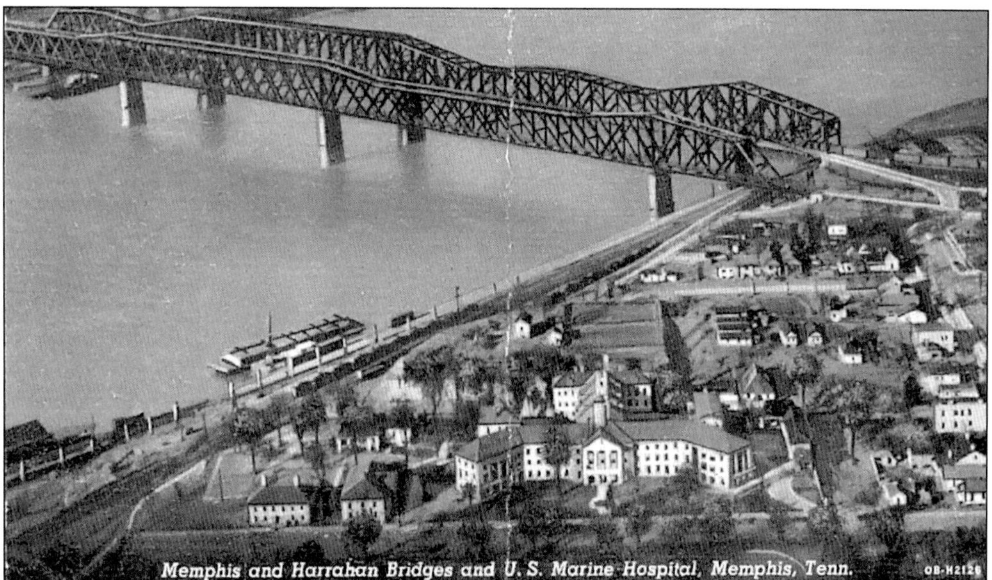

Memphis and Harahan Bridges and US Marine Hospital. This 1944 postcard shows the proximity of the Memphis and Harahan Bridges as well as the former Marine Hospital. More importantly, it shows this area, just south of the downtown area, as it used to be. (Curt Teich Archives.)

Three

Cotton

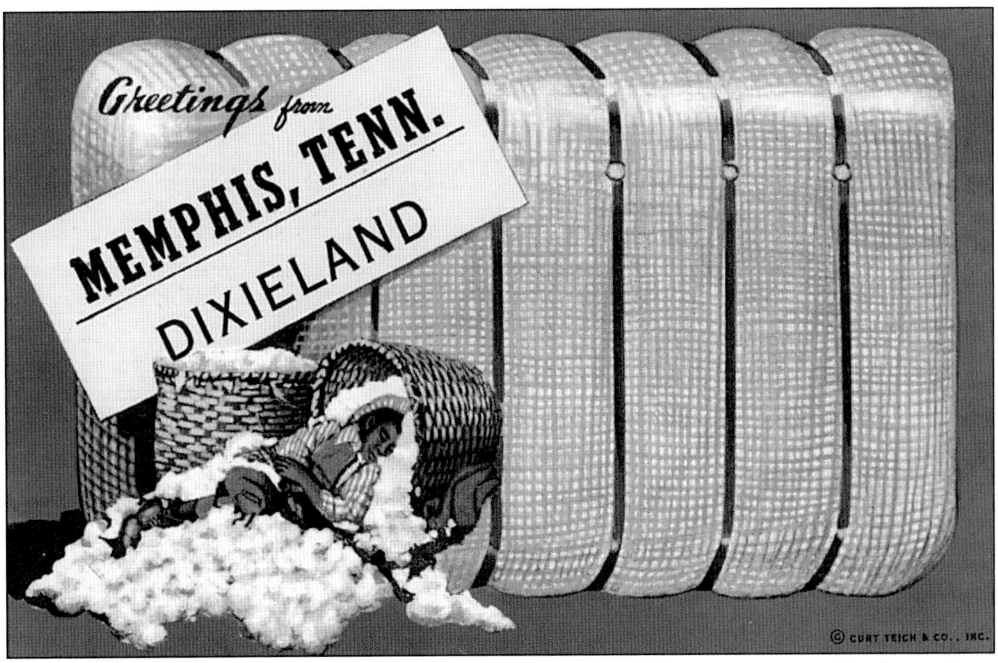

Greetings from Memphis, Tennessee, Dixieland. Only New Orleans, possibly, has a closer association with cotton than Memphis, and that is due solely to the fact that cotton was moved downriver to be loaded for transport to Europe and other places. This 1941 postcard shows a tired field worker taking a well-earned nap, presumably after having picked cotton all day. (Curt Teich Archives.)

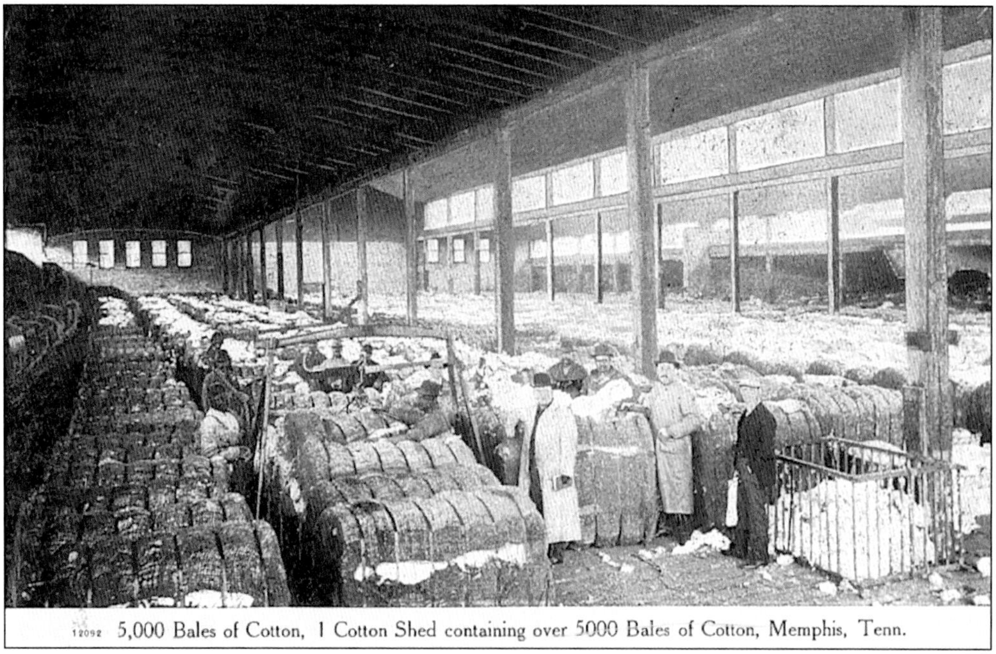

5,000 Bales of Cotton. This 1910 postcard shows one shed containing in excess of 5,000 bales of cotton awaiting shipment.

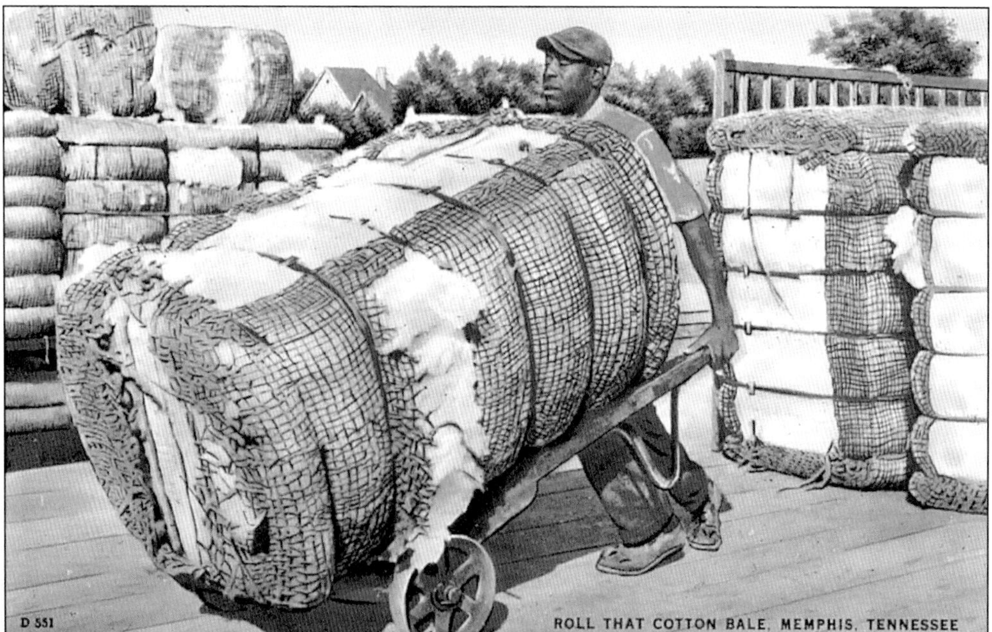

Roll that Cotton Bale. In the days before forklifts and other heavy equipment, cotton bales were moved around the warehouses and loading docks by hand on wooden carts.

Cotton Press. This 1909 postcard depicts the cotton press, an important last stage of preparation of cotton for shipping. The cotton was compressed into bales, wrapped in burlap, and bound with metal straps.

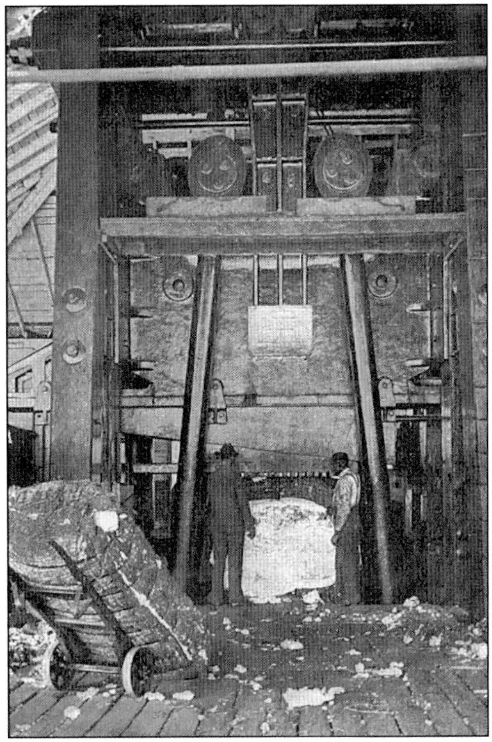

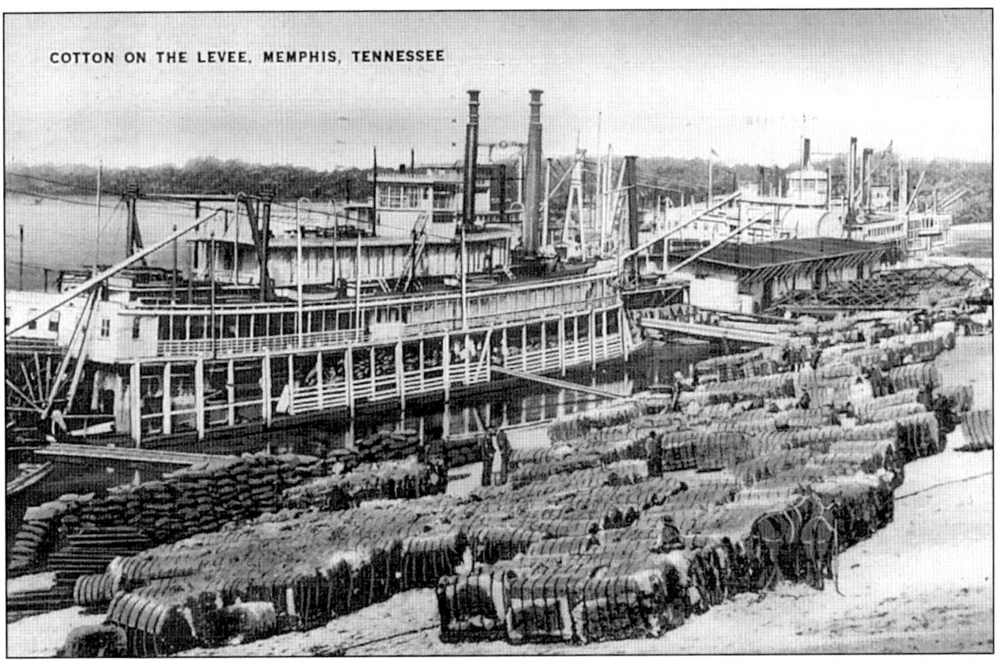

Cotton on the Levee. This postcard from 1945 shows a flat-bottomed stern wheeler waiting to load cotton. The hulls of these boats were flat and displaced very little water in order to allow the navigation of the constantly shifting Mississippi River. Sand bars can appear or disappear literally overnight. Today, goods of all types are still transported on the river.

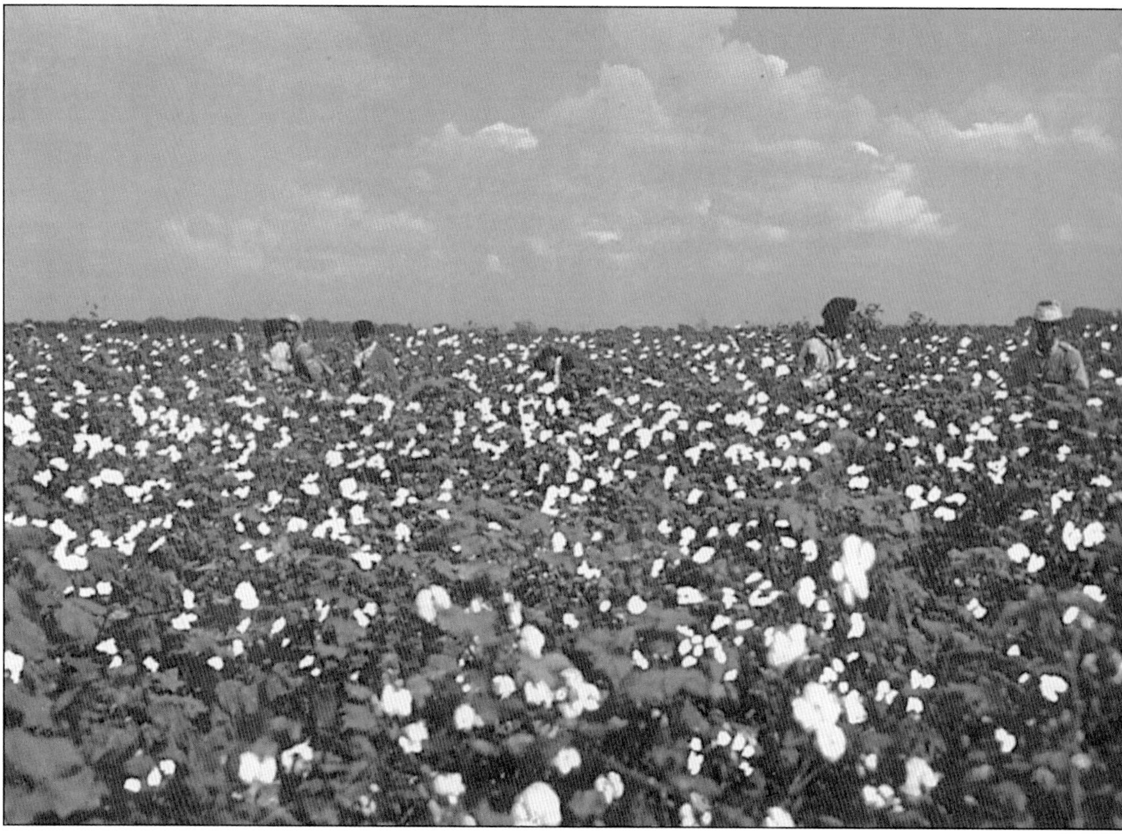

COTTON PICKING. This 1958 postcard shows how cotton was picked until the middle of this century. It was hard, back-breaking labor, performed by hand.

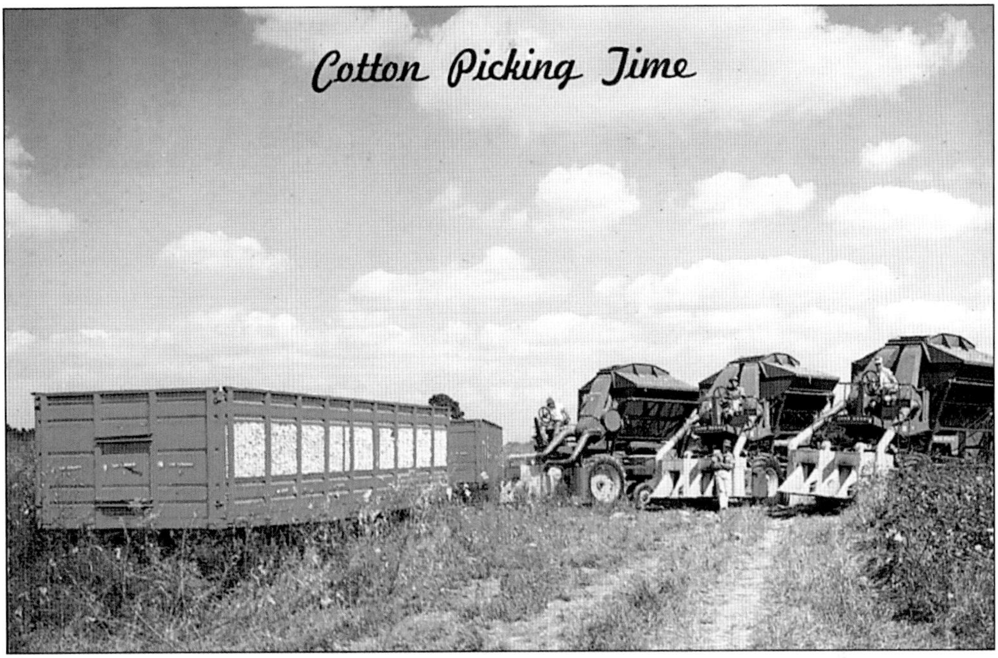

Cotton Picking Time. The modern machinery pictured here can perform the work of literally dozens of men, formerly required by hand picking, in a fraction of the time. The bad news is that thousands who made their living in the cotton fields lost their jobs.

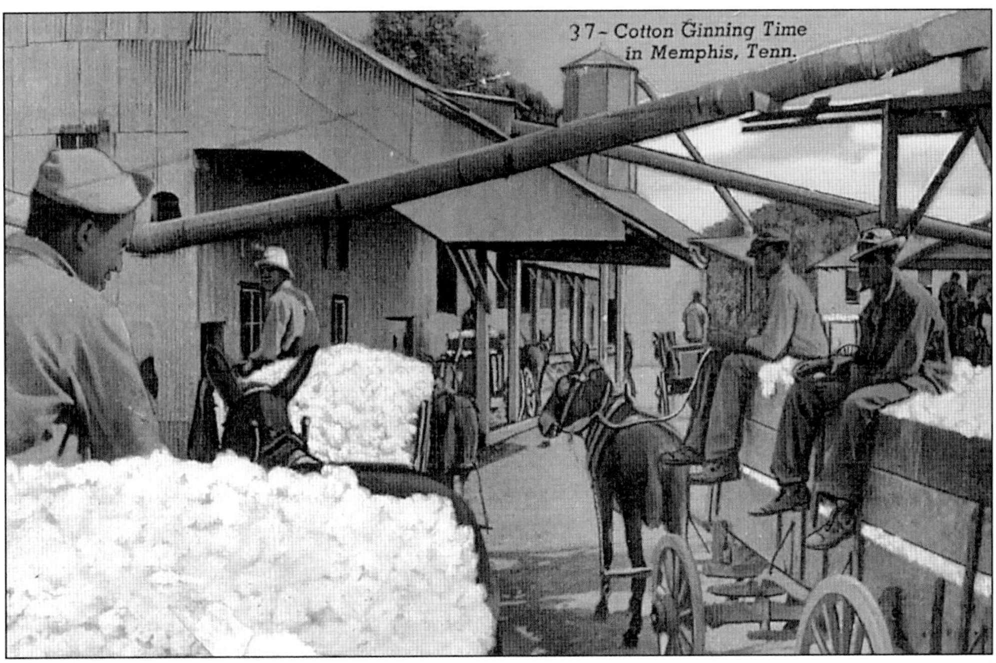

Cotton Ginning Time. At the time the image for this card was made, in 1943, cotton was still transported to the gin by mule-drawn wagons. (Curt Teich Archives.)

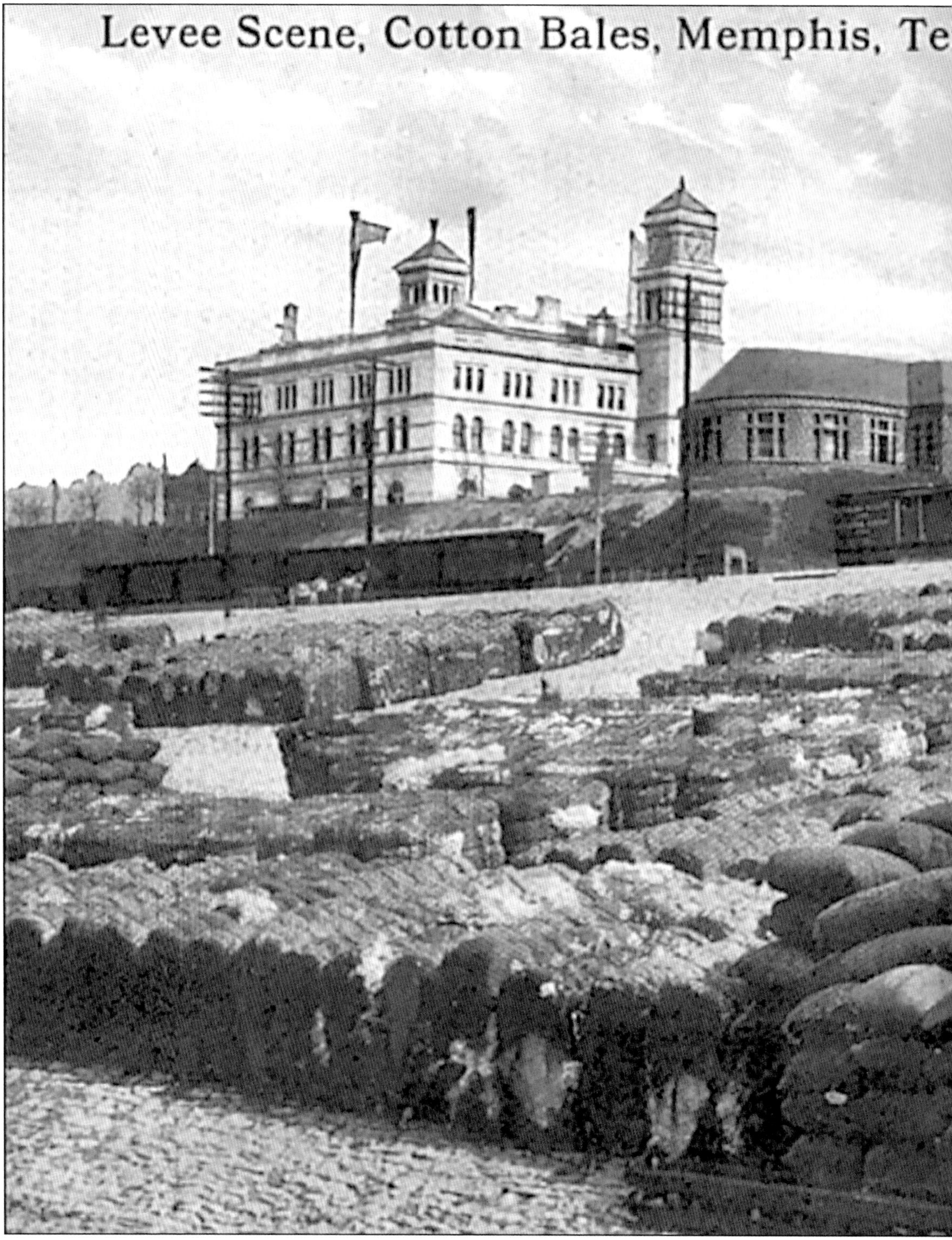

Levee Scene, Cotton Bales. This 1912 postcard depicts hundreds of cotton bales stacked on the river banks waiting to be loaded onto steamboats and transported elsewhere. Above the levy,

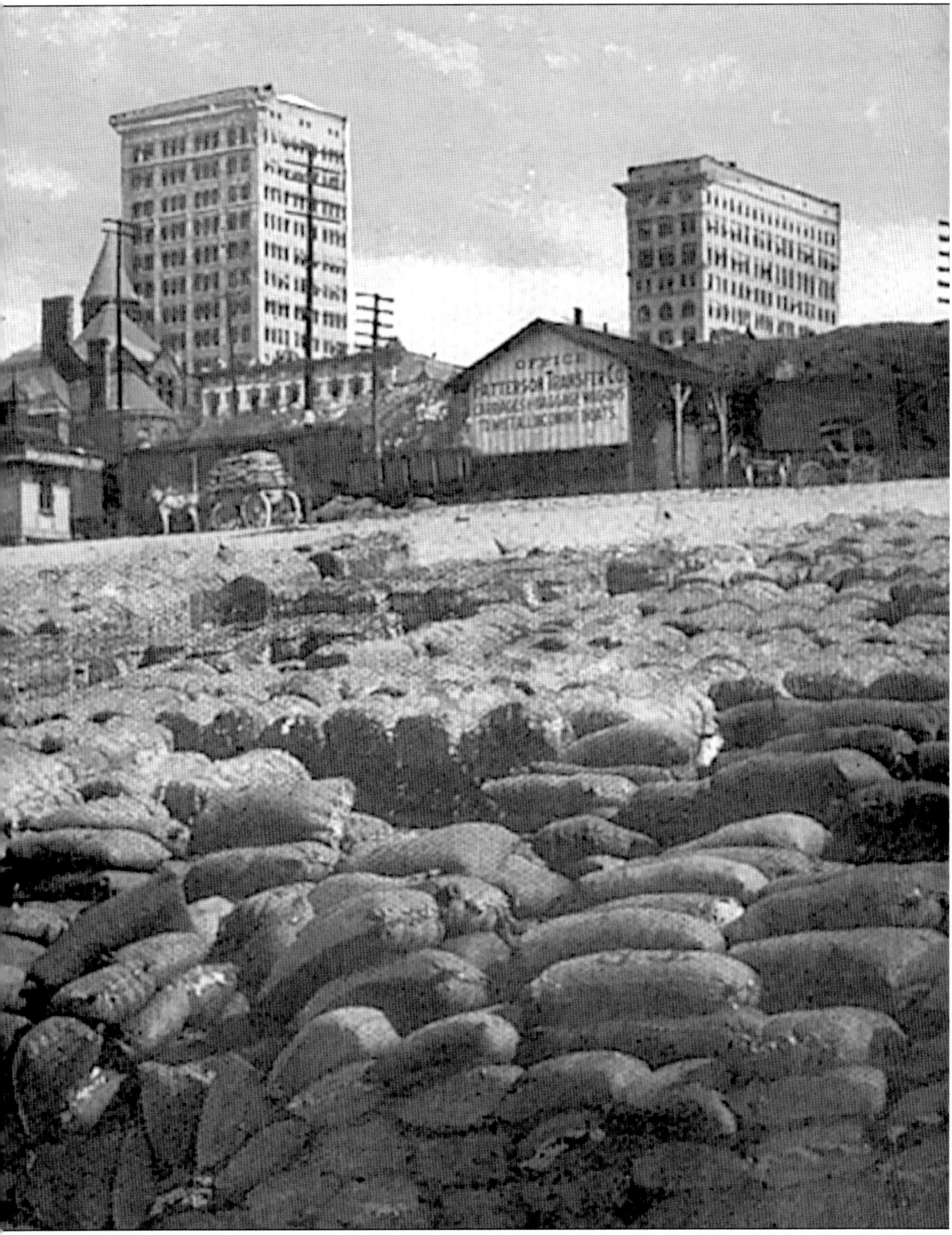

the early city of Memphis stands proudly on the bluff. Even at this early date, the prosperity of the city shows in the architecture pictured here.

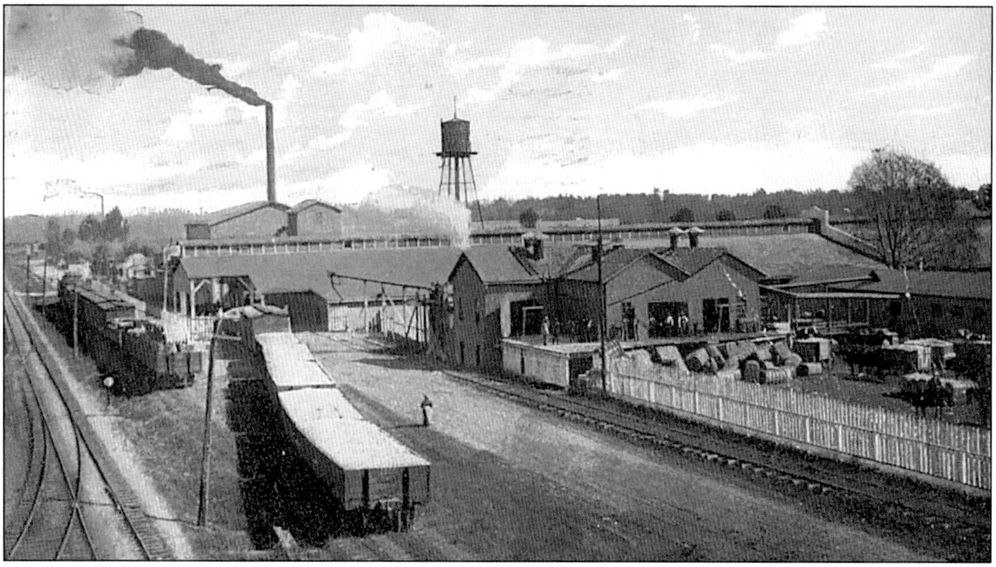

Cotton Seed Oil Mill. Cotton seed oil is among the products produced from cotton. The old cotton seed oil mill is seen in this 1911 postcard.

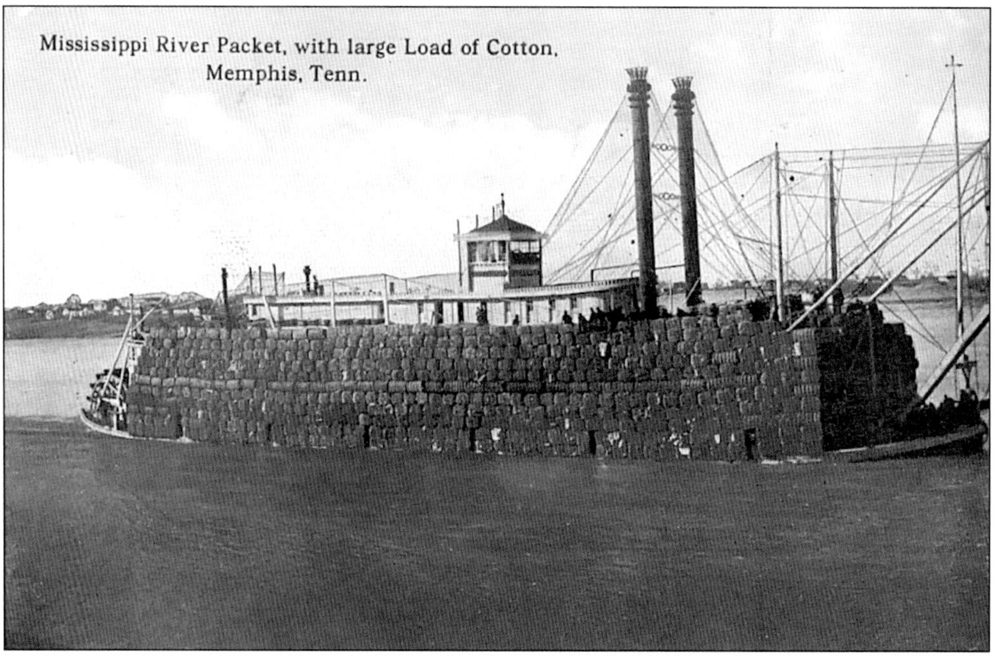

Mississippi River Packet with Large Load of Cotton. This method of transporting cotton was still used along the Mississippi River when this postcard photo was taken in 1912. The particular steamboat pictured here was dangerously overloaded, with the side decks literally below the waterline. Steam-powered riverboats of this era were little changed from those used during the War between the States, and as such, they were wooden and frequently destroyed by fire or boiler explosions.

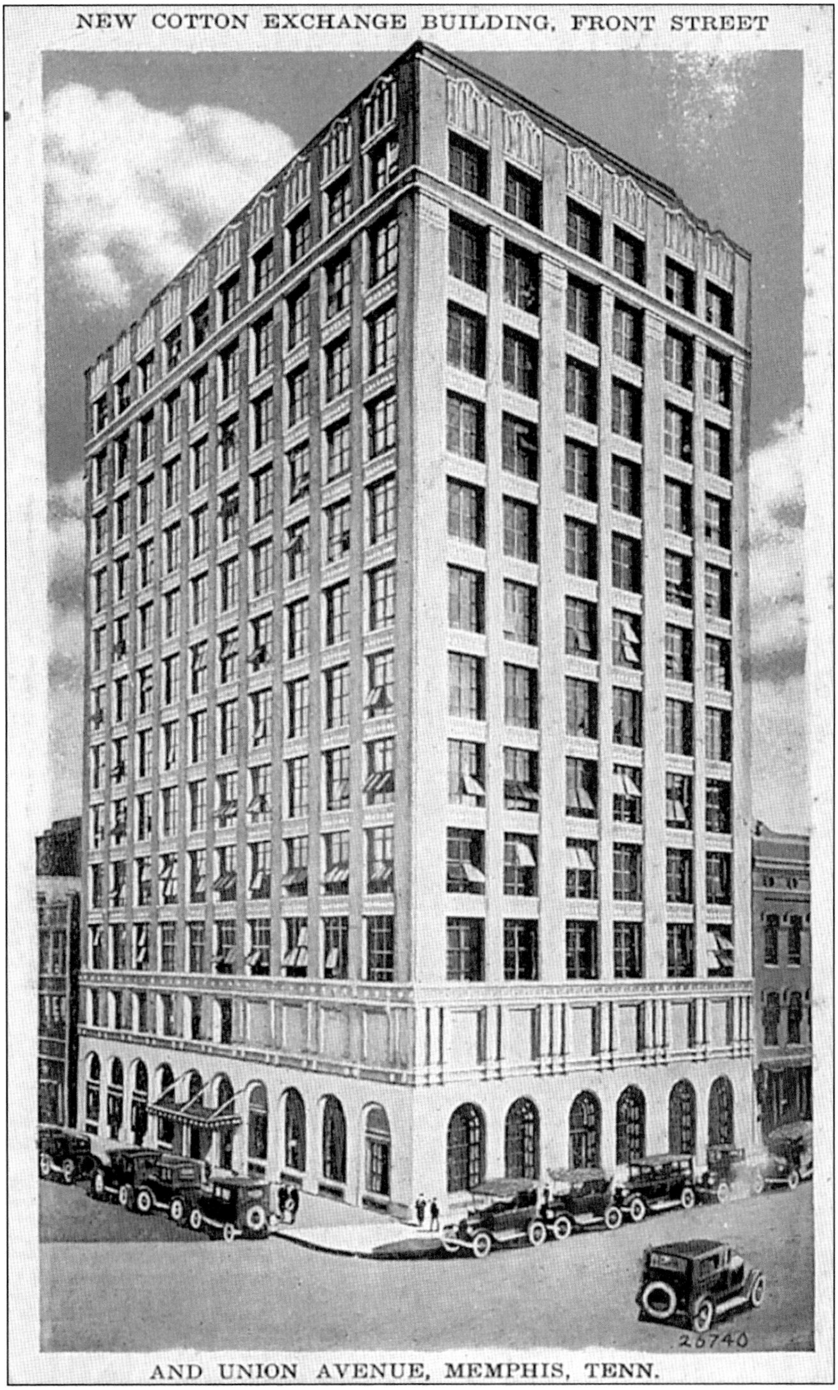

New Cotton Exchange Building. The so-called 'New' Cotton Exchange Building was built in 1925 at the intersection of Front and Union Streets. The Cotton Exchange is sort of a miniature and slower-paced version of the New York Stock Exchange. It is here that cotton is traded. The building pictured in this 1930 postcard has simple but elegant lines. Note the building's open windows.

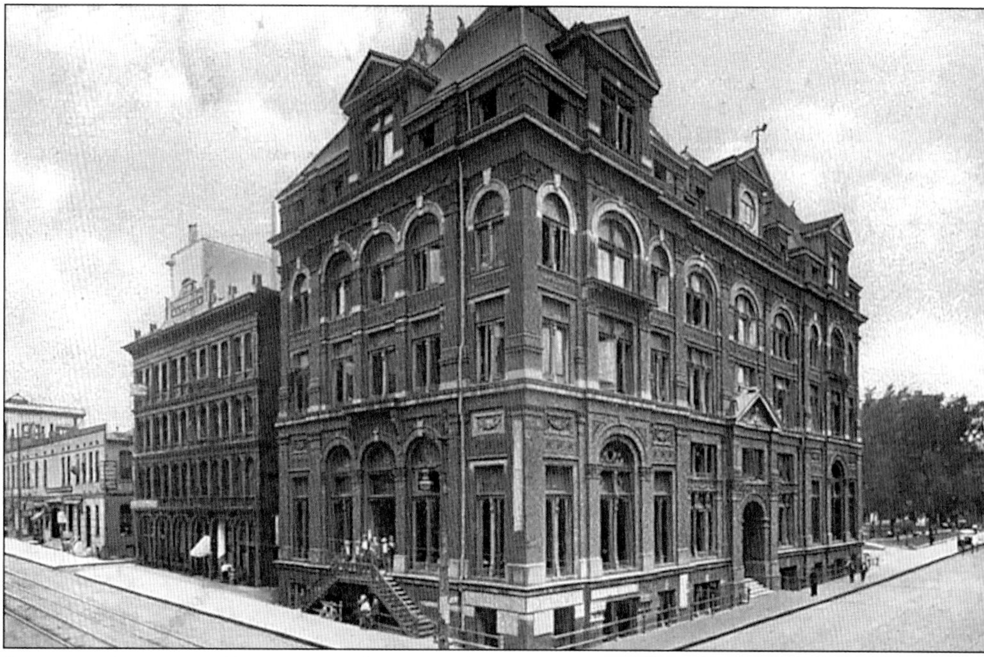

Cotton Exchange Building. The original Memphis Cotton Exchange building seen in this 1908 postcard was constructed in 1885, at the corner of Second and Court (Madison). It was superceded by a larger building at the same location in 1910. In 1925, the Cotton Exchange moved to a new building on Front Street.

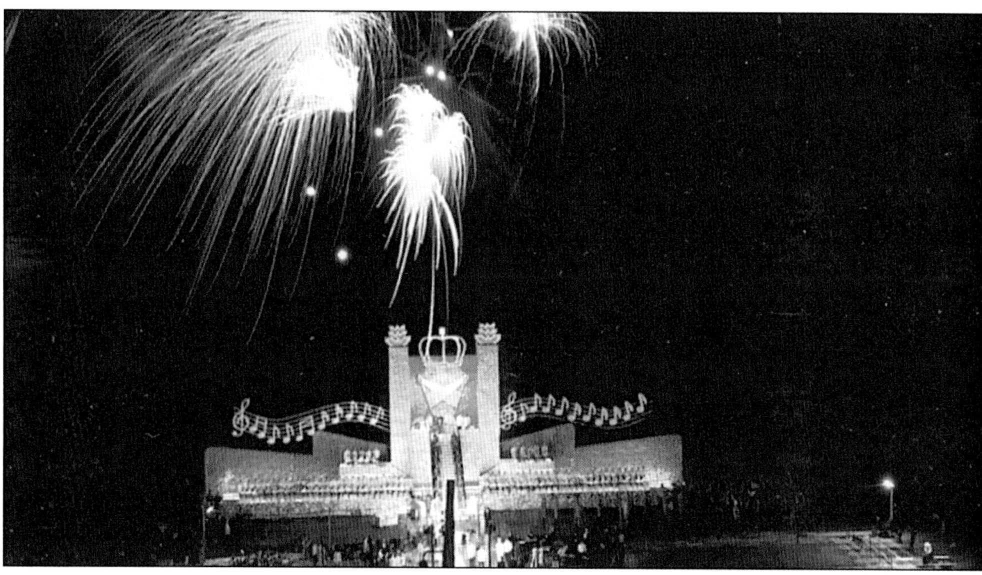

Cotton Carnival. The city's largest celebration, the Cotton Carnival, began on March 1, 1931, and took place every spring. Its purpose was to promote the awareness and use of cotton, as well as the city of Memphis. The opening event was the landing of the royal barge, a great riverfront pageant in which the Cotton King and Queen would arrive by barge on the Mississippi River, much the same as the arrival of Rex in New Orleans' Mardi Gras. The main event was a public parade, followed by a night of partying on a grand scale.

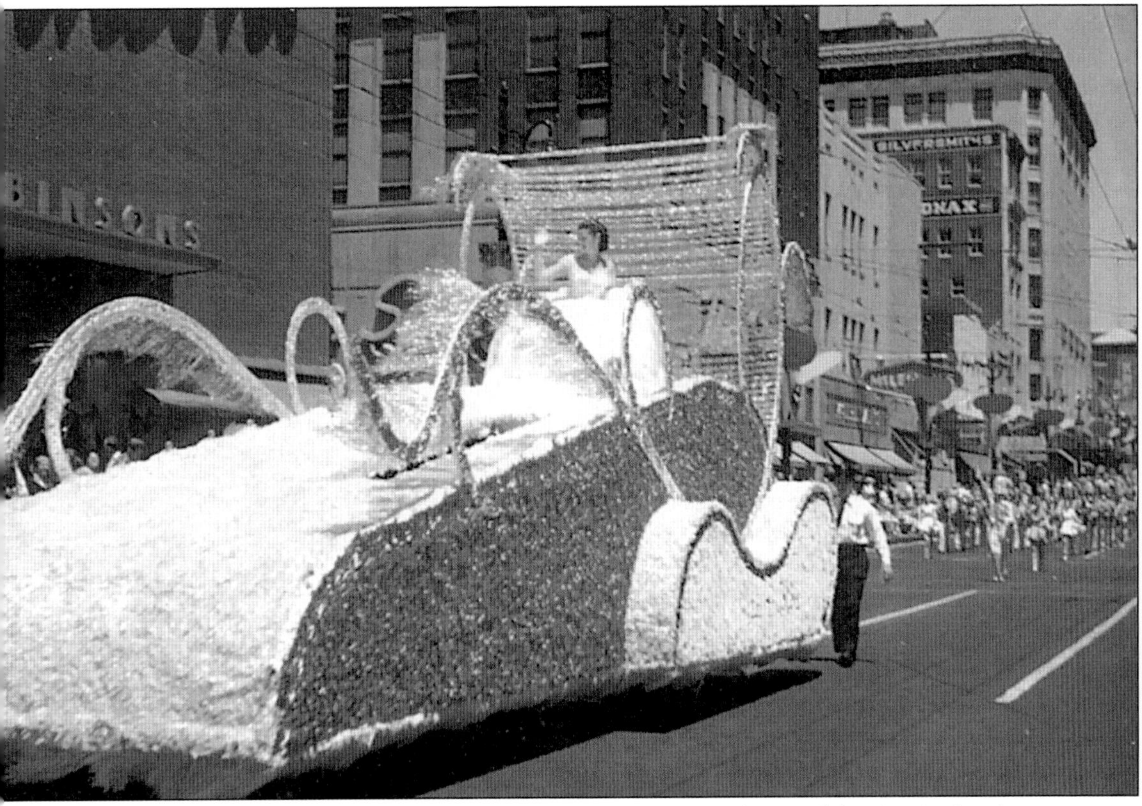

COTTON CARNIVAL. Cotton Carnival was, in its day, the most significant celebration in the city. It was, no doubt, heavily influenced by Mardi Gras, both in New Orleans and Mobile. Here, the Cotton Queen salutes her many admirers along the Main Street parade route.

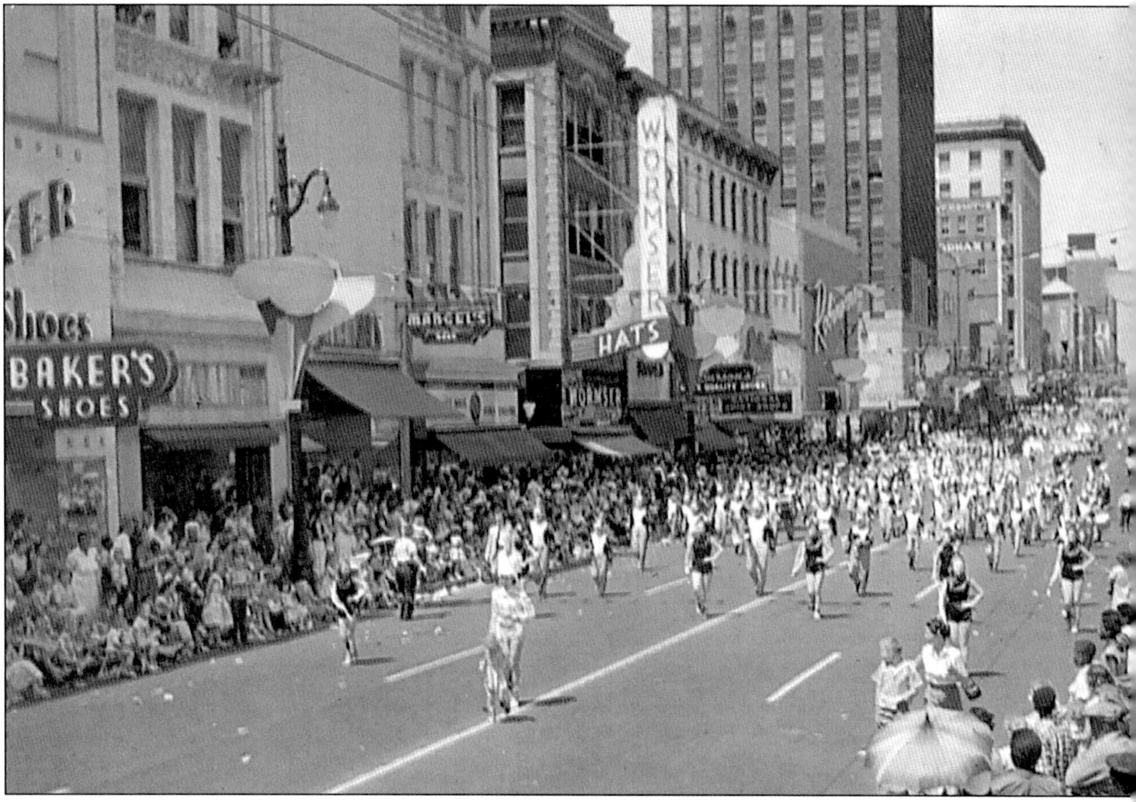

COTTON CARNIVAL. The letter on the back of this postcard says that the senders ". . . are all at the Memphis Bible Students Convention." Actually, this is another view of the parade on Main Street.

Four

Downtown Streets

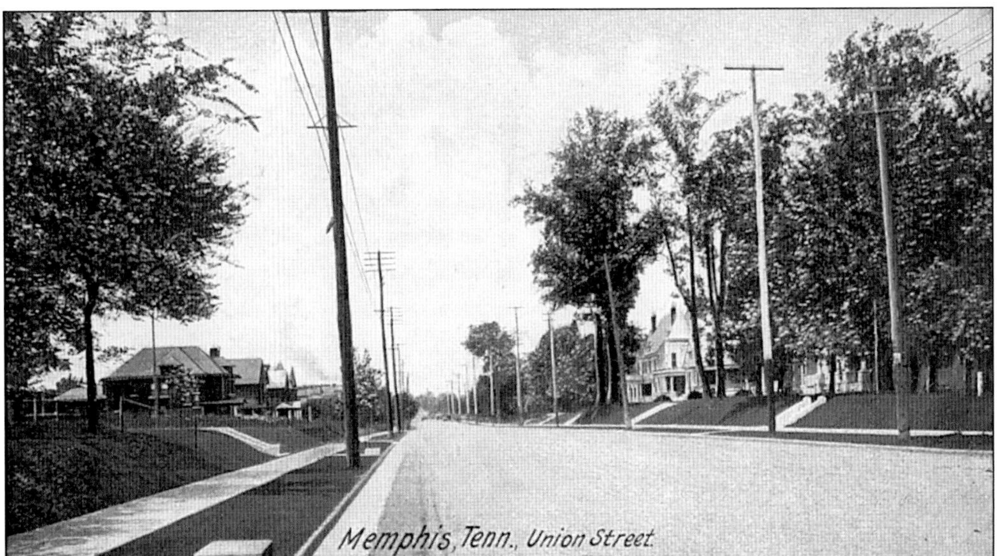

Union Street. Union Street, which runs from east to west, is one of the city's most significant commercial streets and maintains a commercial atmosphere all the way from Front Street to Parkway, several miles away from the river. At the time this postcard image was made, around 1920, Union was a residential thoroughfare. At that time, people with money built extravagant houses right in the middle of the city. The presence and encroachment of government and commercial buildings was not, at the time, considered undesirable to area residents.

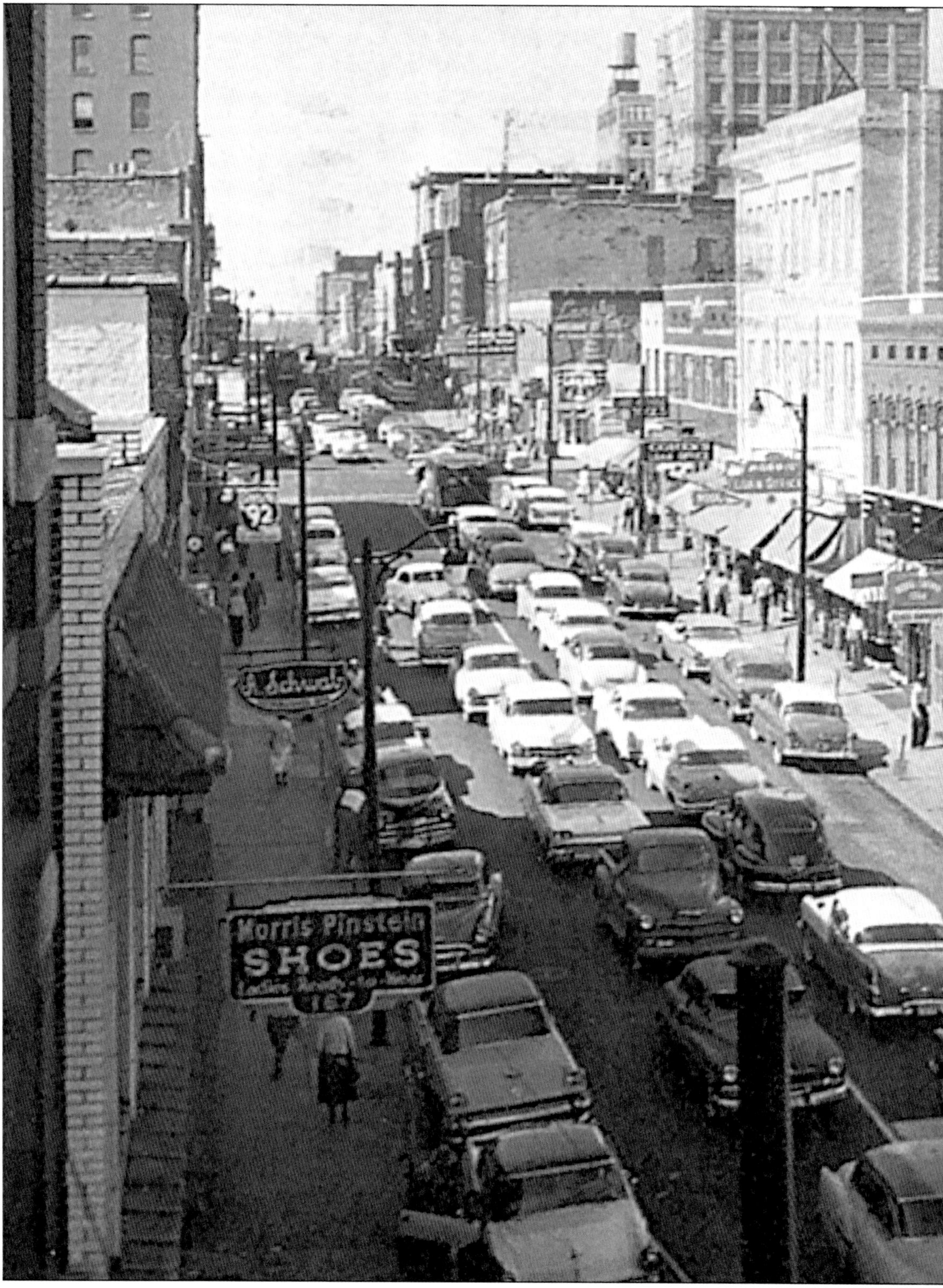
92
Morris Pinstein
SHOES

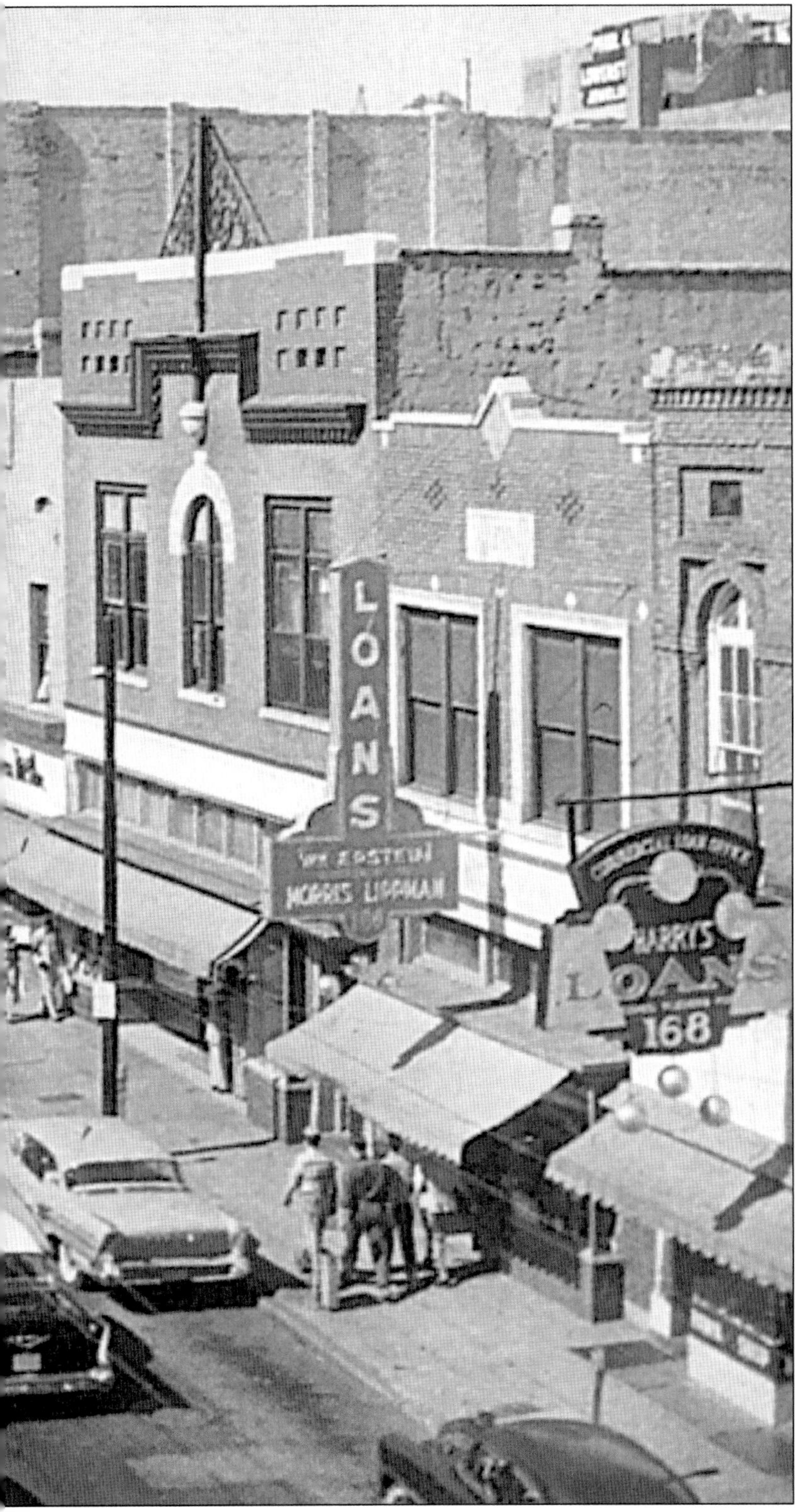

Beale Street. Beale Street, as pictured in this late 1950s postcard, was at the time, as this card says, the "social and economic capitol for Negroes of Mississippi, Arkansas, and West Tennessee." It was the black center of commerce, music, and society. But that was before the street was "restored" in the 1970s and 1980s. It took a while after that for it to regain some degree of its lost glory, and today Beale Street is again thriving, but the real, predominantly black atmosphere, where the blues were born, no longer exists.

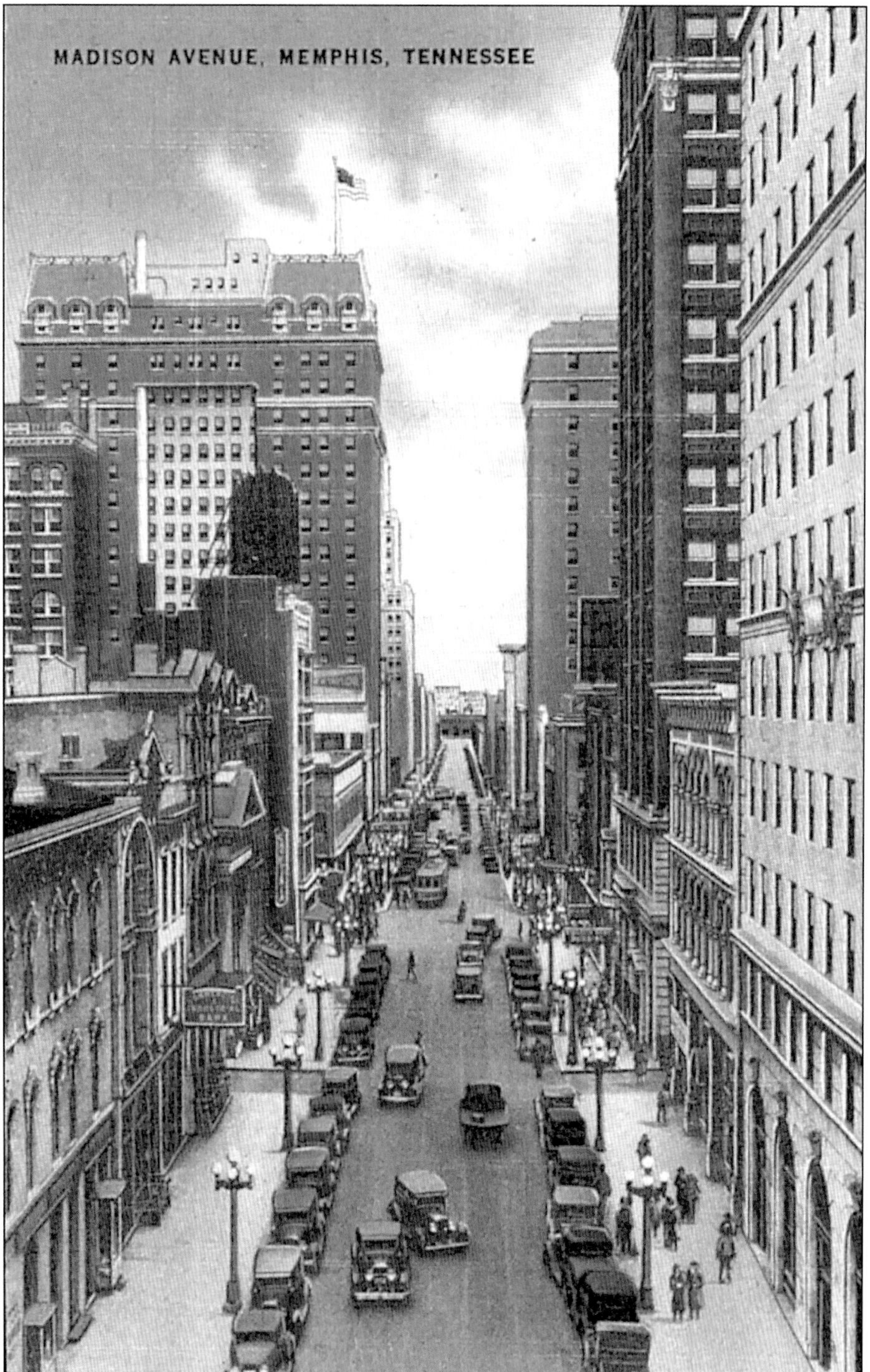

MADISON AVENUE. Madison Avenue is one of the city's main thoroughfares and runs west to east, ending at Front Street on the banks of the river. This view in the early 1930s shows a busy downtown.

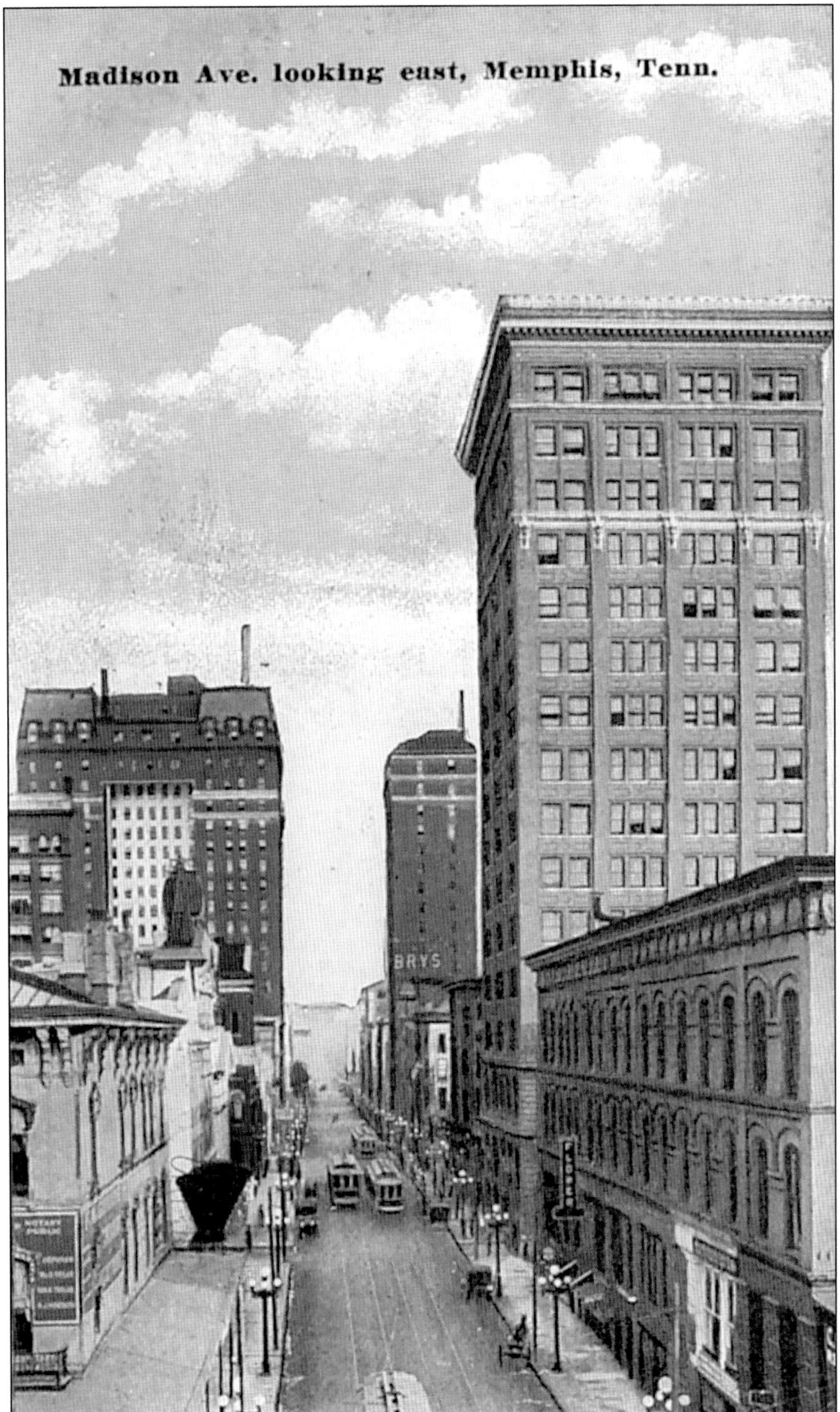

Madison Avenue Looking East. By 1915, the postmarked date on this card, Memphis was a thriving city and was already a major commercial center. Madison Avenue came to be called the "Wall Street of the South."

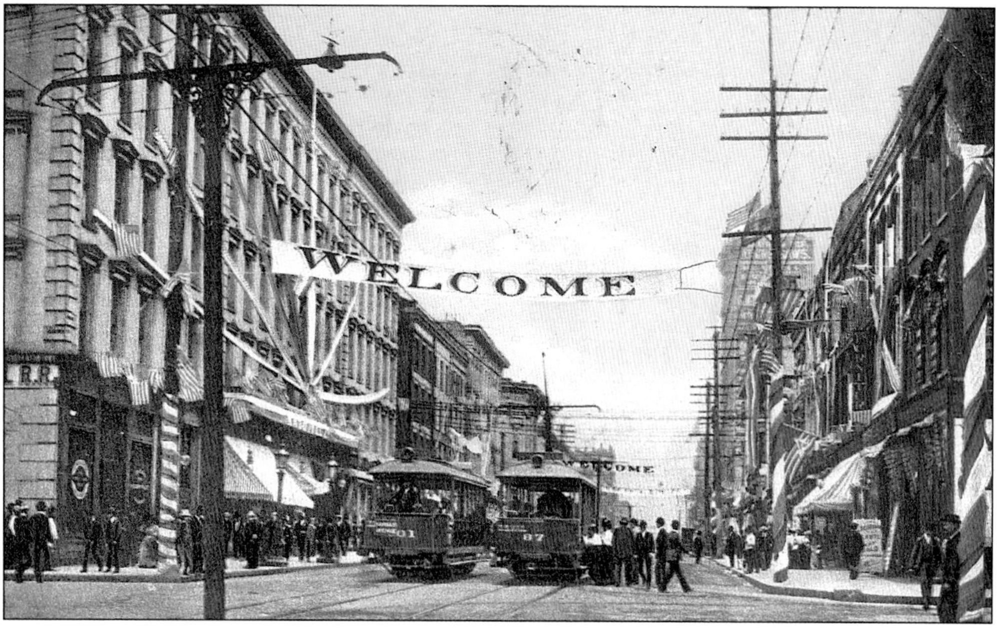

Main Street with Welcome Sign. By 1906, the date this postcard was mailed, electricity had been firmly established in Memphis. The power and trolley lines, even at this early date, were already a part of the growing city landscape.

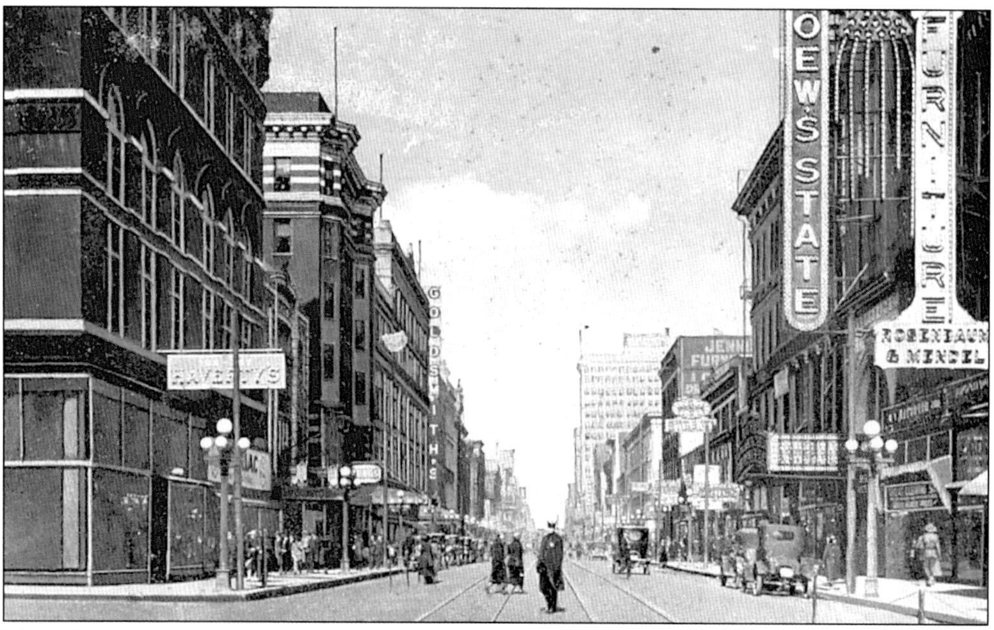

Main Street Looking North from McCall Street. The distinctive striped crown of the Gayoso Hotel is clearly visible on the left side of this 1908 postcard. Just beyond, and also on the left, Goldsmith's Department Store may be seen. Goldsmith's would eventually take over the Gayoso Hotel and use it as warehouse space. (Curt Teich Archives.)

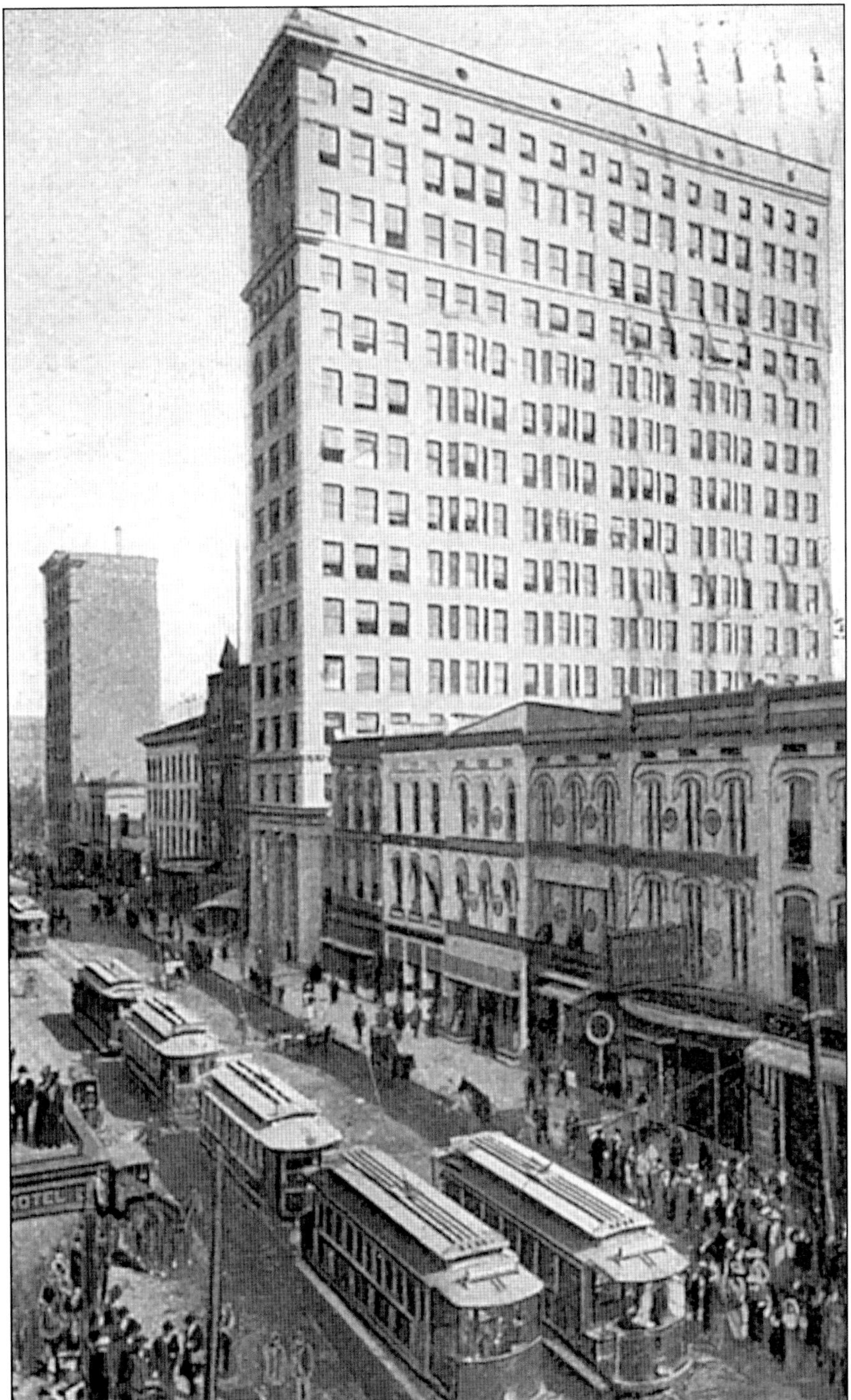

Main Street (Looking North). This 1909 view from South Main shows the new 1904 Memphis Trust Building, known as the Bank of Commerce and Trust Company by the time the following image was made.

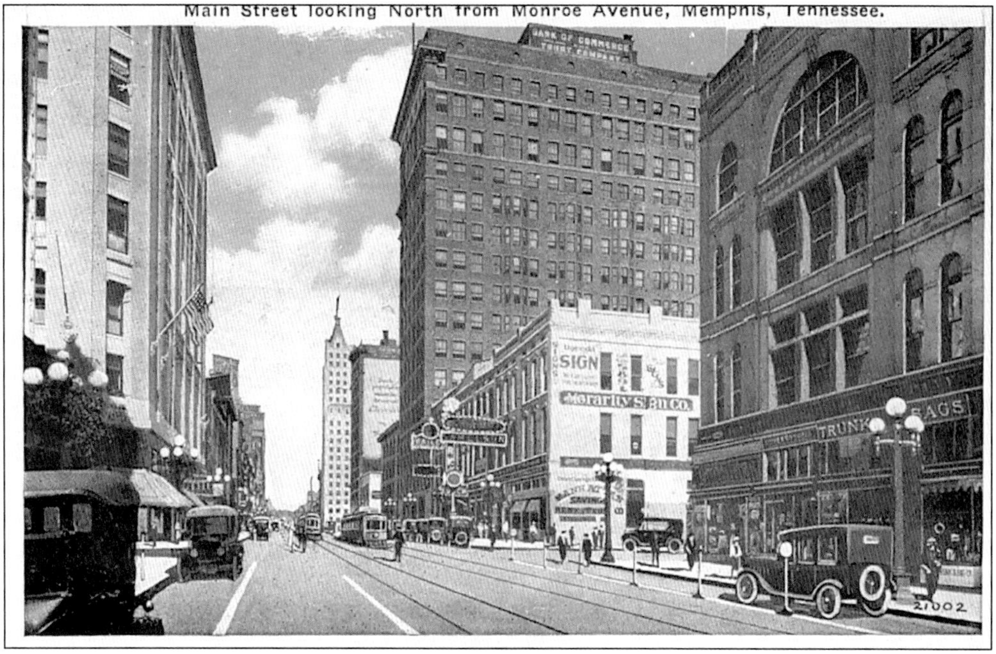

Main Street Looking North from Monroe Avenue. The Bank of Commerce is the large dark building in the center of this picture, with the spire of the Columbian Mutual Tower in the distance in this 1920s downtown Memphis street scene.

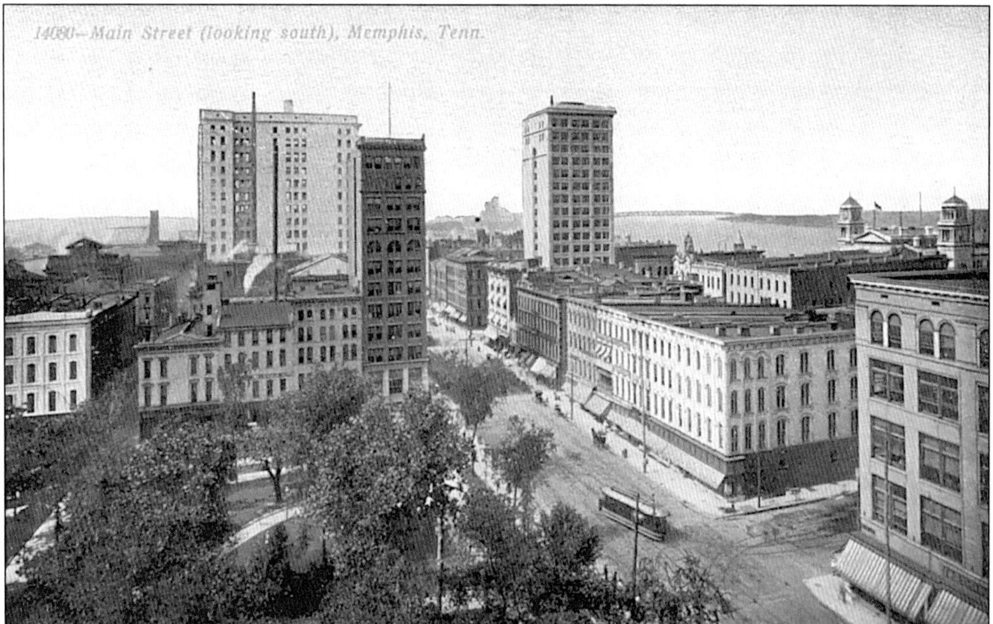

Main Street (Looking South). This view of Main Street looking south shows the city's first modern buildings, with Court Square in the foreground and the Mississippi River in the background.

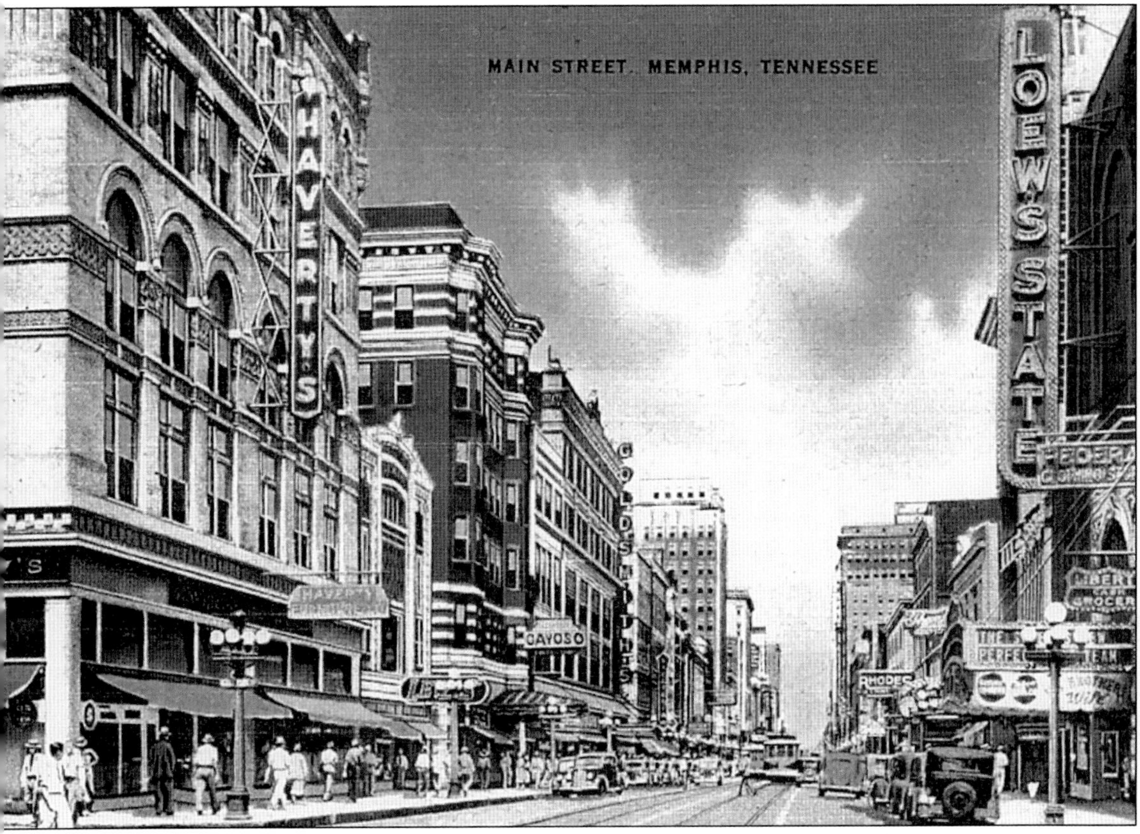

MAIN STREET, MEMPHIS, TENNESSEE. By the time this postcard was made in the late 1930s, Main Street had become the epicenter of the Memphis business district.

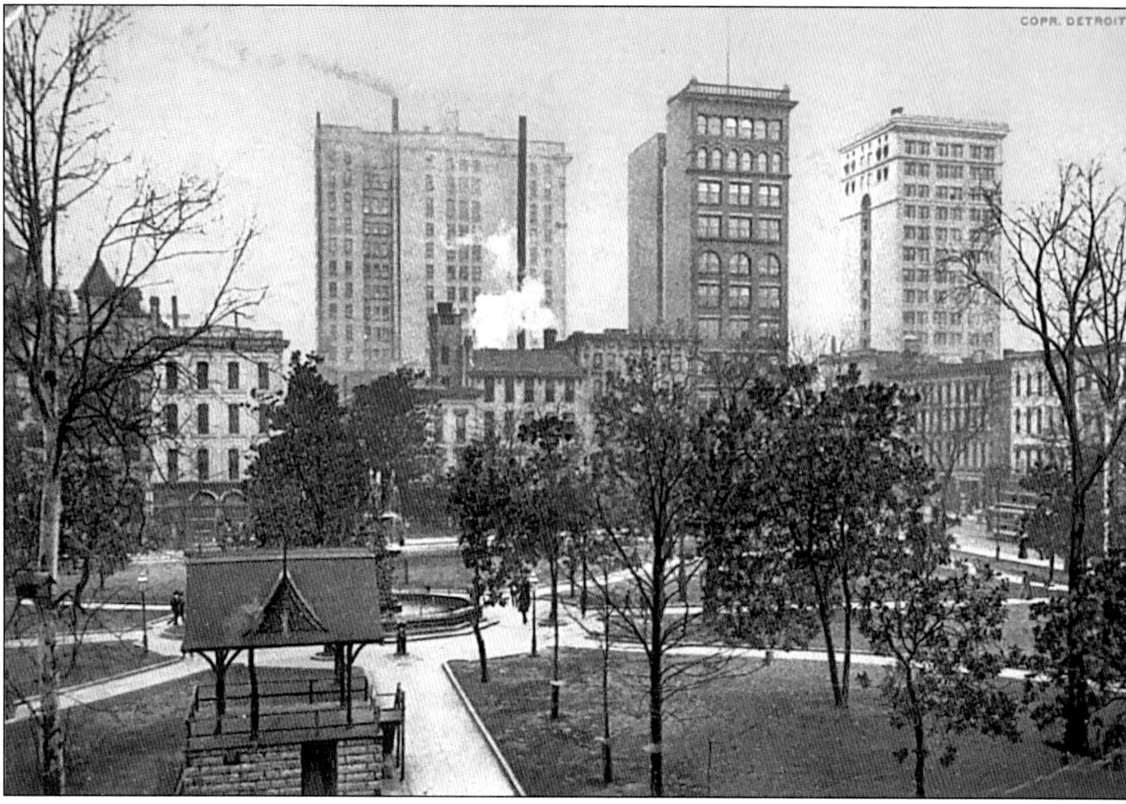

Court Square and Skyscrapers, Memphis, Tennessee. This close-up of Court Square shows the buildings surrounding this city oasis as they appeared in 1909.

Five

Hotels

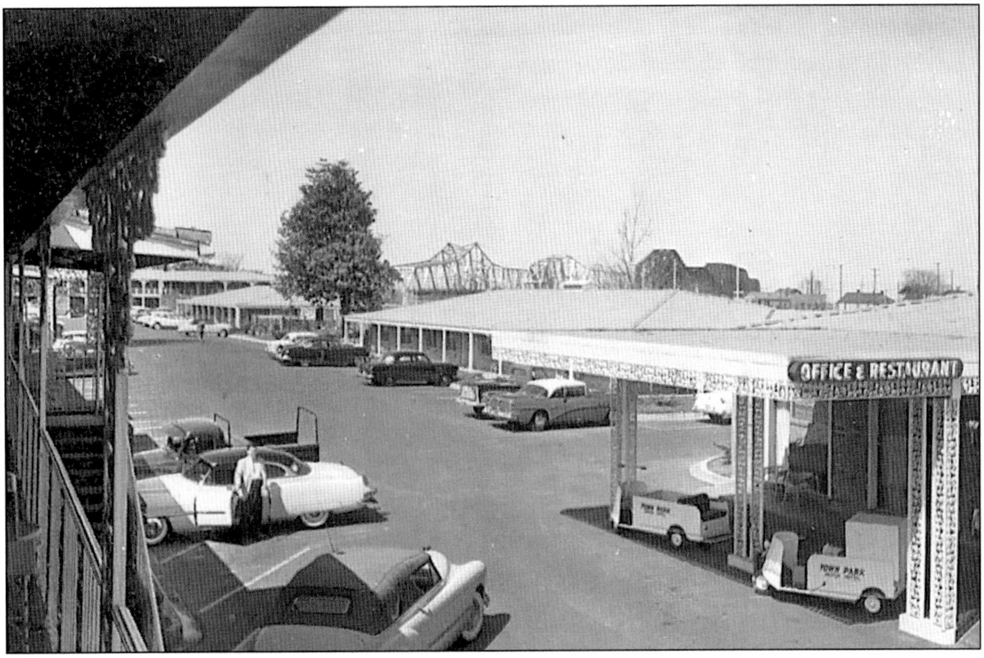

Town Park Motor Hotel. The Town Park Motor Hotel was typical of the new, more easily accessible motels which began dotting the American landscape after World War II. While not as formal as traditional hotels, these new motels offered much more convenience. Since it was now possible to park outside one's room, loading and unloading suitcases became much easier. It was no longer necessary to have to wait for the car to be retrieved from the parking garage, and tipping the parking attendant and the bellboy also ceased to burden the traveler.

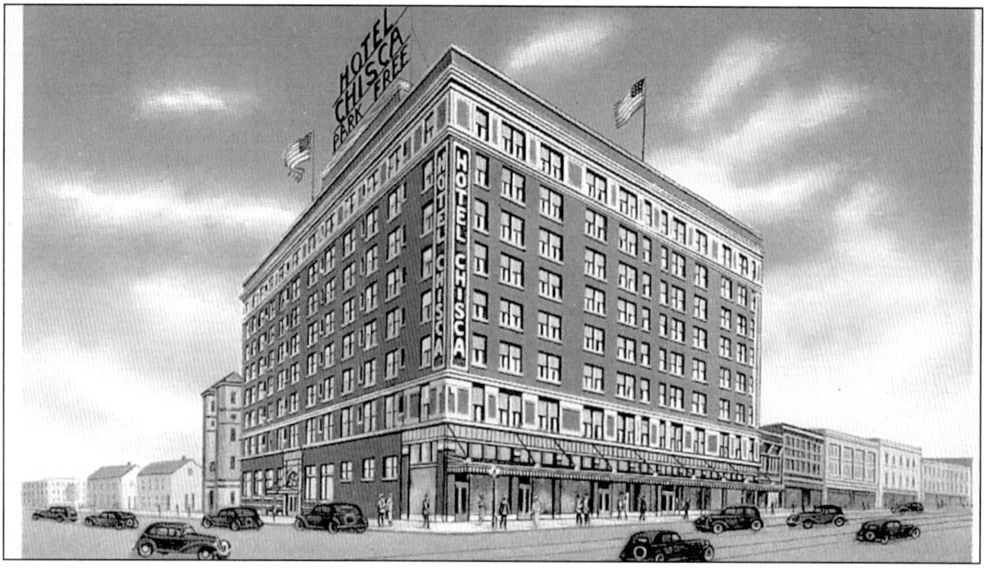

CHISCA HOTEL. The Hotel Chisca, which was named for a Chickasaw village, is pictured in this 1933 postcard. It opened in 1913 and advertised itself as Memphis' most popular-priced hotel. It offered home-style Southern cooking, 400 outside rooms, and air-conditioned guest rooms. The hotel often catered to Vaudeville-type performers and entertainers who worked at nearby theatres such as the Orpheum. In the early days of American cities, first-class hotels usually provided stables for their guests. As the public began to own automobiles, downtown hotel parking became a problem, and many of these former stables were converted into garages. (Curt Teich Archives.)

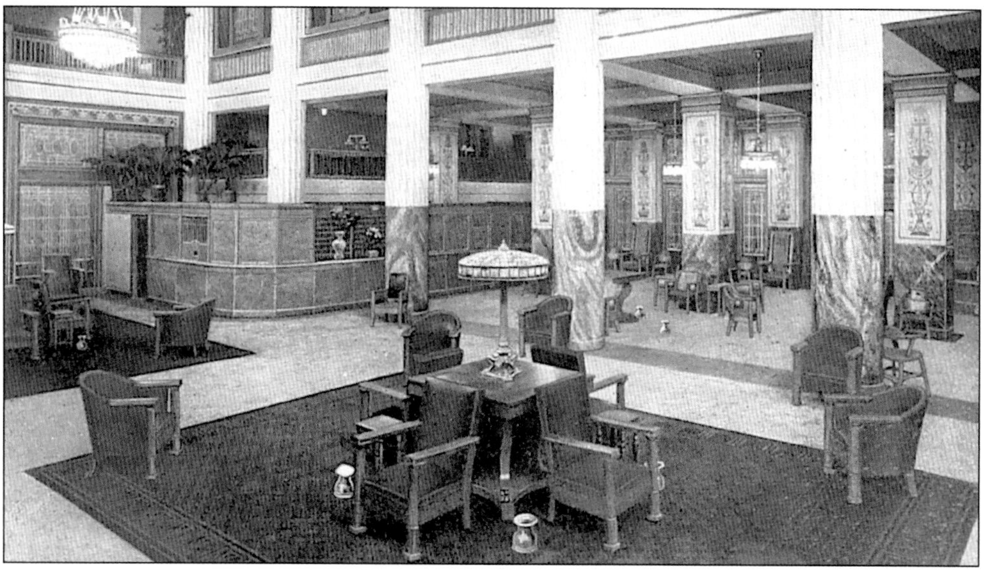

LOBBY, HOTEL CHISCA. The formal lobby of the Chisca is characteristic of the elegance which adorned the great hotels in major cities. A typical first-class hotel lobby often included a main floor surrounded by a second-level mezzanine, as was the case here. The same design may also be seen at the Peabody Hotel and also at Chattanooga's Read House. In addition to the visual appeal, the mezzanine also affords an opportunity for socializing. (Curt Teich Archives.)

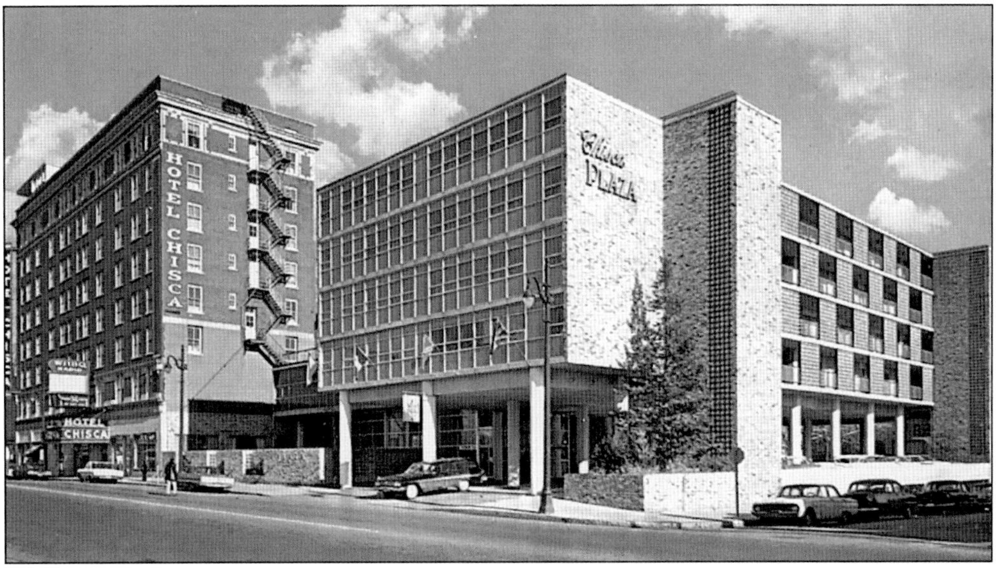

Chisca Plaza Motor Hotel. By the time this postcard image was made in the mid-1960s, many hotels in downtown cities throughout the nation had added motor lodges as annexes. The motor lodges usually offered a swimming pool, parking, and more modern amenities, which the older hotels lacked. The new annex announced in 1959 was designed by Tom Windrum and provided an additional 200 underground parking places. During the same period, the main hotel underwent significant renovation and modernization, including expanded gym and health center facilities, as well as the city's first hotel office suites for patrons. The hotel eventually closed and became the headquarters building for the Church of God in Christ.

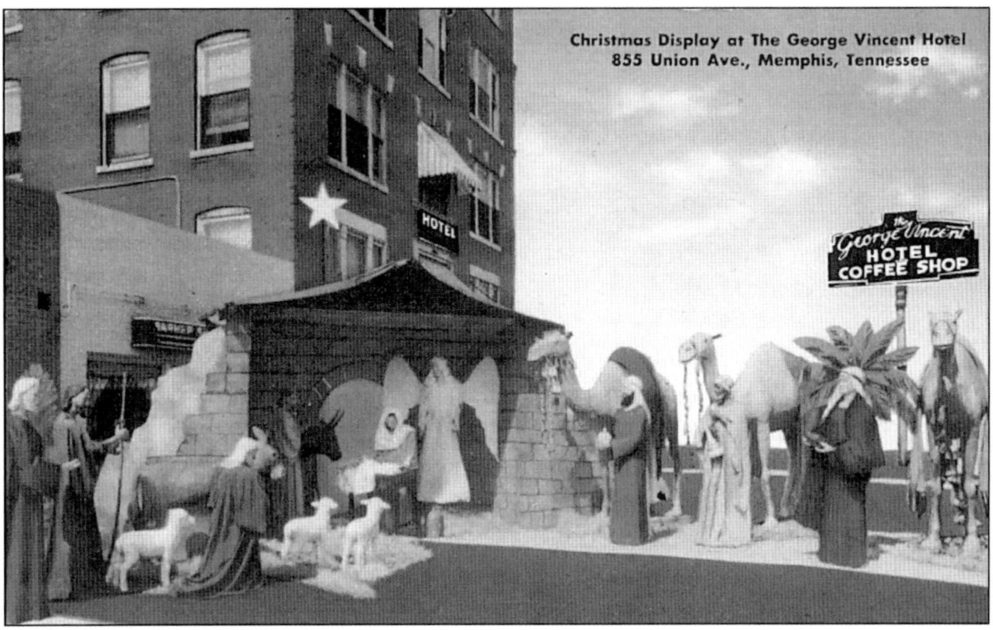

George Vincent Hotel Christmas Display. The George Vincent Hotel was located at 855 Union, one of the city's main arteries. This Christmas depiction of the nativity was made of papier mâché and was a popular holiday display.

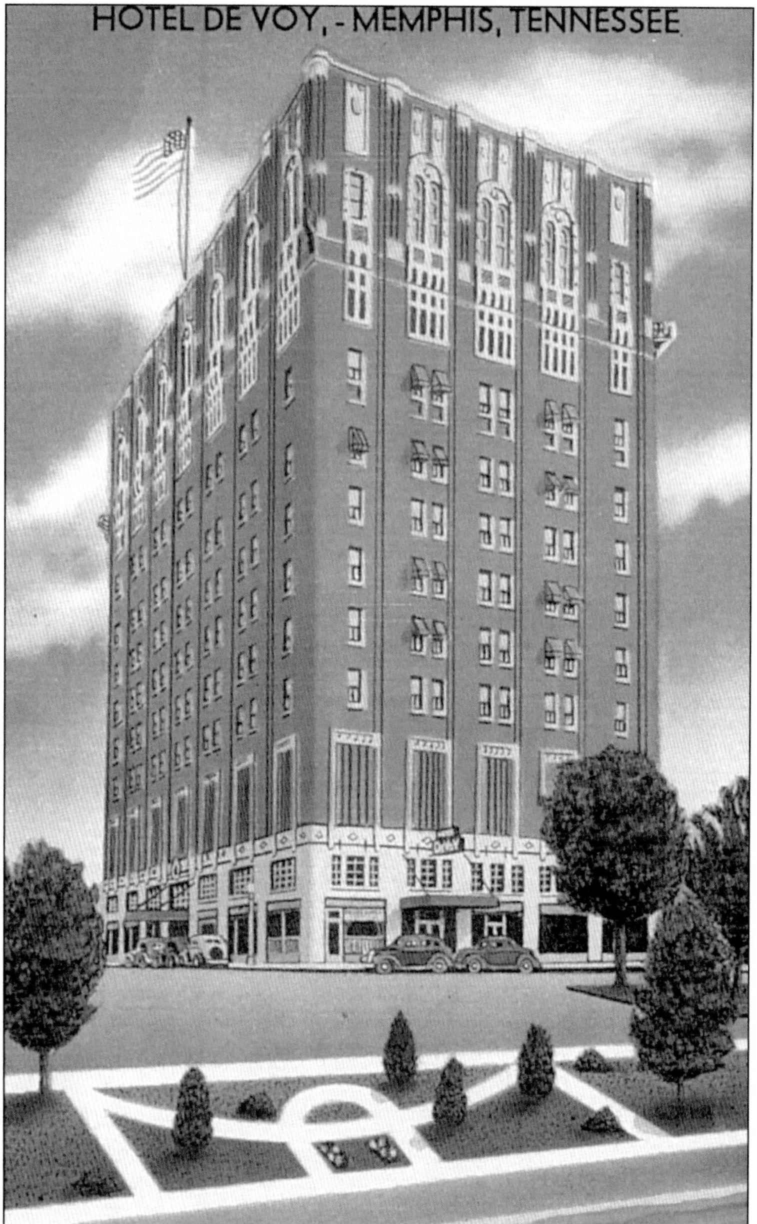

Hotel De Voy. Memphis' golden age of hotels can be acknowledged to have taken place in the 1920s. The Peabody, Claridge, and Parkview immediately come to mind. Another great hotel of the era was the Hotel De Voy. It was built at 69 Jefferson Street in 1925, at the exorbitant cost of $1,400,000, and was first called the Elks. It was renamed in 1939 in honor of Clarence De Voy, a former exalted Elks Ruler. While hotels like the Peabody and the Parkview emphasized luxury, the De Voy advertised "safety and comfort without extravagance." The 150-room hotel was equipped with a gym, swimming pool, and bowling alley, as well as a squash and handball court. In short order, the De Voy would become the King Cotton. A look at the two hotels will show identical architecture. Note the stylized rendering of Confederate Park in the foreground.

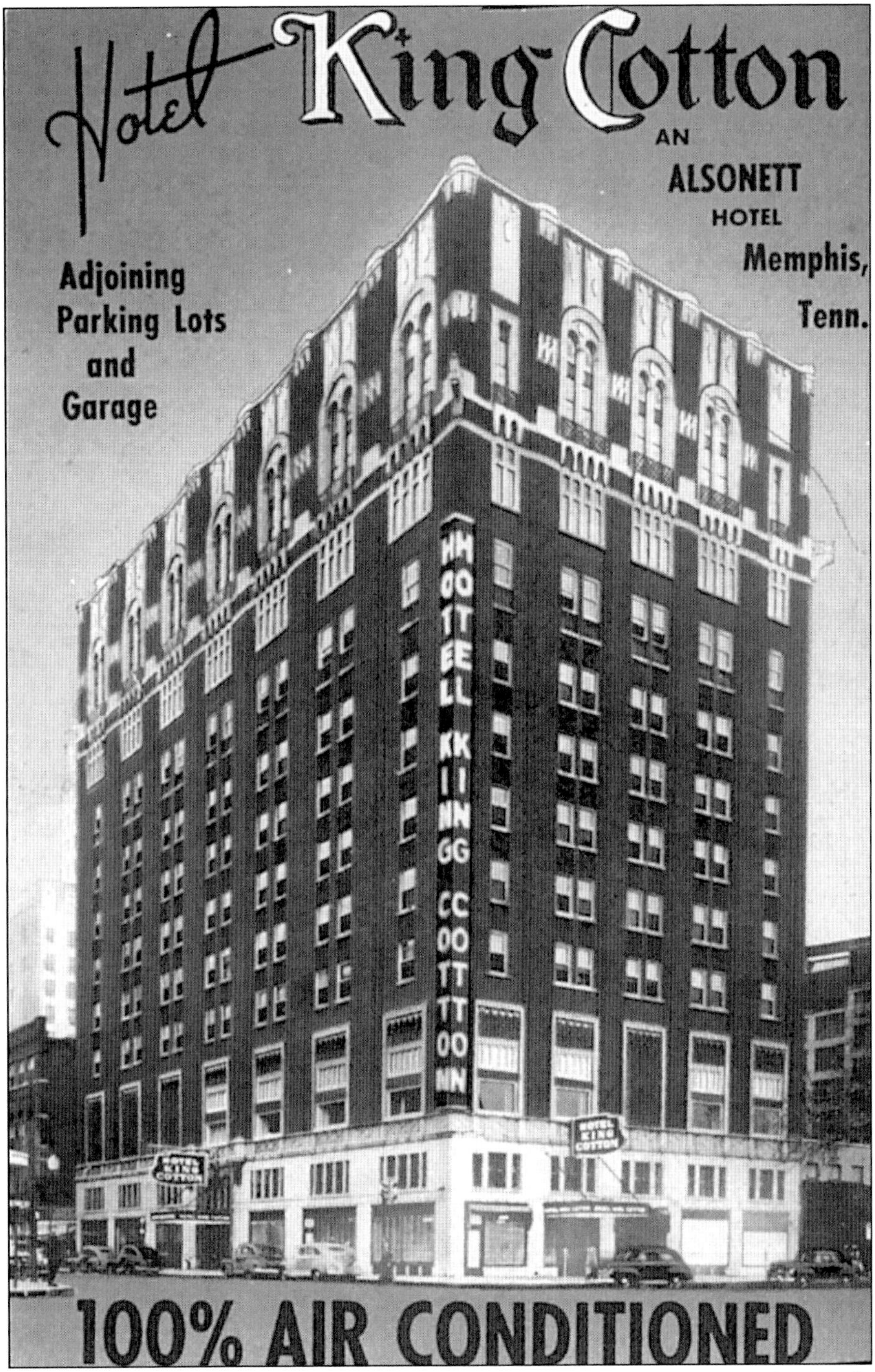

King Cotton Hotel. The King Cotton Hotel symbolized, by its very name, the significance of cotton to Memphis. It was located at the corner of Front and Jefferson Streets, overlooking Confederate Park. It featured a private bath for every room, three channels of radio, and a restaurant overlooking the river. It was also the home of the 'Army-Navy' Club.

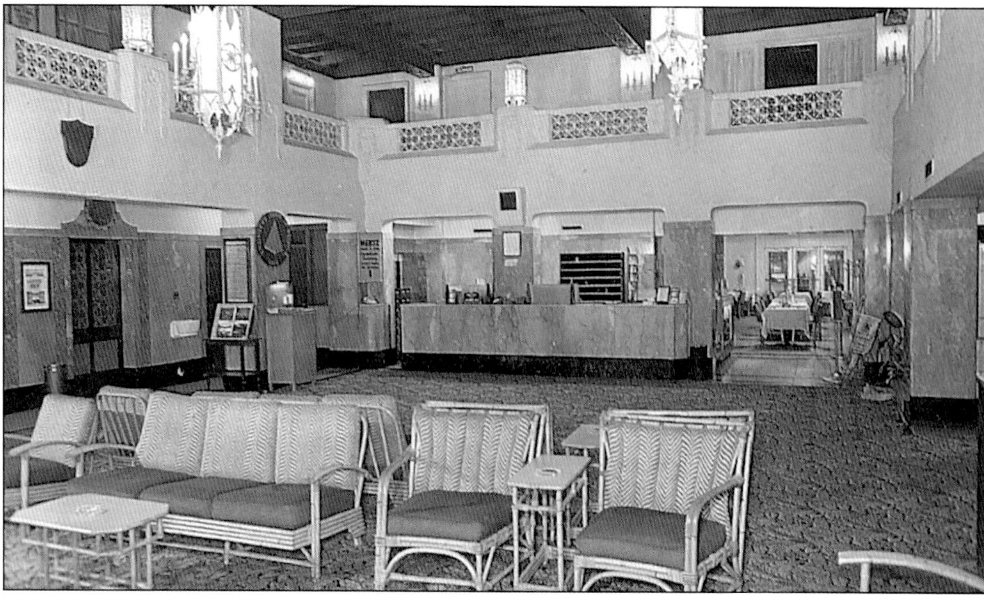

KING COTTON HOTEL LOBBY. The lobby of the King Cotton, as pictured here, certainly lacks the grandeur and opulence of the Peabody Hotel, and yet, during its day, the King Cotton was considered to be a desirable destination for any traveler to the Bluff City. It was sold to the Cindarella House of America hotel chain in 1963 for $1,500,000, and plans were announced to turn it into a residence for women operating along the same lines as a college dormitory. The hotel passed to the Alsonett hotel chain before being sold again in 1965. Eventually the hotel was razed.

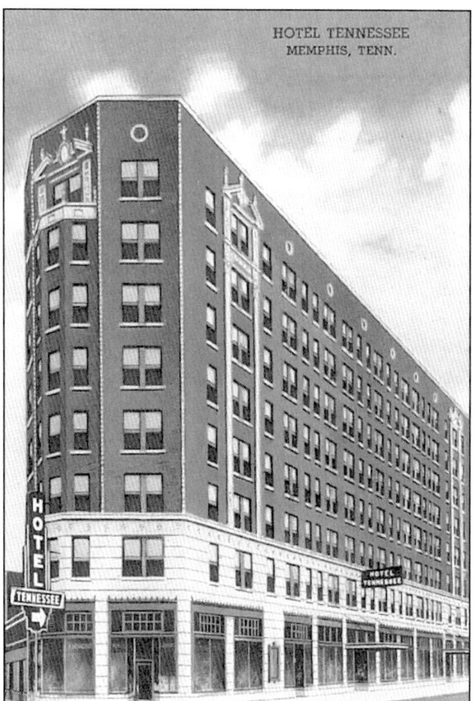

HOTEL TENNESSEE. The Hotel Tennessee was originally built in 1927 at the corner of Third and Union and boldly proclaimed to have 200 rooms and 200 baths. While its design is typical of the period, the building obviously lacks the grace and grandeur of contemporaries like the Parkview and Peabody. Today, a part of the original Hotel Tennessee remains within the lobby of the new Radison. (Curt Teich Archives.)

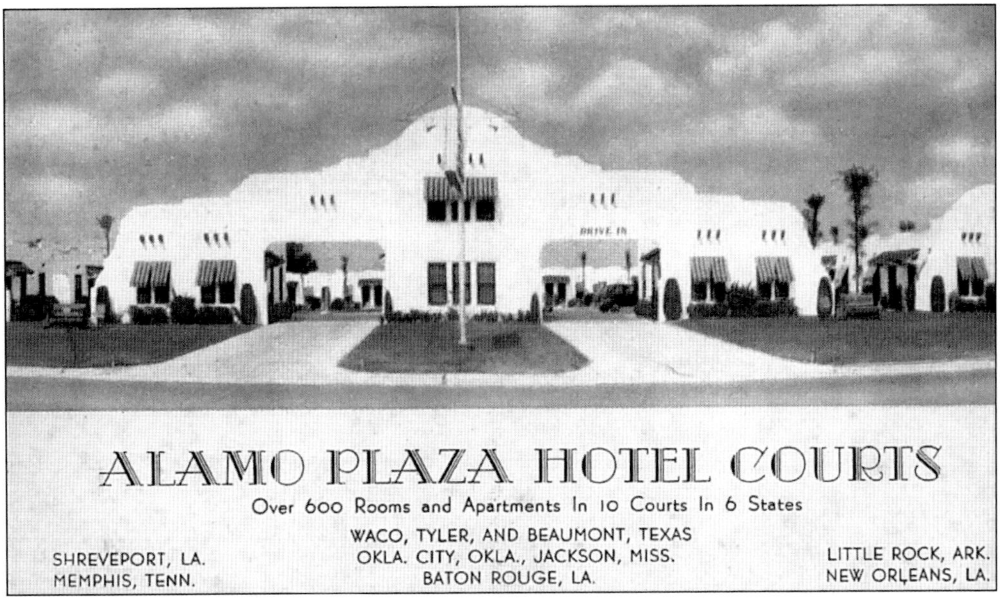

ALAMO PLAZA HOTEL COURTS. The Alamo Plaza Tourist Courts opened in Memphis in 1939 as the seventh link in a national chain started in 1929 by Alamo Torrence. This location on Summer Avenue, with its Spanish architecture, followed the same design as the other motels. The Memphis Alamo Plaza offered 48 deluxe units, each with its own garage.

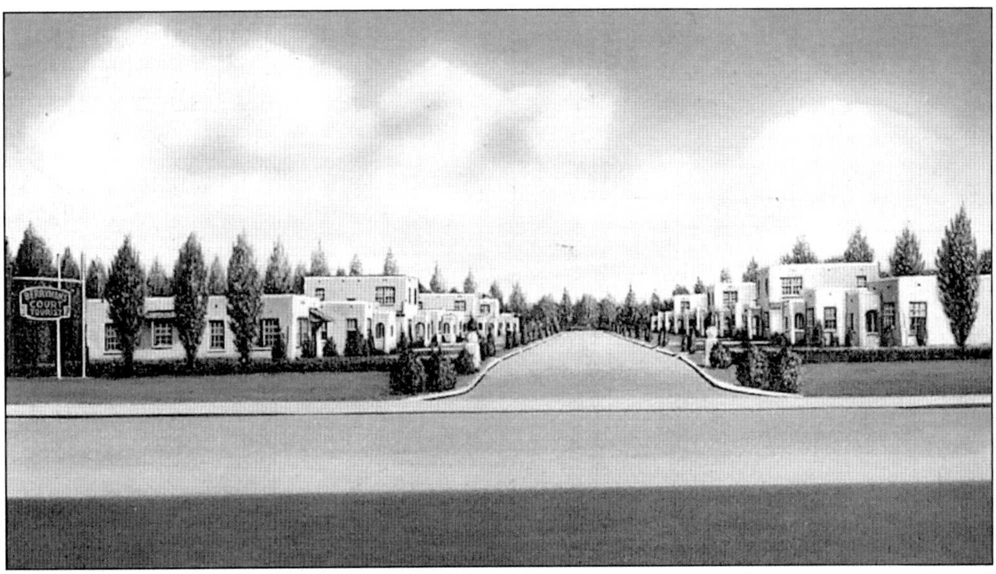

BERRYMAN'S TOURIST COURT. Berryman's was located in South Memphis on Highway 61 until the early 1990s, and for nearly 60 years it was well known to travelers between Memphis and Mississippi. It featured classic individual art deco cottages, each with its own covered parking garage affixed to the side. By the 1980s, the place was still in business, but after a strange manner. The windows of every cottage had been painted so that it was impossible to see in or out. Rusting 1950s vintage cars rotted away in crumbling garages. It met its fate in 1992 and was torn down, a victim of an expanding highway and a decaying surrounding neighborhood. (Curt Teich Archives.)

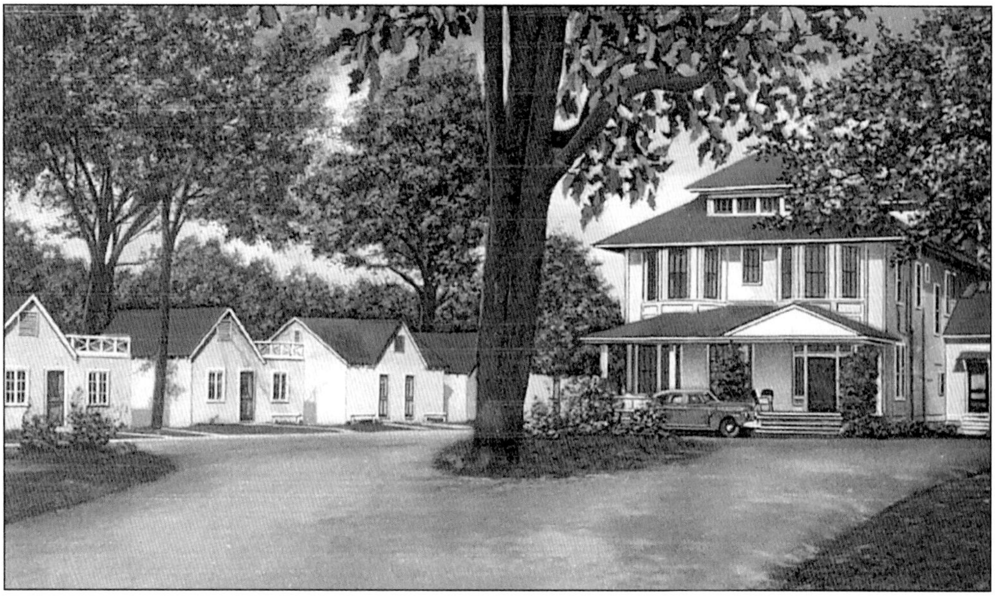

Leahy's Tourist Court. Leahy's Tourist Court is located at 3070 Summer Avenue, and today, over 50 years later, it looks very much the same as seen in this 1948 postcard. It is typical of the cottage-style structures clustered around a larger central building that in many cases was a residence, which served as an office and usually contained a restaurant. (Curt Teich Archives.)

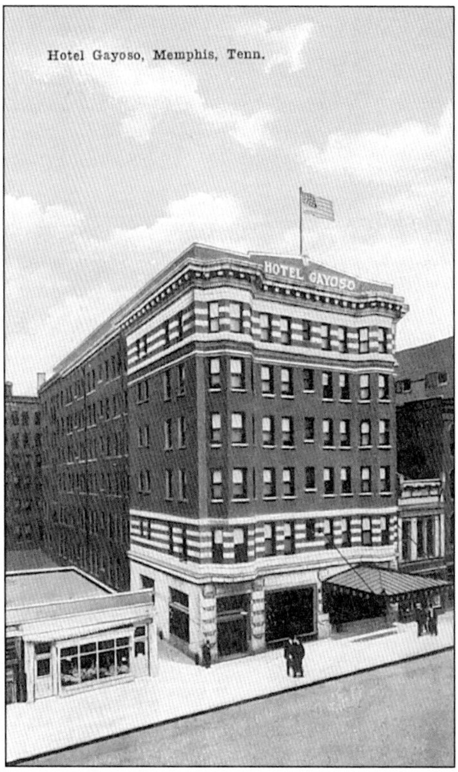

Hotel Gayoso. The Hotel Gayoso, on Front Street, was one of the city's most famous hotels. The first section was built by businessman Robertson Topp in 1842, prior to the War between the States, and overlooked the Mississippi River. It was designed by James Dalin, a prominent New Orleans architect, a first for a Memphis hotel. An addition in 1857 enlarged the structure, which was by then a magnificent Greek Revival building. On April 23, 1861, the hotel's manager unfurled the Confederate flag on top of the hotel. Later, during the war, the building served as Union Headquarters. During Nathan Bedford Forrest's raid on Memphis in 1864, his brother, Captain William Forrest, rode his horse into the hotel lobby demanding Union General Stephen Hurlbut. According to legend, the Union general, in his haste to depart, left without his uniform. Forrest had it cleaned and pressed and returned to the general by way of courier. The Union General returned the courtesy by having enough material sent to Forrest to have uniforms made for himself and his staff.

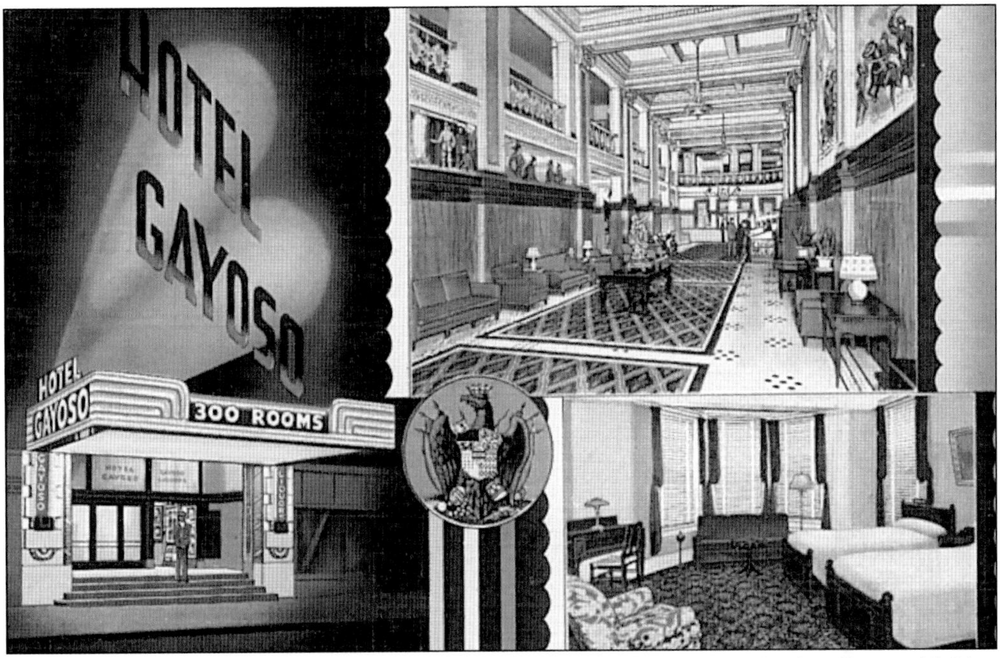

HOTEL GAYOSO. This collage of the Gayoso Hotel shows the entrance, the hotel's grand lobby, and what would appear to be a typical room. Most of the rooms were not this large and lacked the bay window seen here. The hotel burned on July 4, 1899, and a new one opened in 1902. It eventually closed in 1962 and was reconfigured as a warehouse for Goldsmith's Department Store. (Curt Teich Archives.)

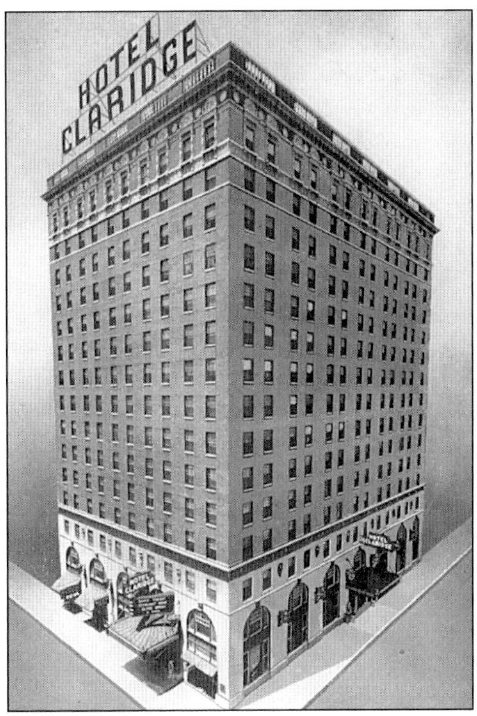

HOTEL CLARIDGE. The Hotel Claridge, located at 109 North Main, opened in April 1924, and for nearly 45 years, served as one of Memphis' well-known hotels. It was converted to apartments in 1968 and renovated in 1983. The hotel's exterior is brick, with the outside surfaces ornamented with limestone, making this an attractive 16-story structure. The hotel featured 400 rooms, each with a private bath, as well as select rooms with air conditioning. Typical hotel amenities included a tap room, coffeeshop, and cocktail lounge. All public space was air conditioned, a significant point considering Memphis' summertime heat.

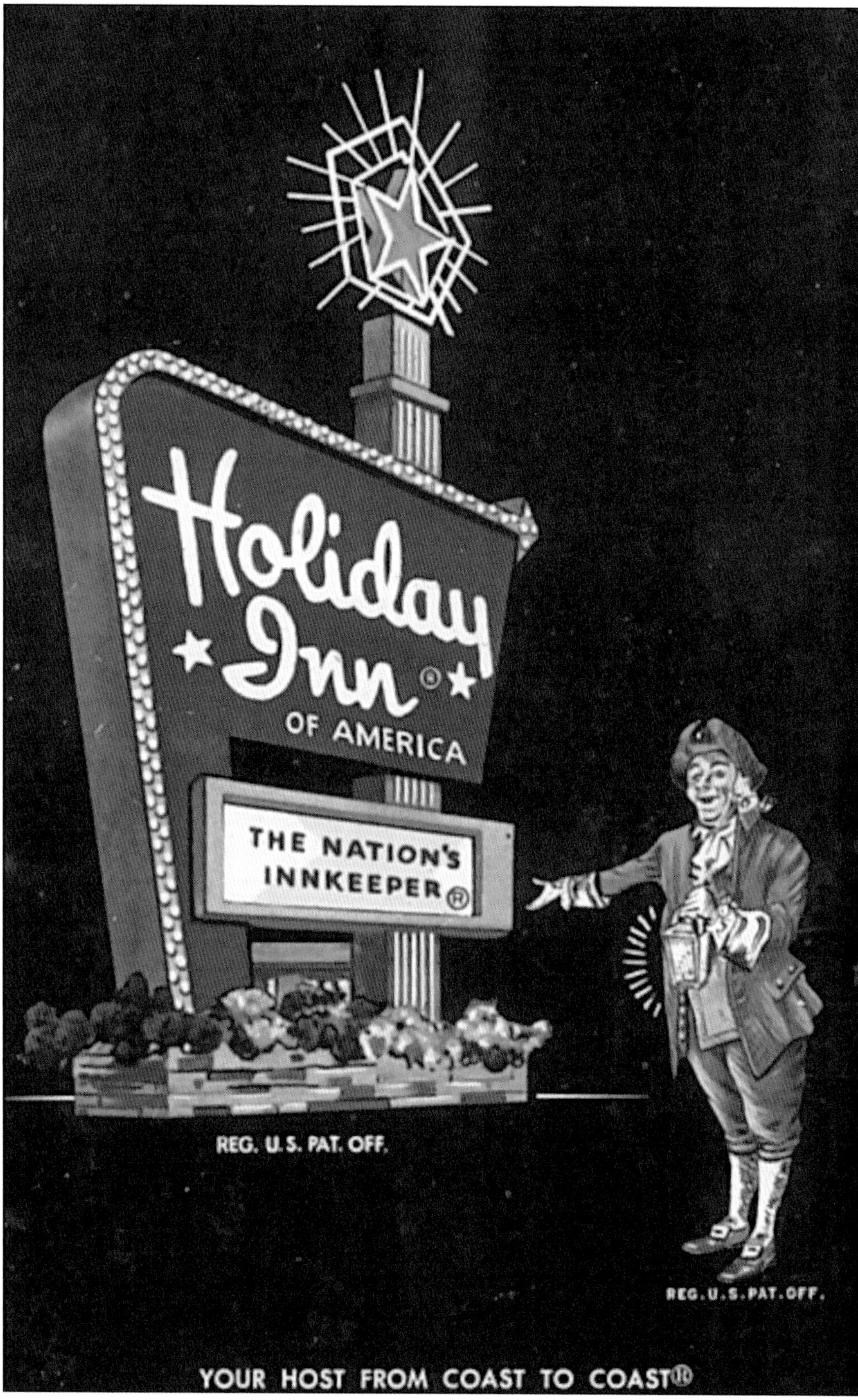

HOLIDAY INN LOGO WITH FIGURE. The famous Holiday Inn hotel chain, the world's largest, started in Memphis in late summer 1952, when Memphis home builder Kemmons Wilson opened the world's first Holiday Inn in the 4900 block of Summer Avenue. This 120-room motel would change the way American families spent vacation nights. (Curt Teich Archives.)

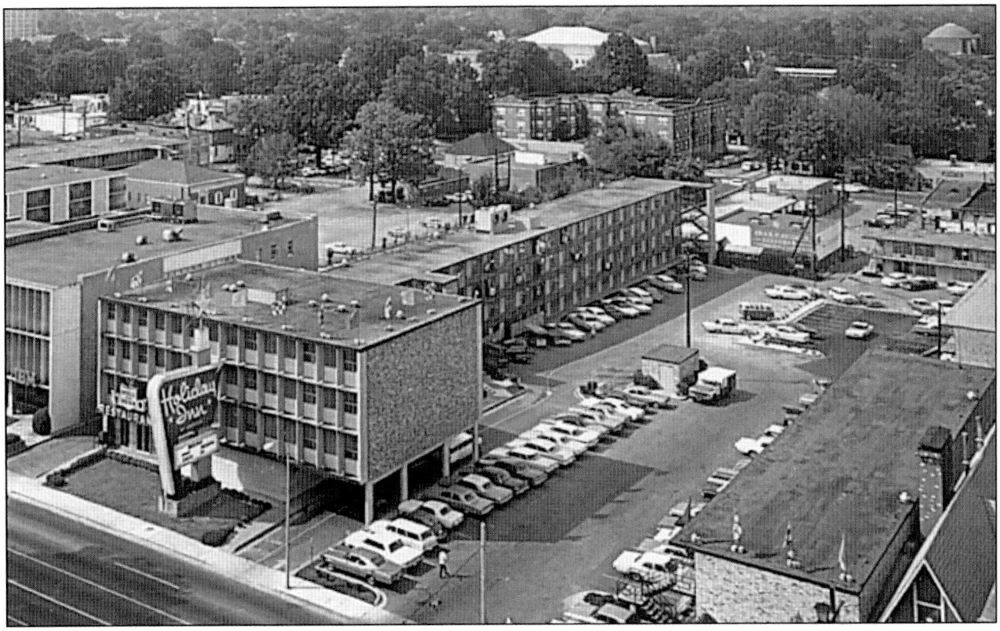

Holiday Inn. The Holiday Inns were opened as the result of an unsatisfactory family vacation that founder Kemmons Wilson, his wife, and his five children had taken to Washington, D.C., in 1951. On this vacation, he found hotels to be expensive, uncomfortable, and unpredictable. When he returned home, he quickly designed what would ultimately become known nationwide as "The Nation's Inkeeper." (Curt Teich Archives.)

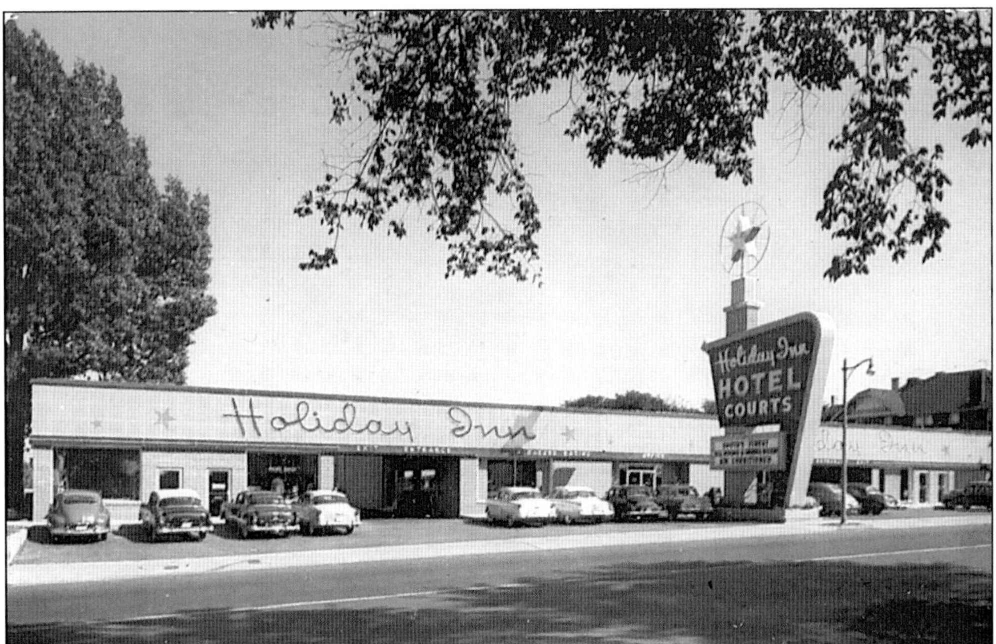

Holiday Inn Hotel Courts. By the time this postcard was made, there were four Holiday Inns in Memphis, with a combined total of 450 rooms. Each room featured air conditioning, steam heat, and a full bathroom.

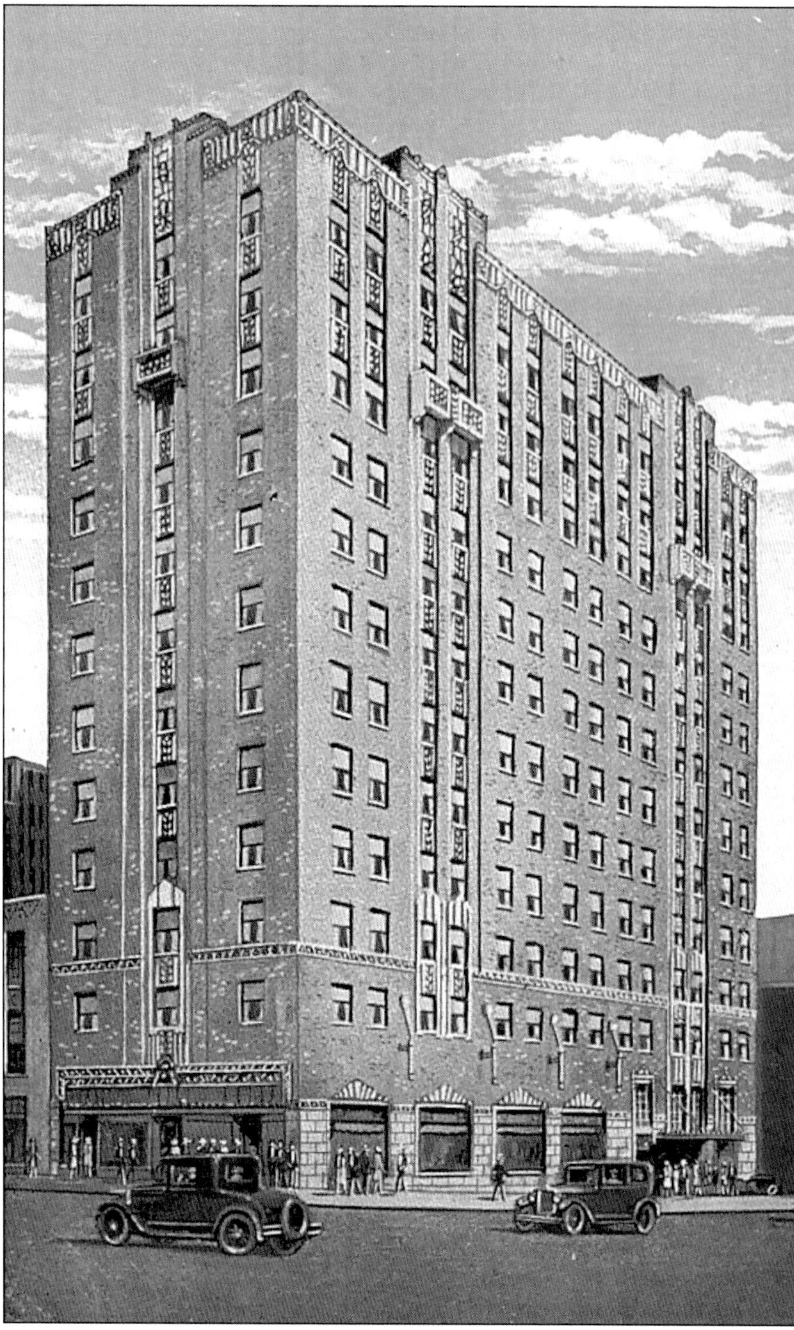

William Len Hotel. The William Len Hotel at 110 Monroe and South Main, opened October 3, 1930, and, as can be seen in this postcard, is a classic example of art deco architecture. It was named in honor of William Len Seaman, a wealthy Arkansas man who had at one time lived in Tennessee. This postcard, from 1930, states on the back that the William Len Hotel had 250 rooms and 250 baths as well as "every modern convenience" and the "finest coffee shop in the South." It was restored in the early 1980s and placed on the National Register of Historic Places in 1984. (Curt Teich Archives.)

William Len Hotel. This photo shows the rear of the William Len Hotel as it appeared in the late 1930s. As you can see from the blatant advertising, rooms started at $2 per night.

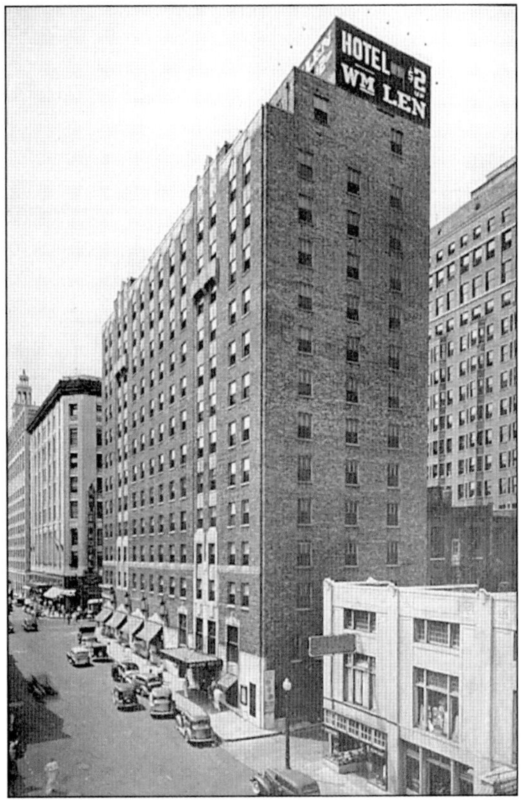

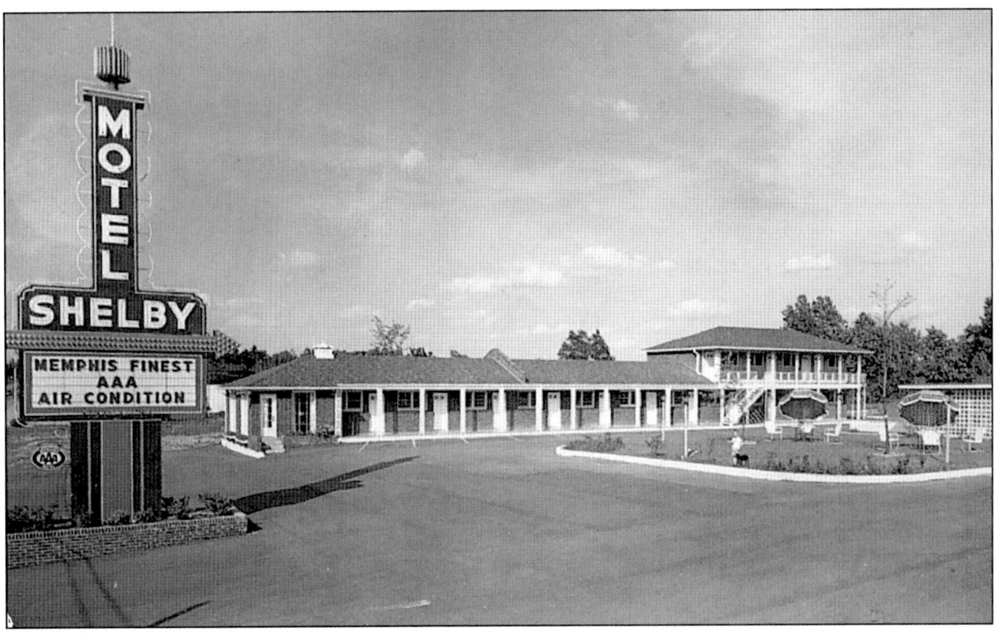

Shelby Motel. The Shelby Motel, named for Shelby County, was built in 1953 and consisted of 25 air-conditioned units, with TV available as an option. The motel was located out from town in an area called Bartlett, now just another part of Memphis.

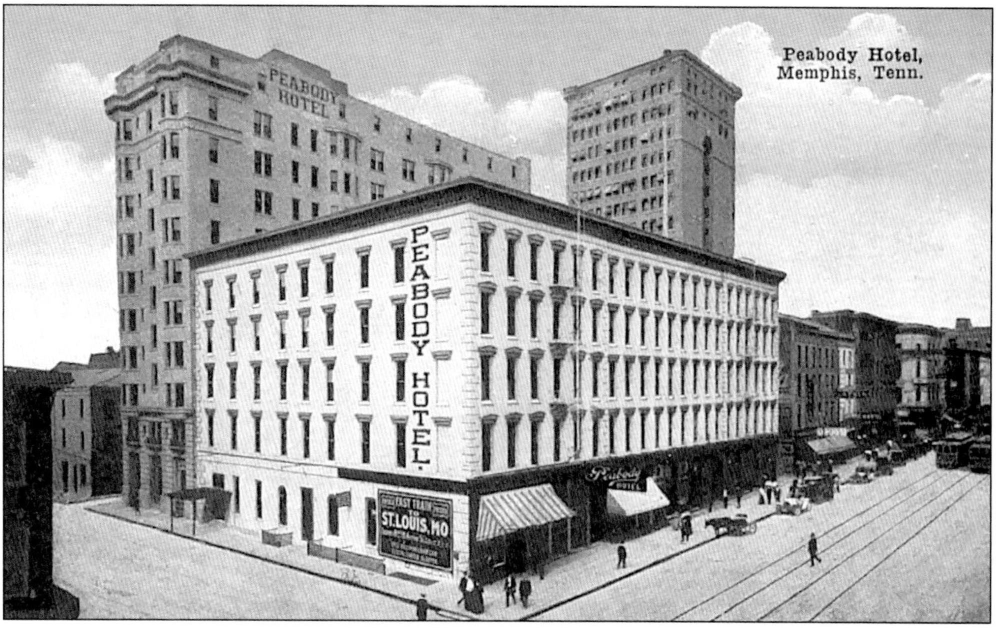

Peabody Hotel. When most Memphians think of the Peabody Hotel, they invariably imagine the current, 1925 Peabody. The first Peabody Hotel opened in 1869, was named for financial wizard George Peabody, and was first managed by D. Cockrell, former manager of the original Gayoso Hotel. Few people today even know that an earlier Peabody ever existed. These two images of the old Peabody Hotel show the same structure from different angles. This was the first Peabody Hotel as it appeared prior to 1923.

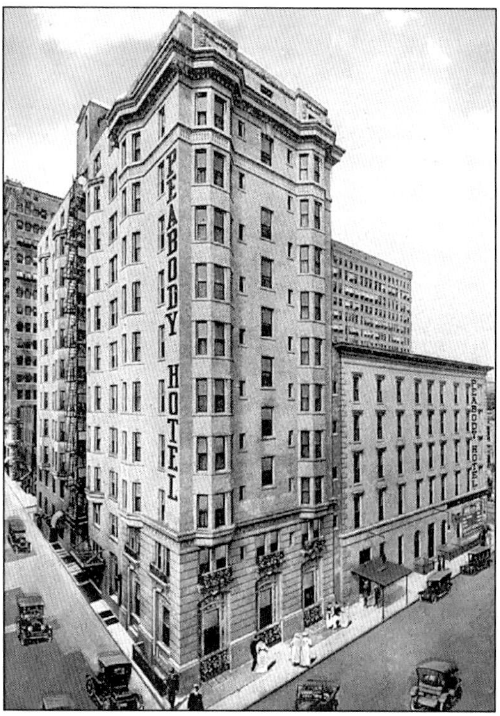

Peabody Hotel. The Peabody Hotel had survived competition from the elegant Gayoso, only to become second fiddle to the newer Chisca. The first Peabody was torn down in 1923 and replaced with Lowenstein's, a department store. The Peabody Hotel's fortunes, both the first and second hotels, ebbed and flowed with the city's fortunes. (Curt Teich Archives.)

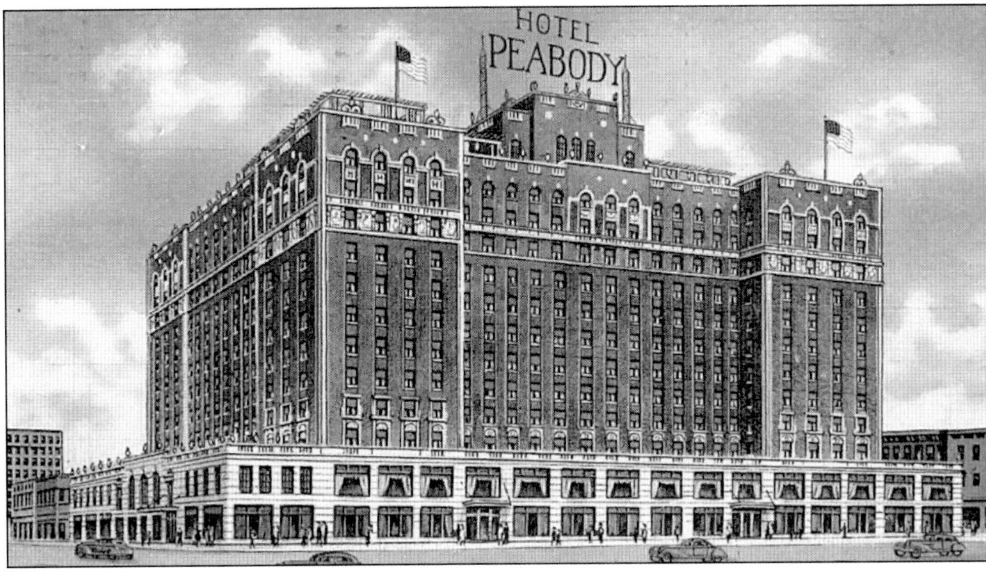

PEABODY HOTEL. The second and current Peabody Hotel, known as the New Peabody, opened in September 1925 with 625 rooms. It was designed by Walter Ahlschlager, a Chicago architect, and remains the city's grand hotel more than 75 years after it originally opened. The proud hotel underwent continuing financial difficulties and was sold several times before closing in April 1975. It sold at public auction for a mere $540,000 and was boarded up, seemingly for good. (Curt Teich Archives.)

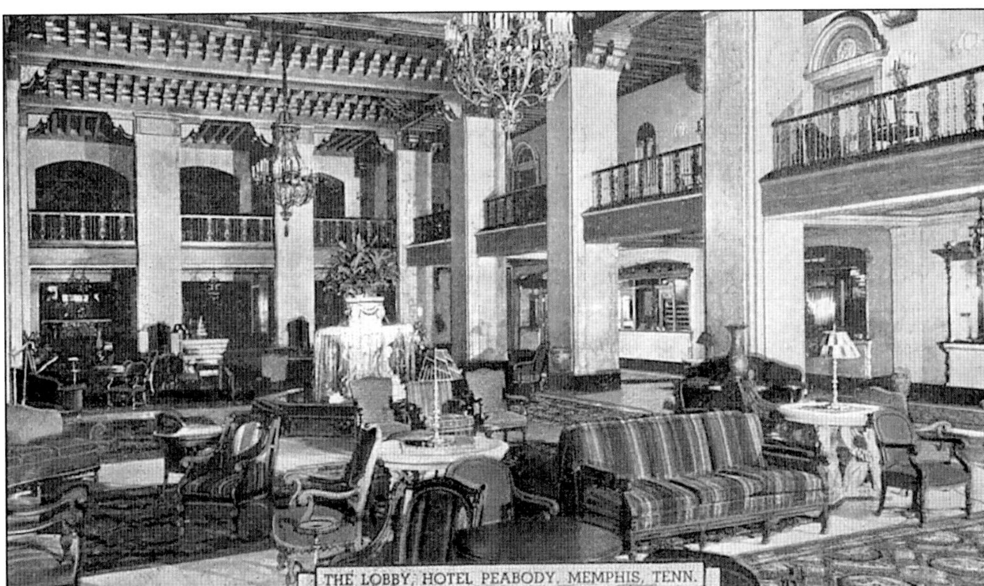

PEABODY HOTEL LOBBY. The elegant lobby of the Peabody Hotel, pictured here in the 1930s, looks much the same as it did 70 years ago. Now, however, there is a bar at the far end of the room. The second level mezzanine leads to spacious banquet and convention rooms. The Peabody Hotel exists today thanks to the work of the Belz Family. They undertook the project and restored it to its original grandeur. For this, the entire nation owes them a great and unpayable debt. It would truly be impossible to imagine a Memphis without the Peabody Hotel.

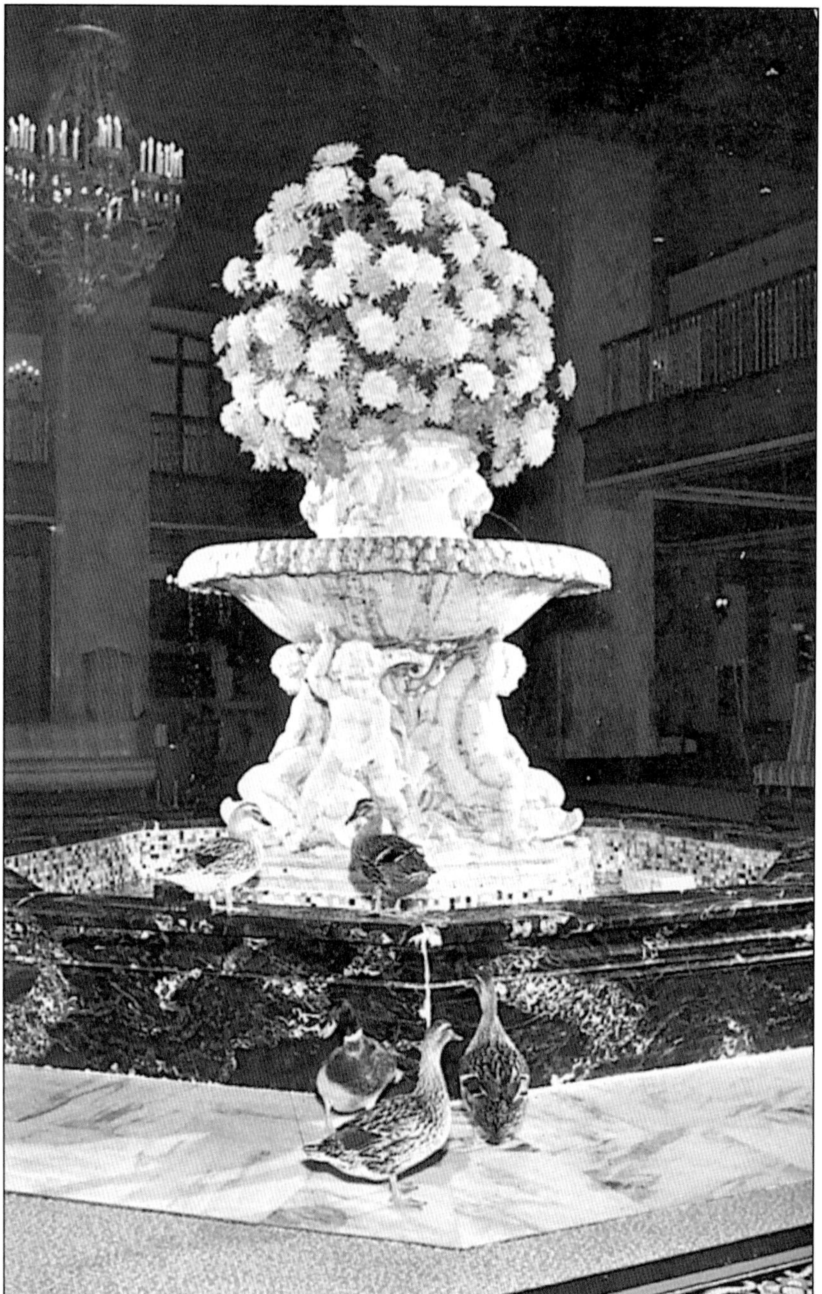

PEABODY HOTEL FOUNTAIN. The Peabody Hotel is known worldwide for its duck-inhabited fountain. The fountain, located in the center of the first floor lobby, was constructed from a single piece of marble. The ducks were first placed in the fountain by hotel manager Frank Schutt in 1932 and have since become a Memphis tradition. Every morning, the ducks are ceremoniously escorted to the ground floor fountain from their outdoor penthouse via elevator and red carpet. Every evening, they are returned by the same route to their place of residence on the hotel's roof.

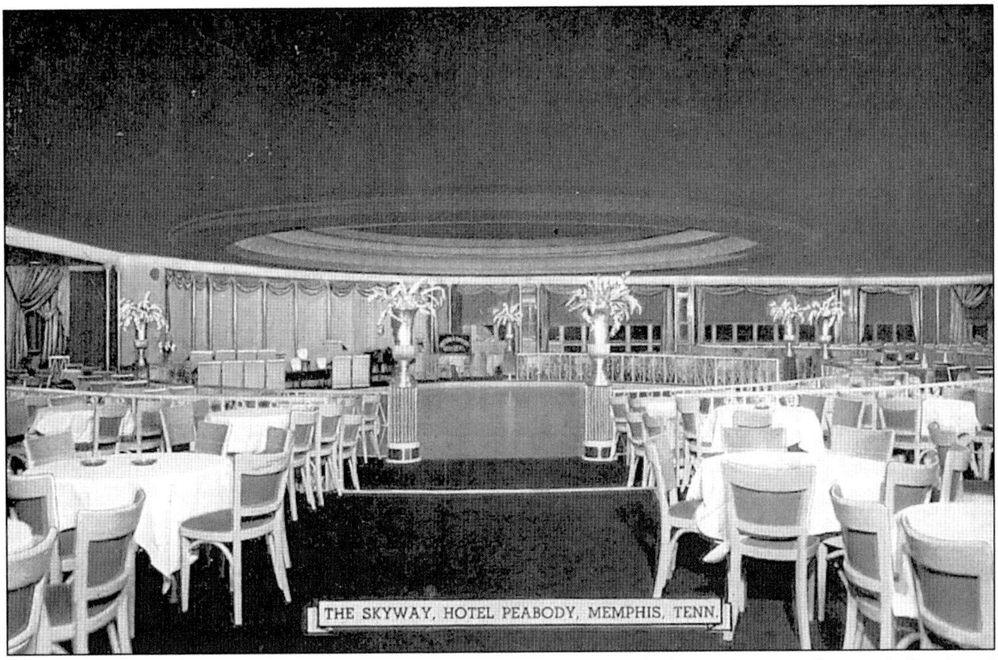

SKYWAY PEABODY HOTEL. The popular Skyway was installed on the top floor of the hotel in 1938 and has, since that time, served as a night club and as a private room for weddings, receptions, and conventions, as well as a concert venue and ballroom. At the time of this picture, the Skyway served as a supper club, with a seated dinner followed by entertainment, referred to in those days as a "floor show."

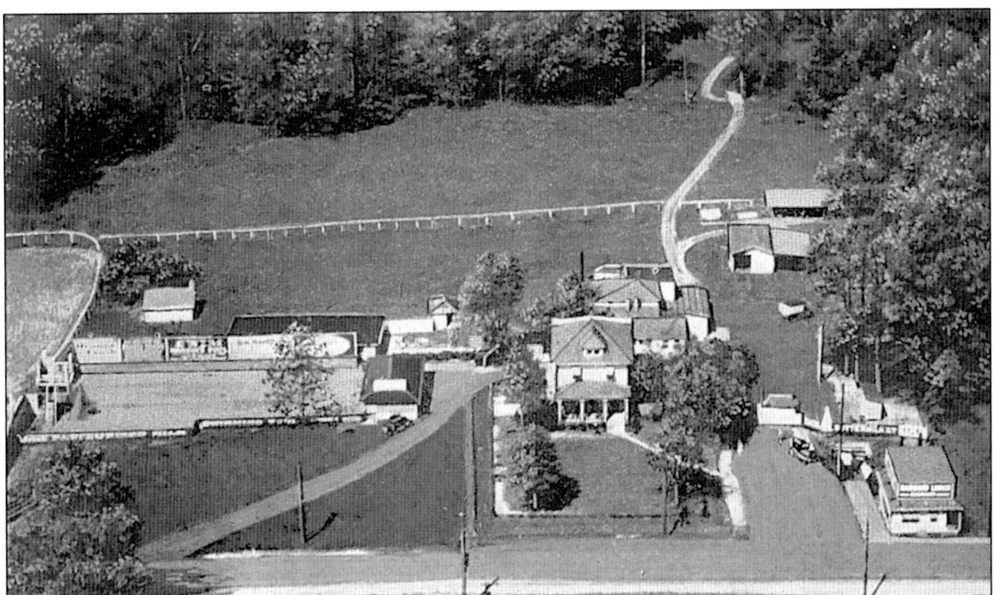

HARBIN'S TOURIST CAMP SWIMMING POOL. Harbin's billed itself as a tourist camp, as opposed to a standard motel or tourist court. It was located on Highway 51, apparently at a converted farm.

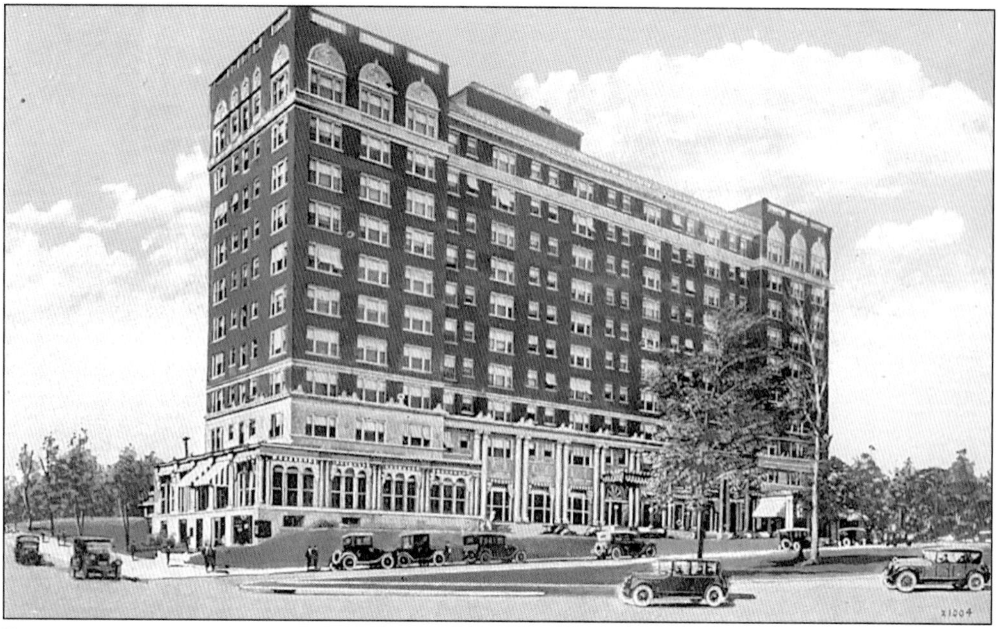

PARKVIEW HOTEL. The Parkview Hotel was at its zenith when this late 1920s postcard image was made. It was quite stunning architecturally and was, during its day, the equal of any hotel in the South.

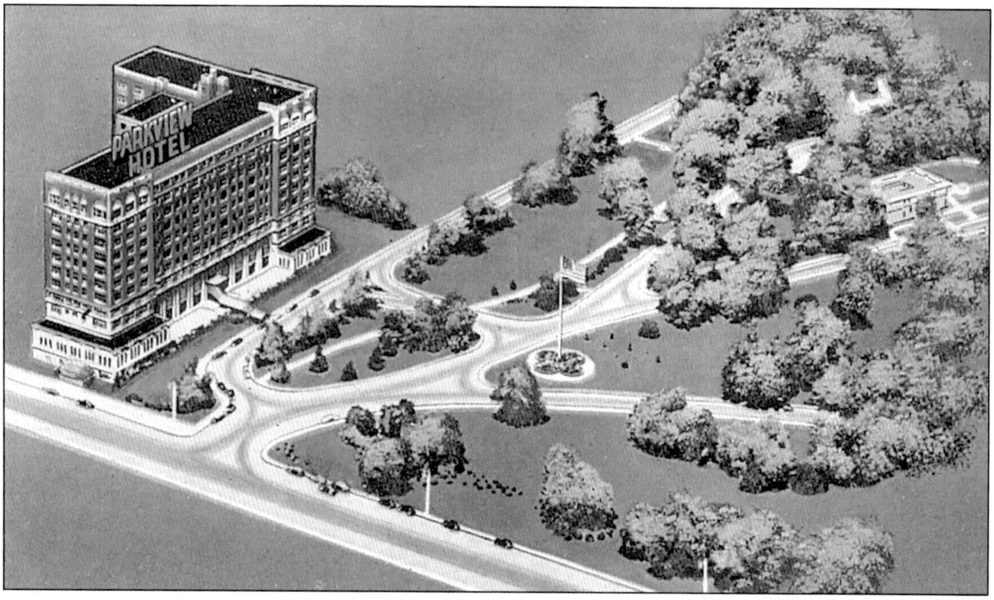

PARKVIEW HOTEL. The Parkview Hotel, as seen in this aerial view, shows its proximity to the golf course and to the Brooks Museum. This hotel, unlike the Peabody, King Cotton, or other notables, was located several miles from downtown. This location, away from the business district, no doubt had an adverse effect on the hotel's fortunes. The Parkview made the transition from hotel to residential hotel to apartments to retirement community. Still, in its day, it was one of the finest hotels in the entire city. Even today it remains a living monument to the type of lodging available in larger Southern cities. (Curt Teich Archives.)

Six

Clubs and Restaurants

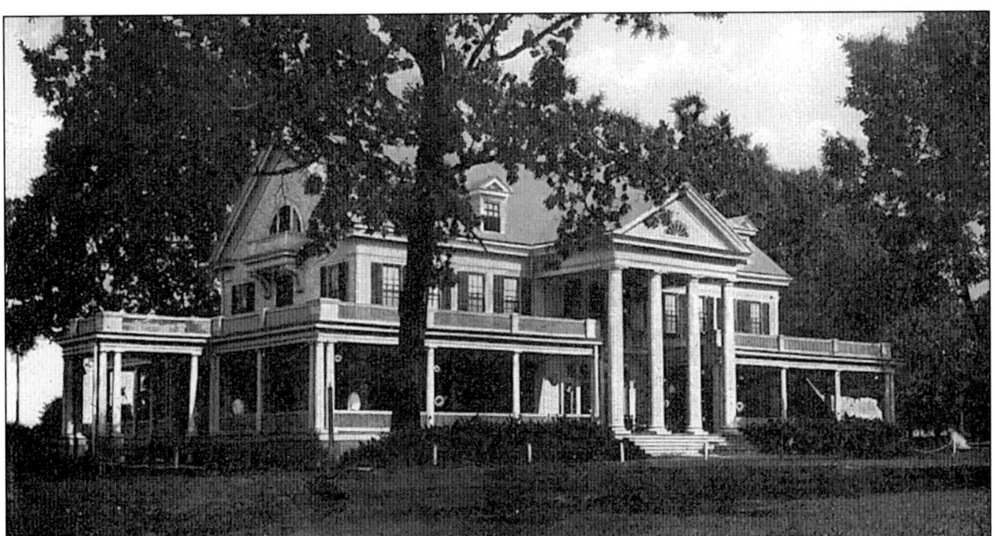

New Country Club. The New Country Club building, pictured here, was actually built prior to the War between the States. It burned in 1910, and a new structure was built on the same spot.

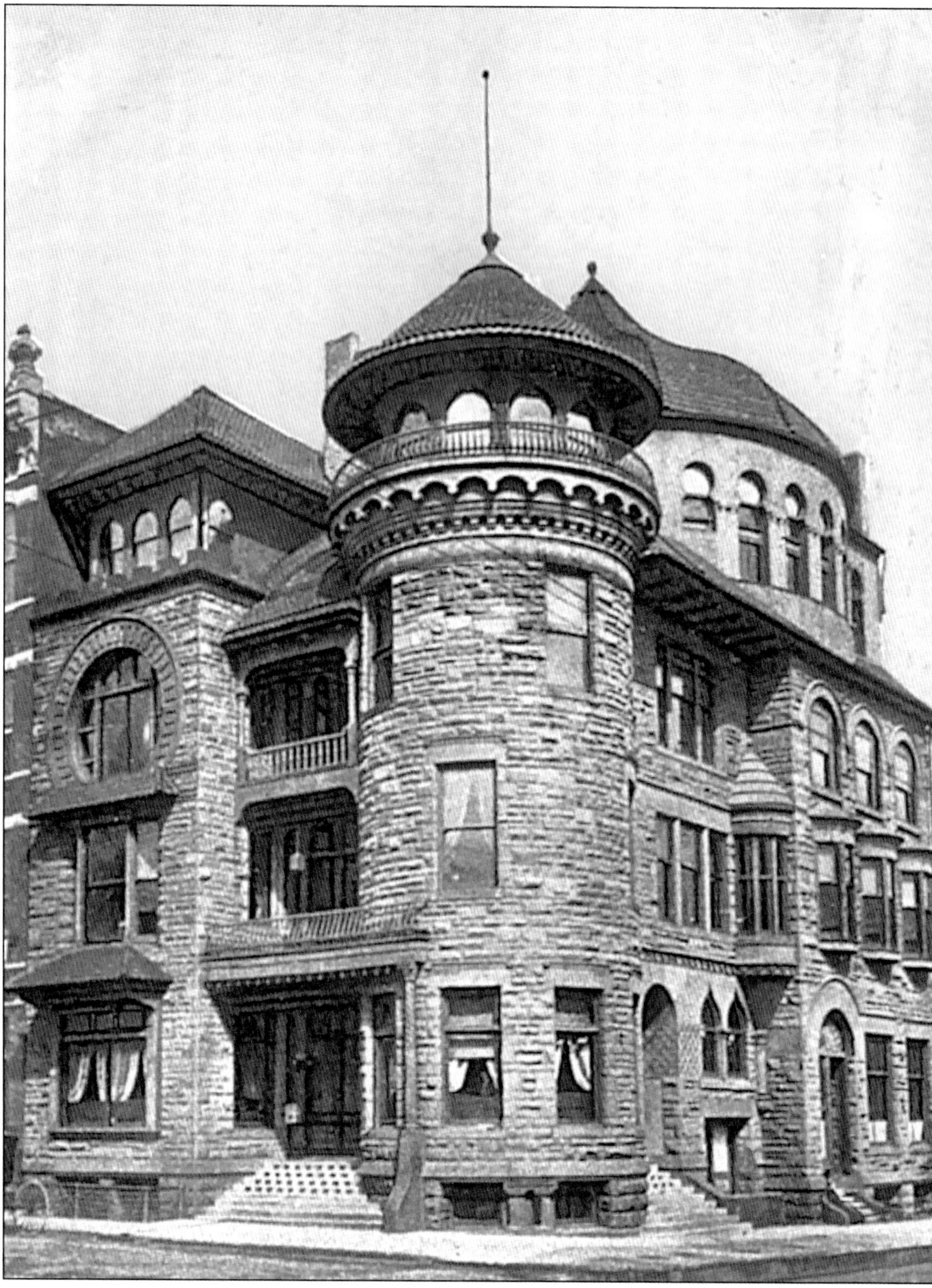

Tennessee Club. This 1907 postcard shows the heavy-looking cut stone Tennessee Club, which still exists today as office space. The massive building, built in 1890, looks more like a castle than anything else and appears to be basically Richardsonian Romanesque in style.

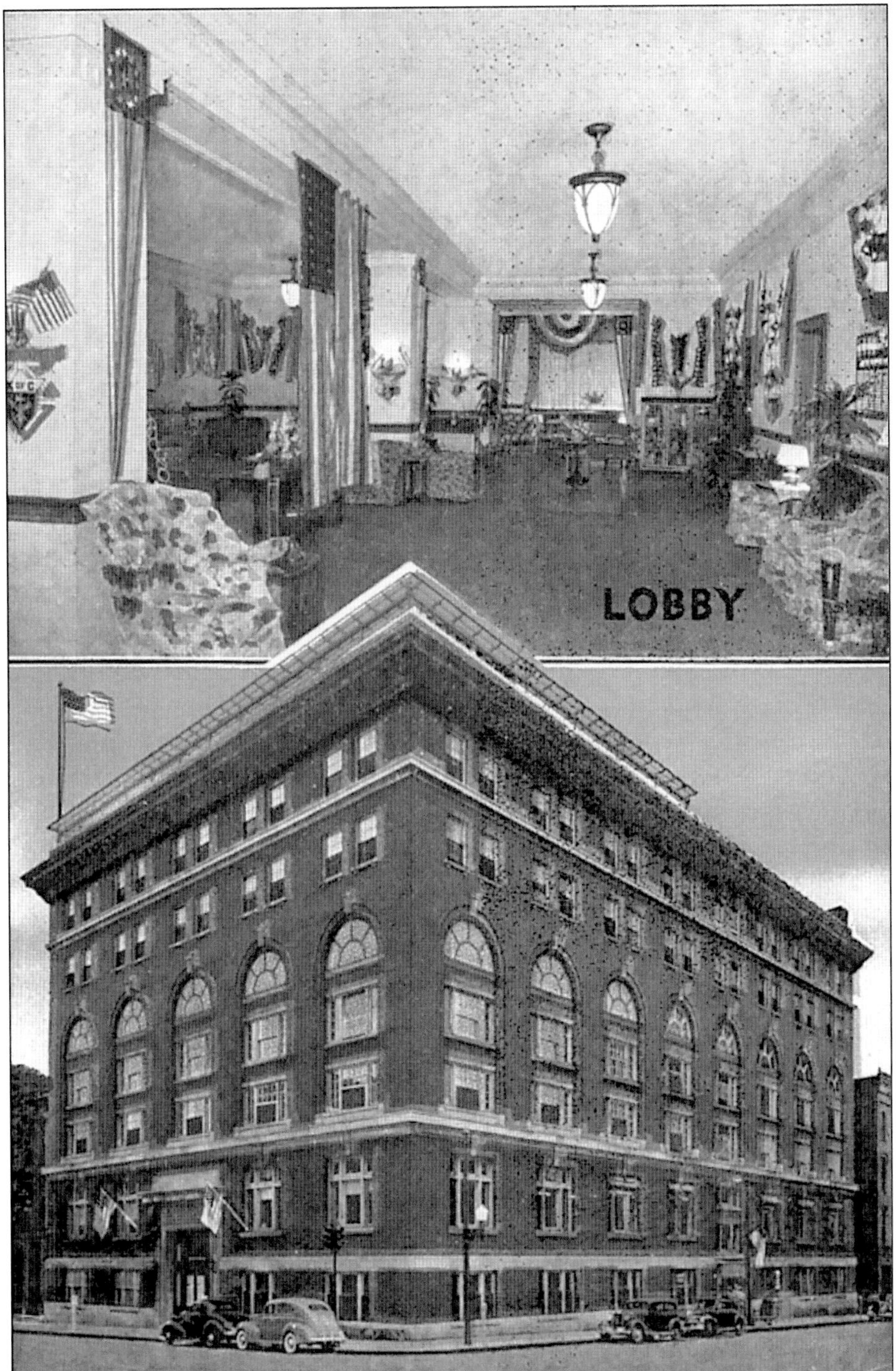

Knights of Columbus and Catholic Club. The Knights of Columbus and Catholic Club Building, seen here in this 1930s postcard, was located at Third Street and Adams. The building itself, along with its formal lobby, resembles a 1920s hotel.

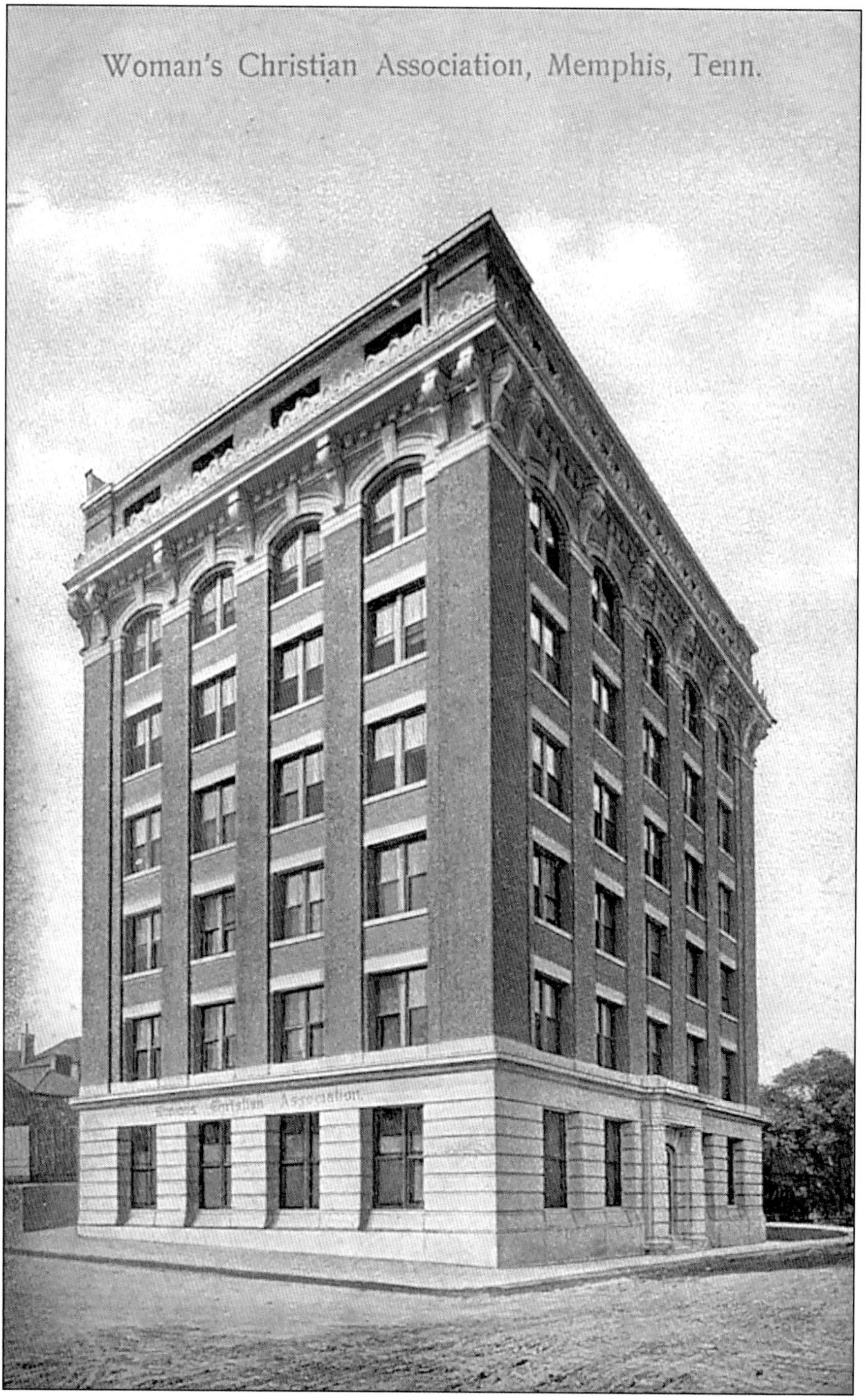

Woman's Christian Association. The seven-story Woman's Christian Association Building, seen here, is typical of the architectural style of the early part of the twentieth century. Buildings of this type, depending upon ownership, usually offered administrative space as well as room for activities and recreation and, in some cases, rooms for lodgers.

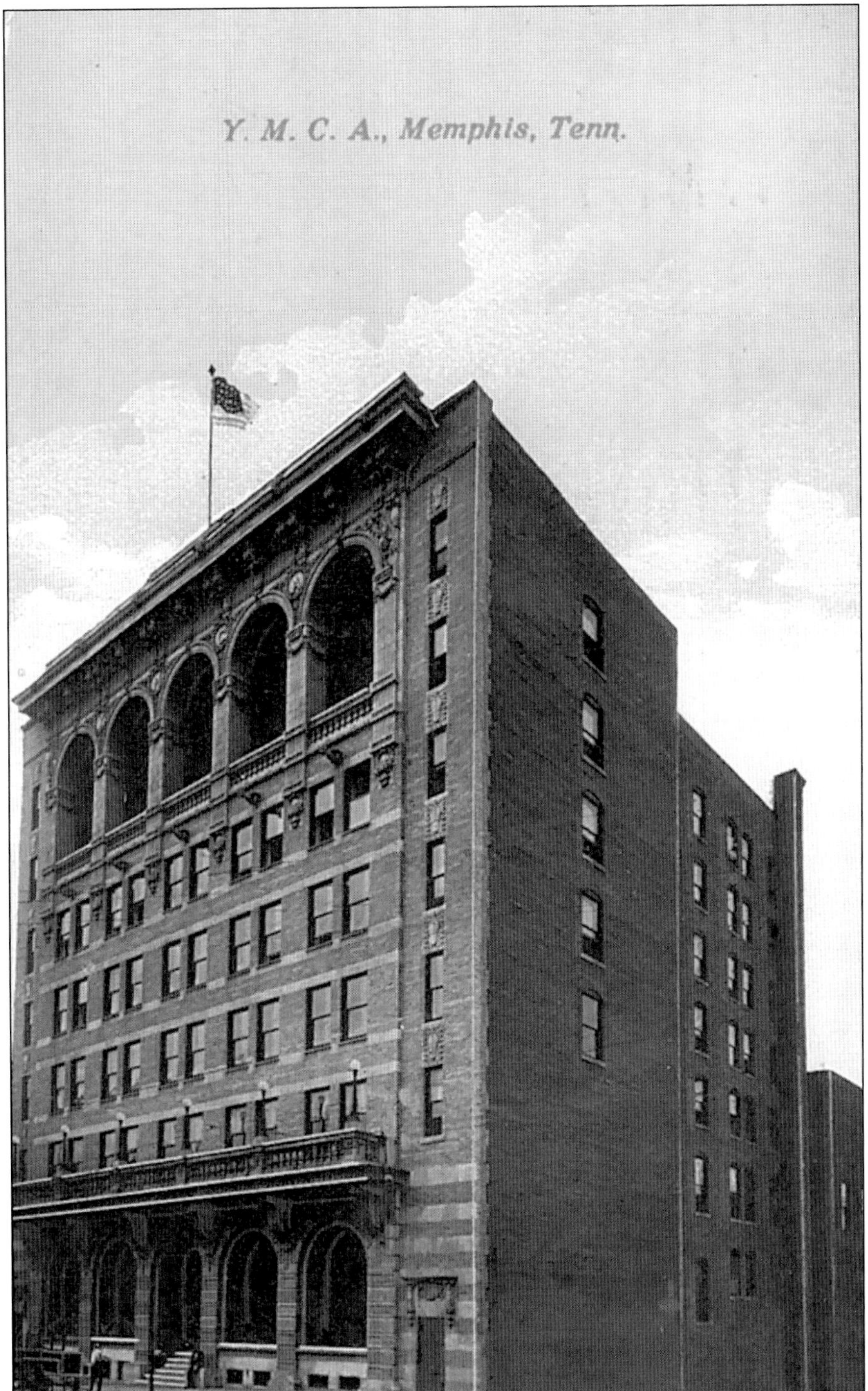

YMCA. This 1911 postcard shows the Young Men's Christian Association Building. The formal facade differs from the rest of the building, and yet, despite its ornate front, the building was, for the most part, utilitarian.

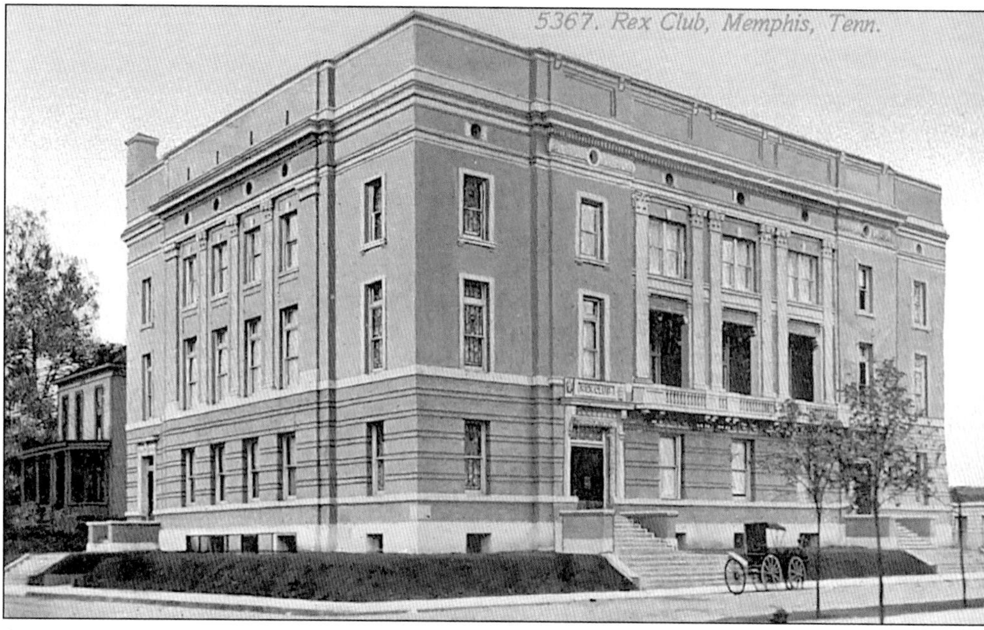

REX CLUB. This postcard of the Rex Club shows a carriage parked in front of the building, but the horse appears to be strangely absent. Note again the juxtaposition of commercial and residential property. In the early history of major cities, most monied people lived within the city limits, actually downtown. Having a giant building immediately next door did not seem to bother the urban dweller.

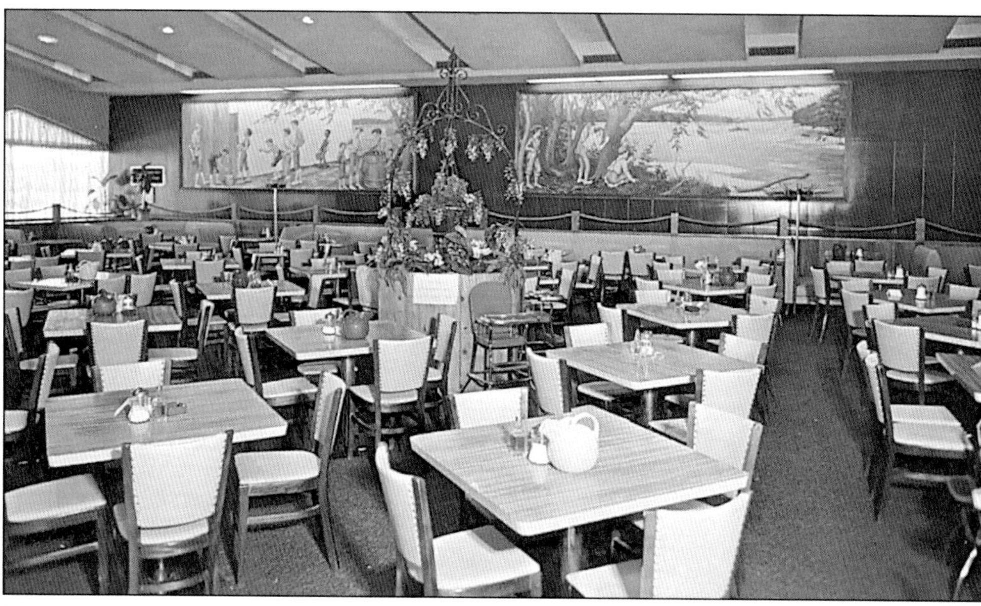

MARK TWAIN. In the South, during the golden age of motoring between 1945 and 1965, many Americans enjoyed prosperity for the first time. This meant cars and travel. The Mark Twain "Family Cafeteria" was located at 4320 Summer Avenue, also known as Highways 64-70-79, one of the main thoroughfares entering or leaving the city. As may be seen from this postcard, its large size was typical of the 1950s and 1960s, the zenith of American cafeterias.

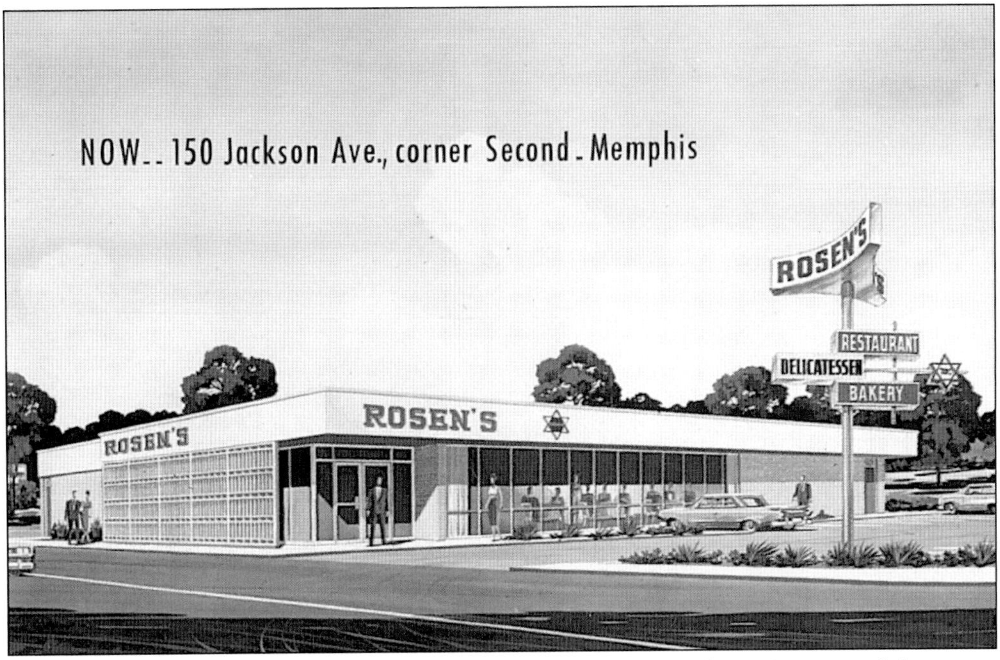

ROSEN'S. Pictured here was Rosen's new, larger building at 150 Jackson Avenue and the corner of Second. This kosher delicatessen, restaurant, and bakery is now just a memory.

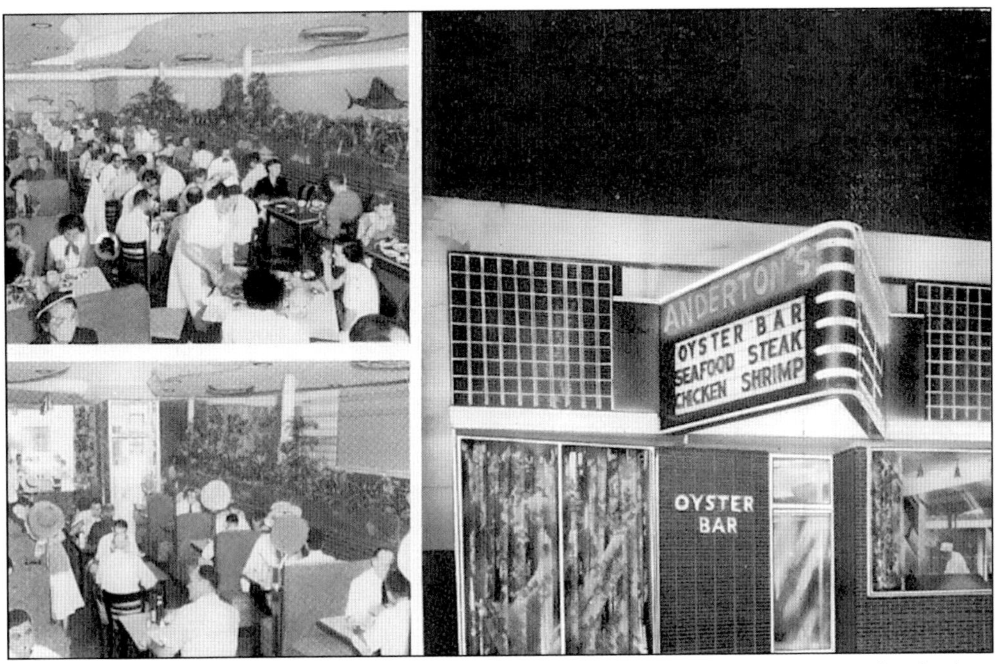

ANDERTON'S. While Memphis has long been famous for its native foods, especially the best barbeque ribs in the world, few restaurant postcards remain. This collage shows Anderton's, one of Memphis' oldest and most famous restaurants. The massive pale-green building is still open for business as pictured at 1901 Madison Avenue in the Midtown area.

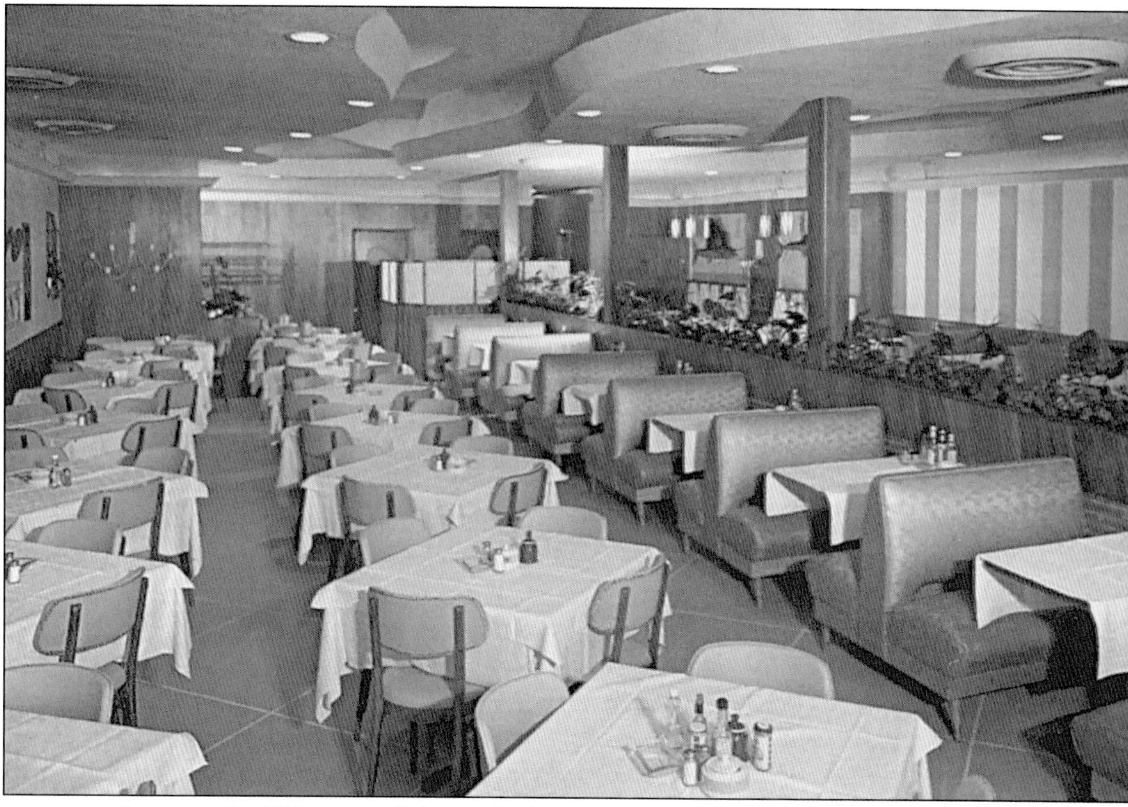

ANDERTON'S. This postcard shows the large interior of this popular Memphis landmark. The inscription on the back of this postcard, as well as on the previous one, indicates that no visit to Memphis is complete without a meal at Anderton's.

Seven

BUILDINGS

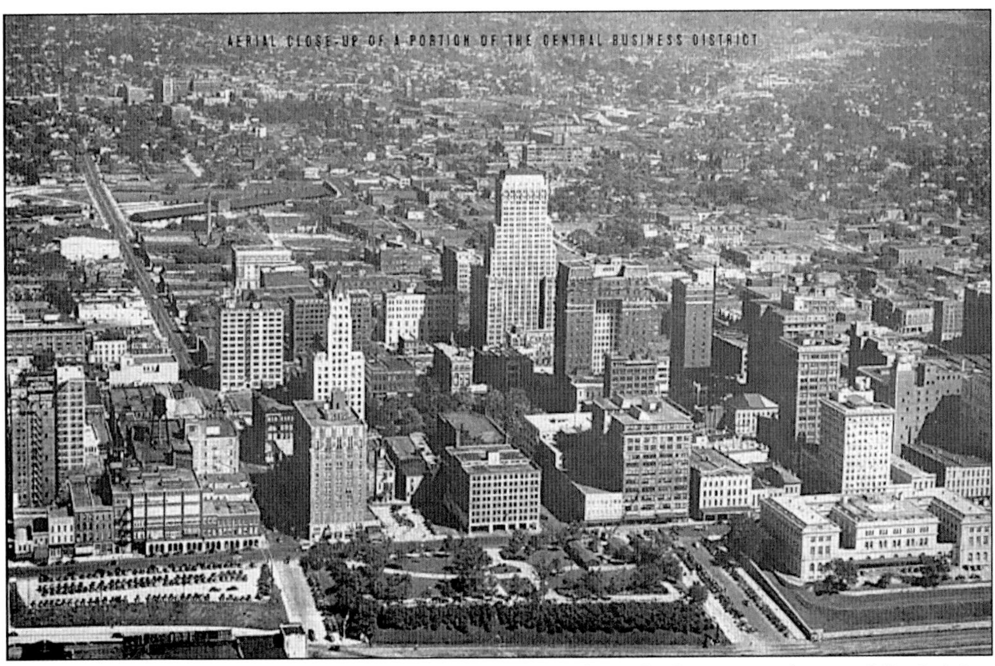

AERIAL CLOSE UP. This wide-angle view of downtown from the late 1930s shows a fully thriving city. Memphis, despite being younger than Nashville, quickly established itself as Tennessee's largest and, many would say, most important city. Most of the city's important buildings can be clearly distinguished here.

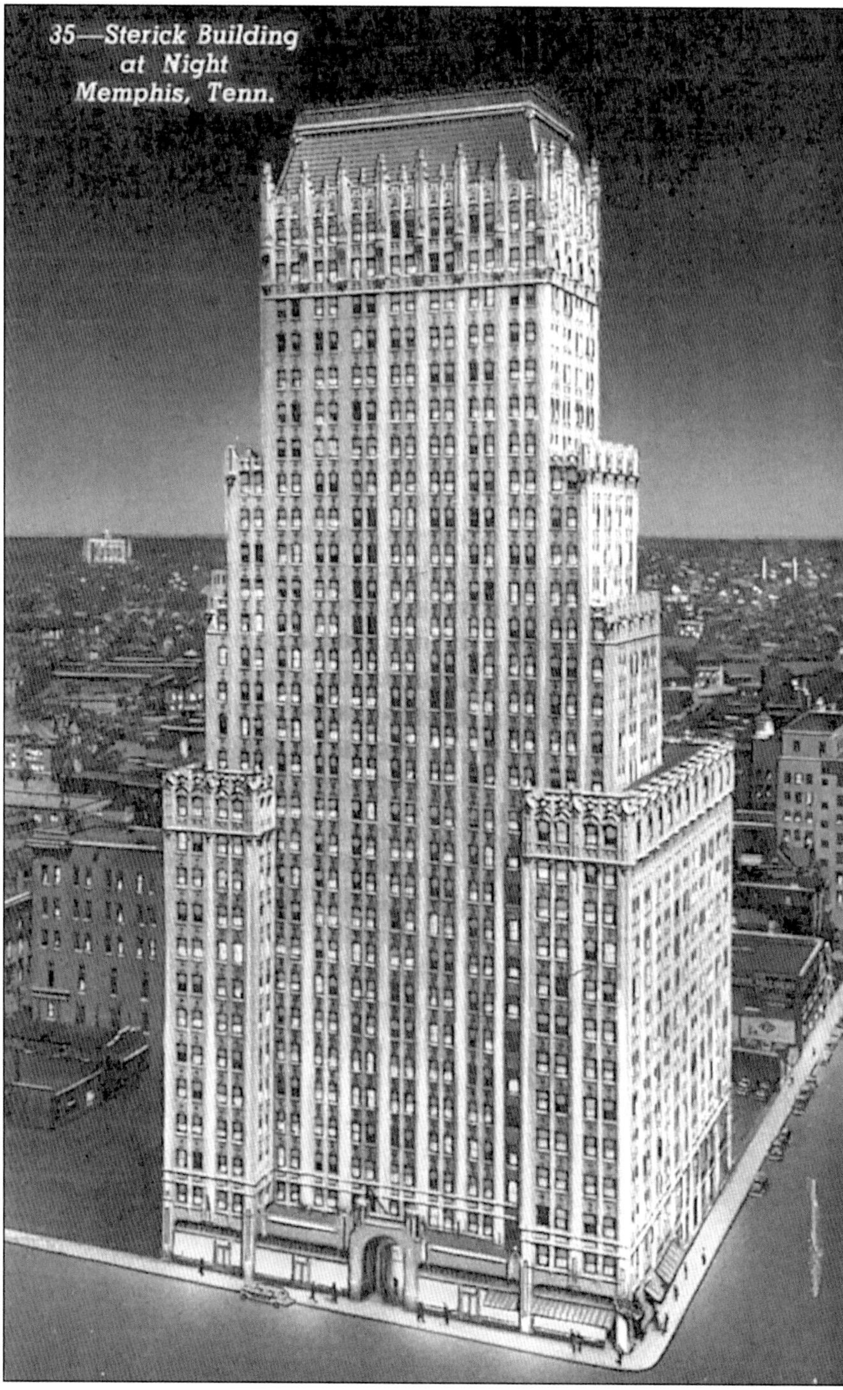

Sterick Building at Night. The Sterick Building, in this 1948 postcard, clearly dwarfs anything in the surrounding architectural landscape. Often postcard images depicting large buildings show the surrounding buildings removed, so as not to distract the eye of the viewer. Perhaps this was considered unnecessary in this case, due to the Sterick's complete domination of the scene. (Curt Teich Archives.)

STERICK BUILDING. There has always been an unspoken competition between Memphis and Nashville. It is interesting to note that when Nashville built its first skyscraper, it was taller than Memphis' tallest building (seen here), but only by one story. This aerial shot of the Sterick Building shows its size as well as its graceful lines.

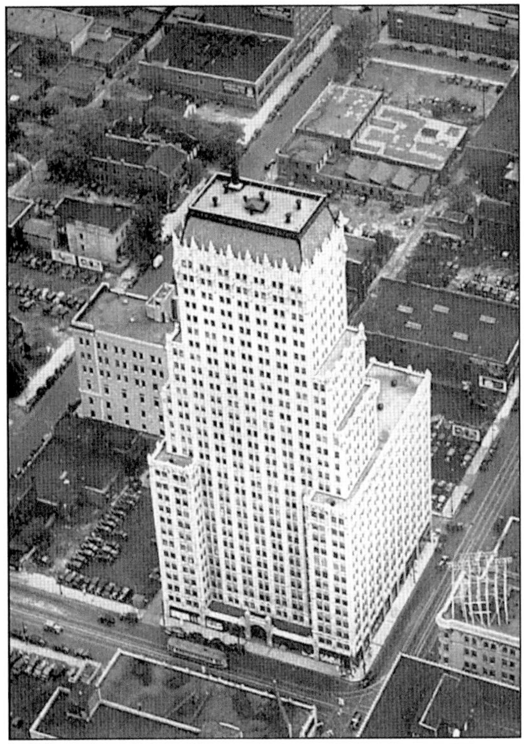

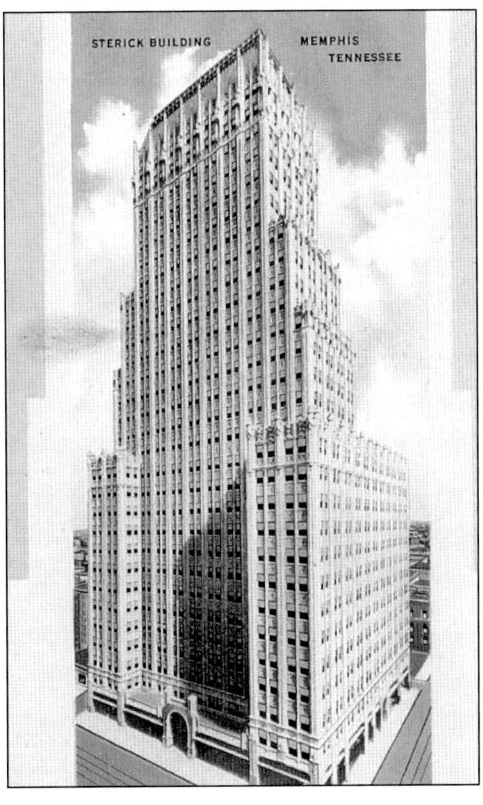

STERICK BUILDING. The 29-story Sterick Tower, as it was known, was completed in 1930 and was at one time the tallest building in the South. Its classic symmetry and elegant lines betray the building's sheer mass. The Sterick Tower is significant in Tennessee architecture in that it was more than 25 years later that Nashville, the state capital, got its first skyscraper with the construction of the 30-story Life & Casualty Building.

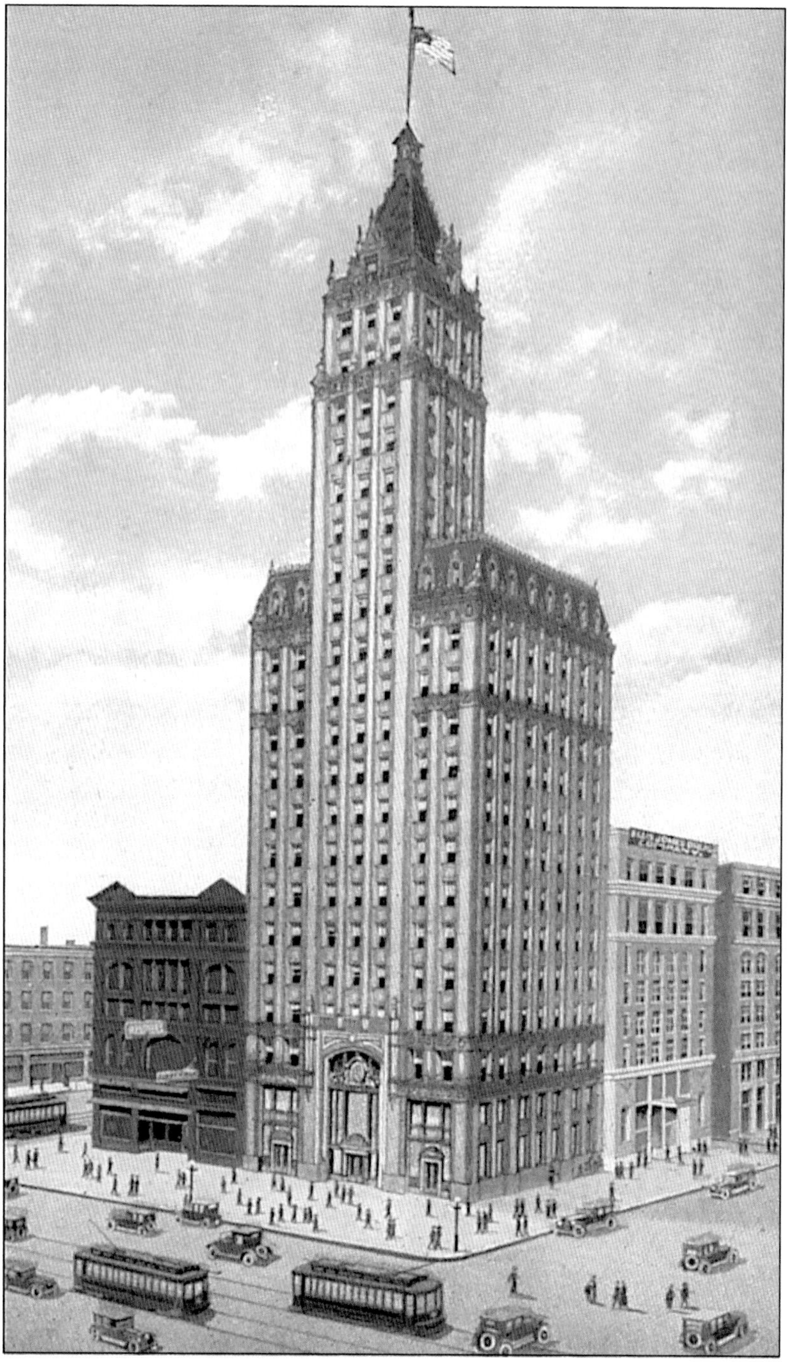

COLUMBIAN MUTUAL TOWER. Now known as Lincoln America Tower, this 21-story, 1924 building, which stands at 60 North Main, was built at a cost of $1,500,000. The building, which contains 266 offices, has long been a Memphis landmark and was, at the time of its construction, the tallest building in Memphis. It was new when this postcard was sent in 1927, and it is typical of early skyscrapers of the time. The green tile roof as well as the symmetry of the building contribute to its timeless elegance. (Curt Teich Archives.)

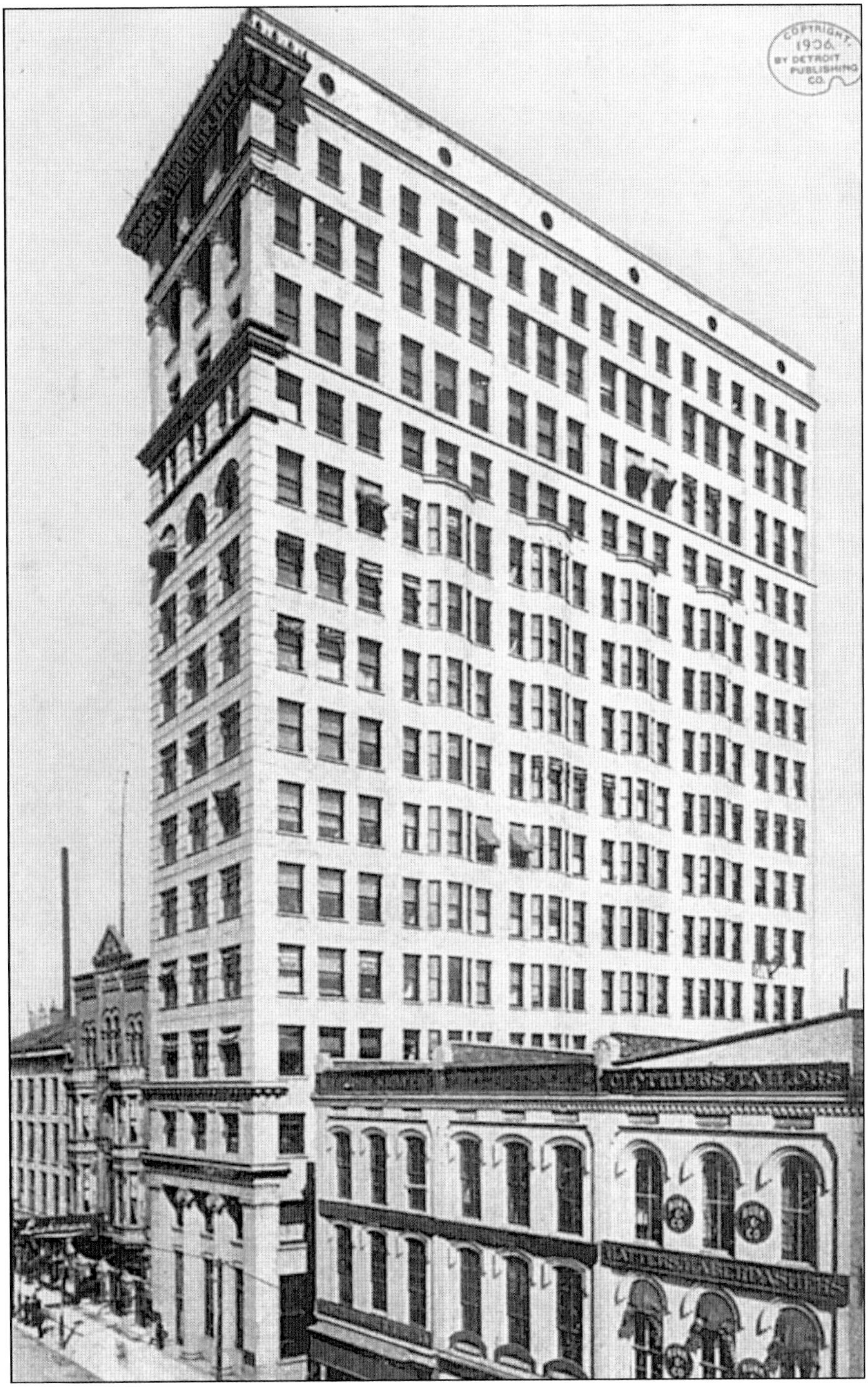

MEMPHIS TRUST CO. One interesting note about Memphis architecture is that many of the larger downtown office buildings have changed ownership over the years. The Memphis Trust Company Building on South Main falls into this category. It was built in 1904 and is now called the Commerce Title Building. This photo was taken in 1906, shortly after it was erected.

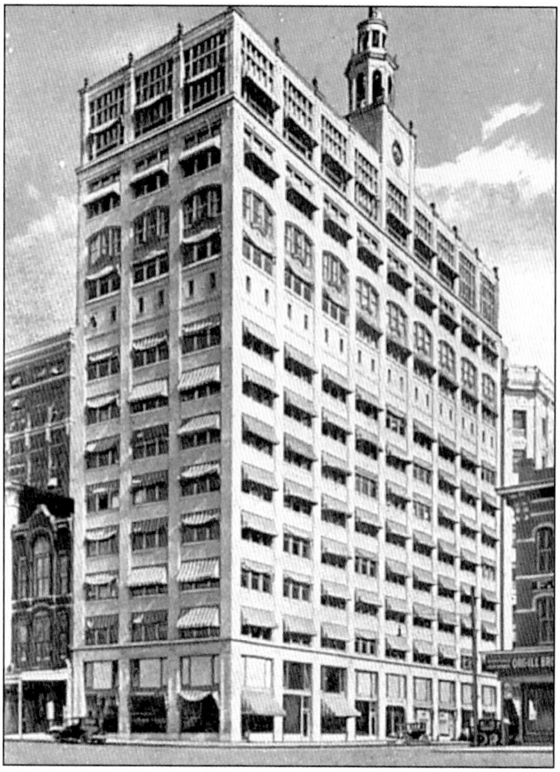

The Shrine Building. The Shrine Building on Monroe was designed to serve as a Shrine temple as well as a commercial building, with stores on the first level, rental office space higher up, and then Shrine use beginning on the ninth floor. The building possessed a rooftop restaurant, billiard room, two-story auditorium, and an underground swimming pool. It is seen here in this late 1920s postcard, shortly after its completion in 1923. The building, as seen here, possessed a multi-tiered rooftop cupola reminiscent to that of the Hibernia Bank Building in New Orleans, though to a much smaller degree. It was subsequently removed, and the building was converted to apartments in the late 1970s. Notice the awnings over the windows. They were functional and helped shield the building's occupants from the summer heat. (Curt Teich Archives.)

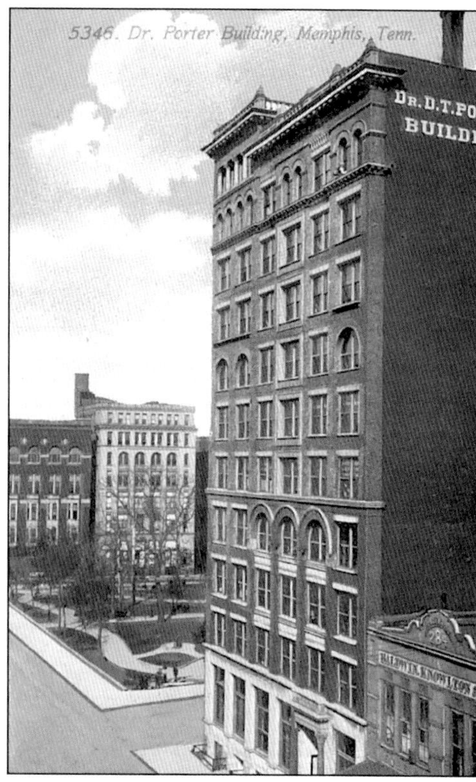

D.T. Porter Building. What became known as the Dr. D.T. Porter Building, at 10 North Main Street, was built in 1895 as the Continental Bank Building and is considered to be the first skyscraper in Memphis. It was renovated in the early 1980s and turned into an apartment building.

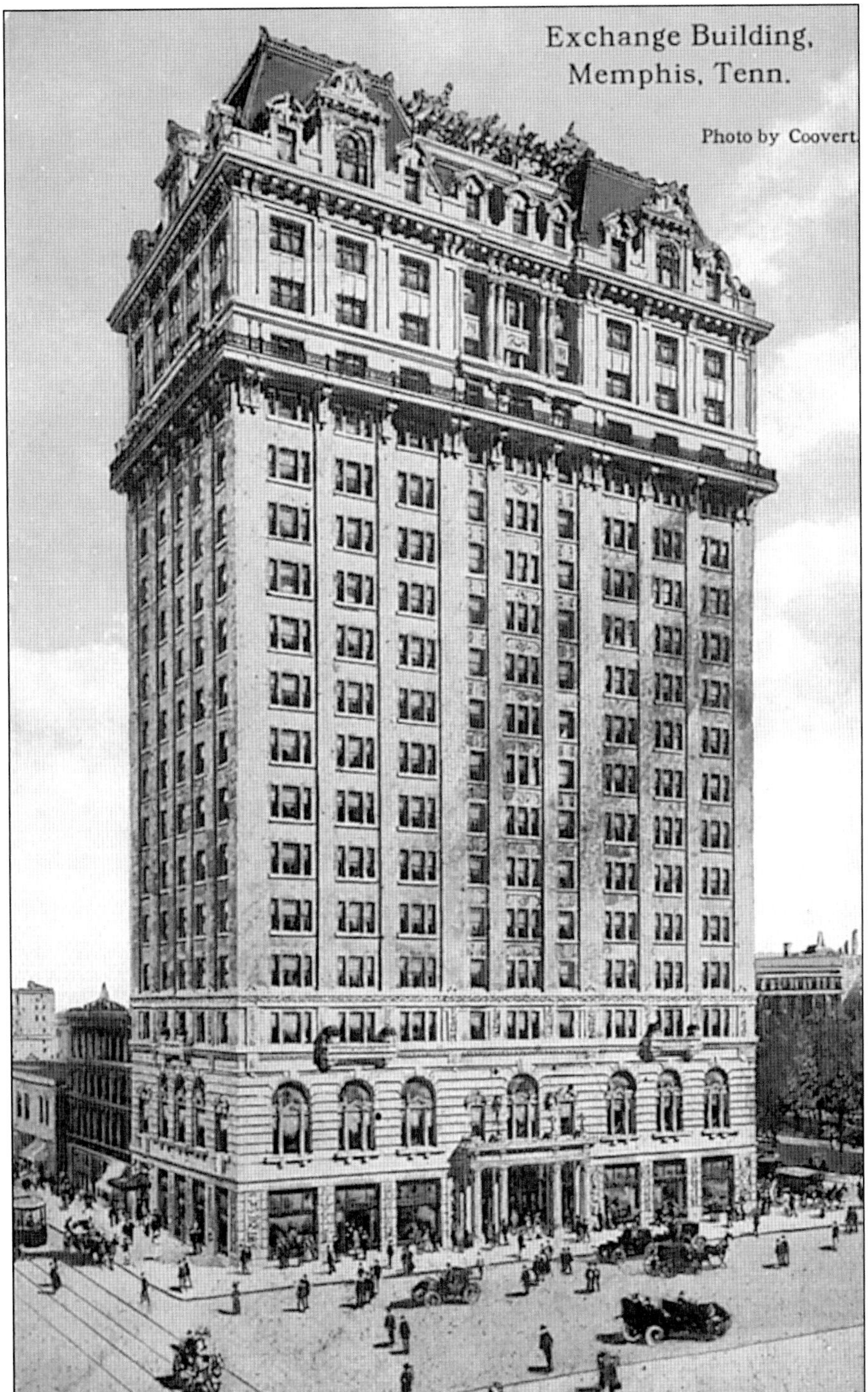

EXCHANGE BUILDING. The ornate 19-story Exchange Building is arguably the most recognizable building in the Memphis skyline. Its green copper French chateau-styled roof, along with the heavy ornamentation on the top levels, immediately catches the eye.

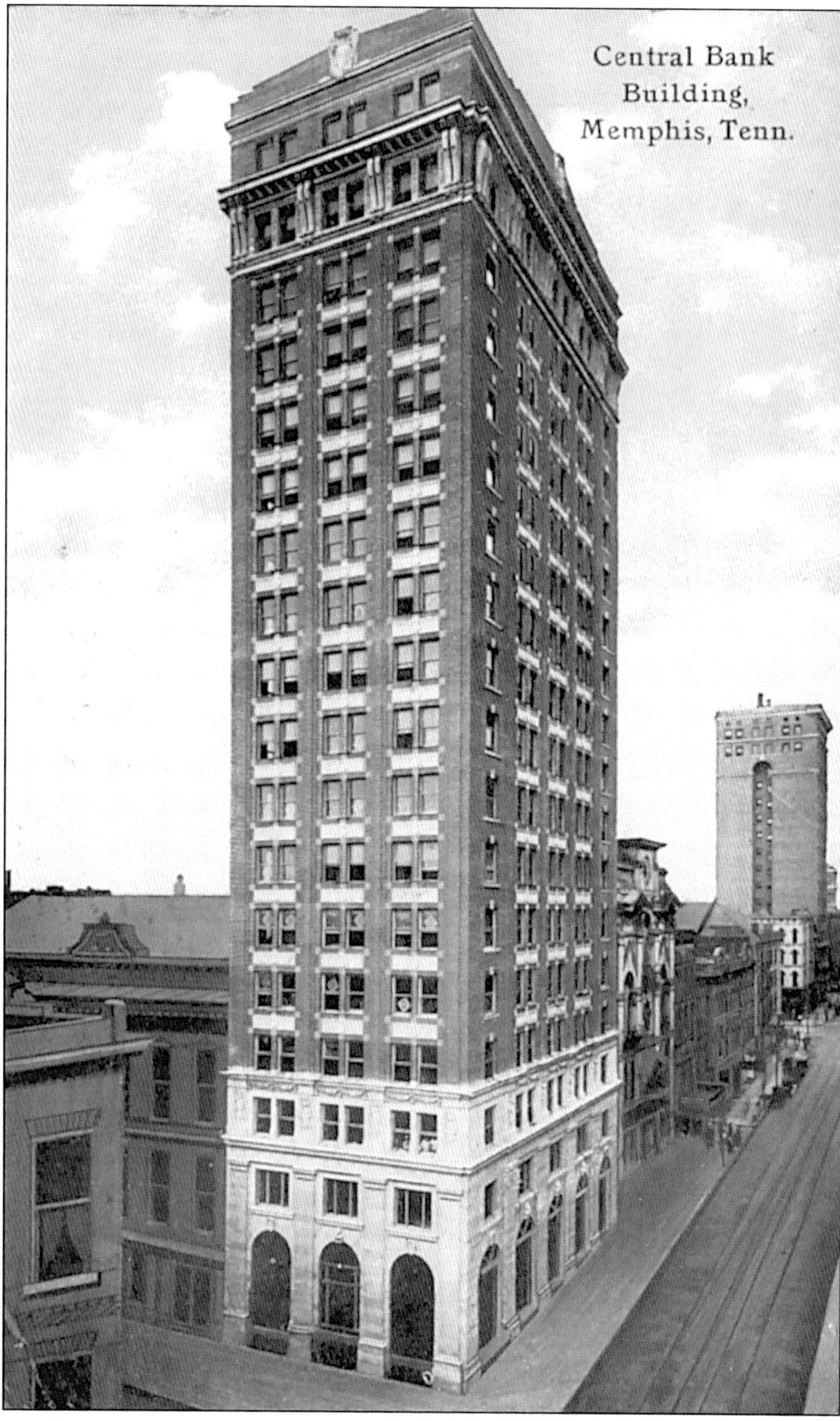

CENTRAL BANK BUILDING. The Central Bank Building was built in 1909 and, as seen in this 1912 postcard, was one of the Bluff City's first skyscrapers.

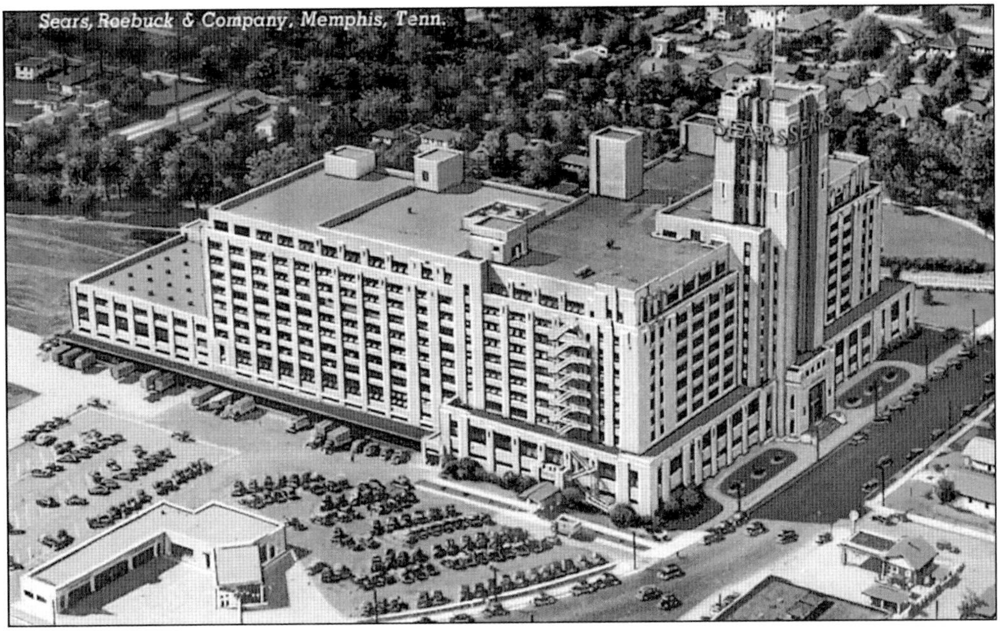

SEARS, ROEBUCK & CO. The immense 1927 Sears, Roebuck and Company warehouse building is located at the corner of Watkins and North Parkway. The classic art deco building was one of the largest in the South in its time and boasted parking for 1,000 automobiles. This massive structure is even more impressive today than it was in 1941, when this postcard was made. (Curt Teich Archives.)

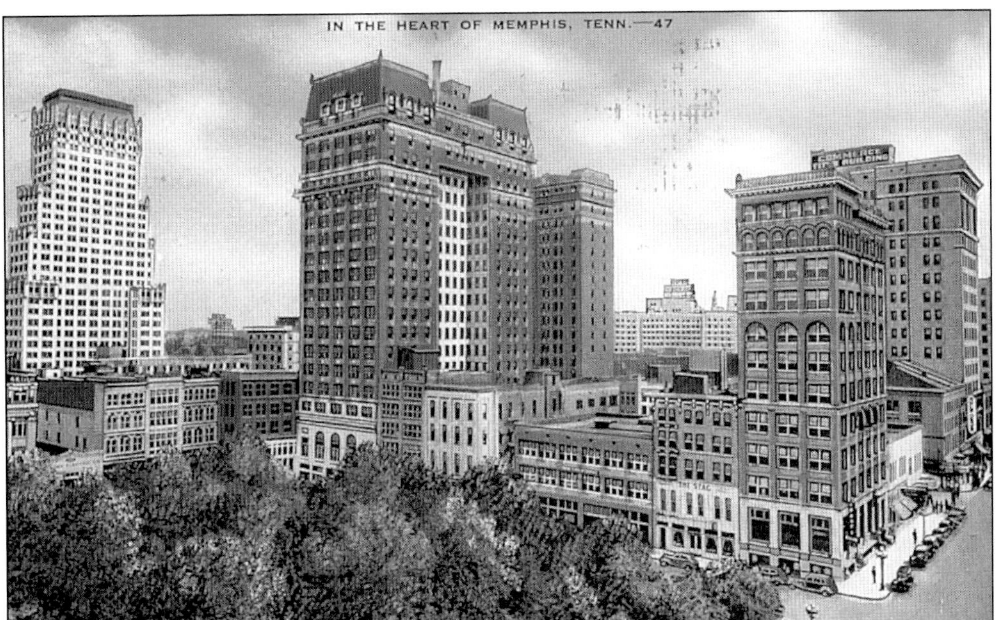

IN THE HEART OF MEMPHIS. This 1945 postcard depicts Court Square, one of the more than 40 parks in Memphis that cover in excess of 1,500 acres and which operate under the jurisdiction of the Memphis Park Commission. The Exchange, Sterick, and Porter Buildings are clearly identifiable.

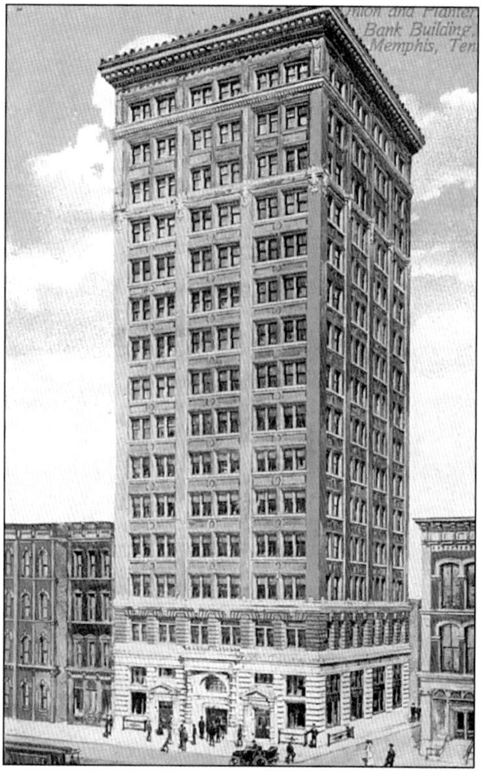

Union and Planters Bank Building. The Union Planters Bank Building, pictured here, is located on South Front Street and was built prior to this 1911 postcard, with subsequent additions and remodeling.

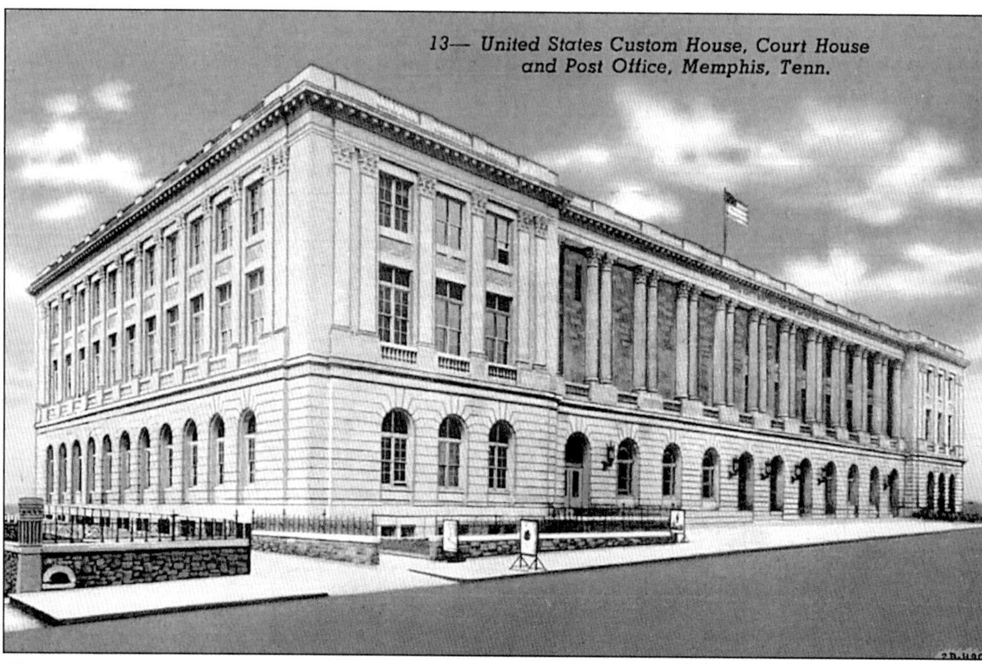

United States Custom House, Court House, and Post Office. This 1942 postcard shows the magnificent U.S. Customs House, which, between 1929 and 1930, was built basically around and over the previously existing building. (Curt Teich Archives.)

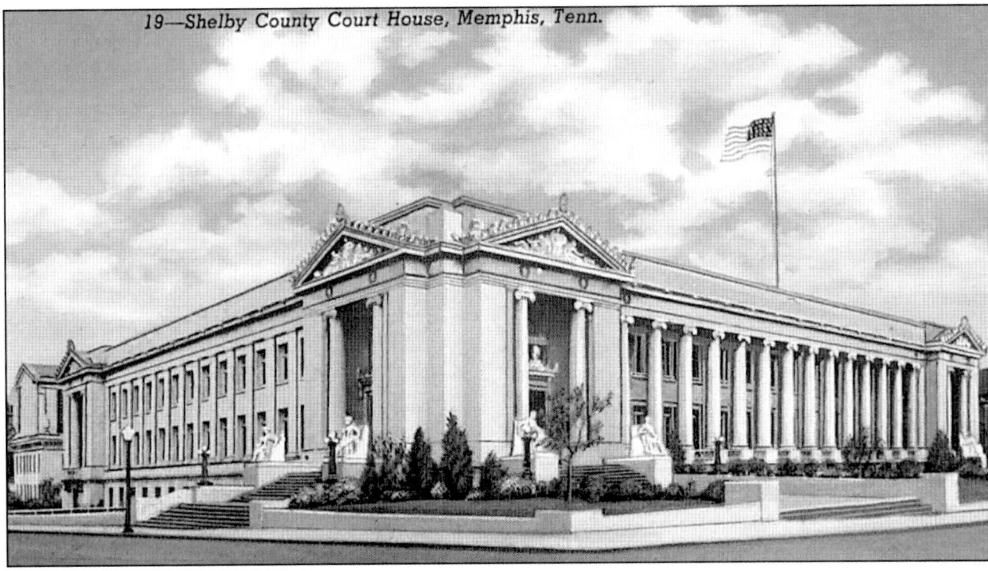

SHELBY COUNTY COURTHOUSE. This 1943 postcard shows the Shelby County Courthouse. The first thing one notices when looking upon this building is its immense size. The massive limestone building occupies a full city block. Like the Brooks Museum, this building was designed by architects James Gamble Rogers and H.D Hale. It is located on Adams, was completed in 1909, and is composed of limestone. Of particular interest are the large carved marble figures next to the steps, signifying prosperity, wisdom, liberty, justice, peace, and authority. If you happen to enjoy magnificent buildings of this era, it is worthwhile to have a look around the public areas of this magnificent structure. Those familiar with the Custom House in New Orleans may feel a kinship between the two buildings, although there is really no similarity other than the fact that they are both massive, and each occupies a full city block. (Curt Teich Archives.)

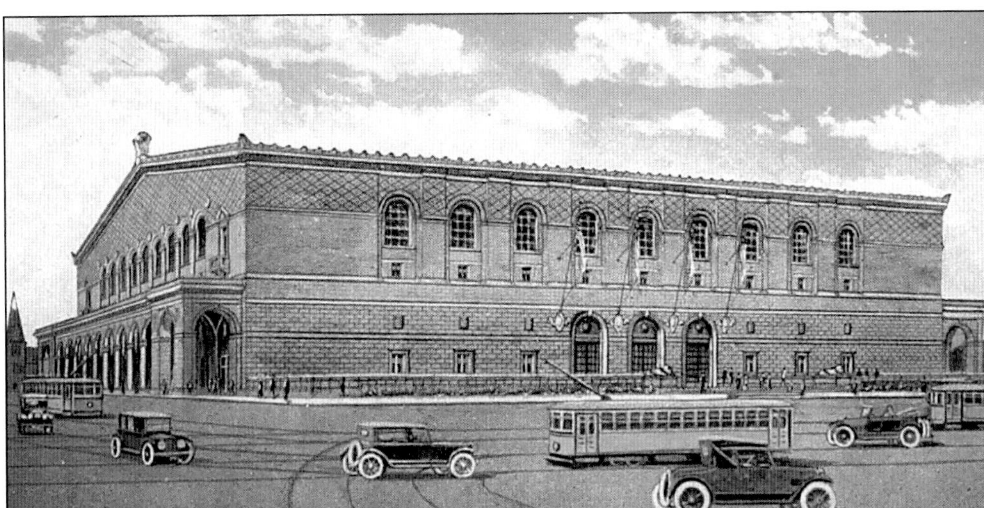

ELLIS AUDITORIUM. The Ellis Auditorium, seen here, was constructed on the site of the former Overton Hotel, built in 1859 at the corner of Poplar and Main. The auditorium was completed in 1924 at an initial cost of $3 million. (Curt Teich Archives.)

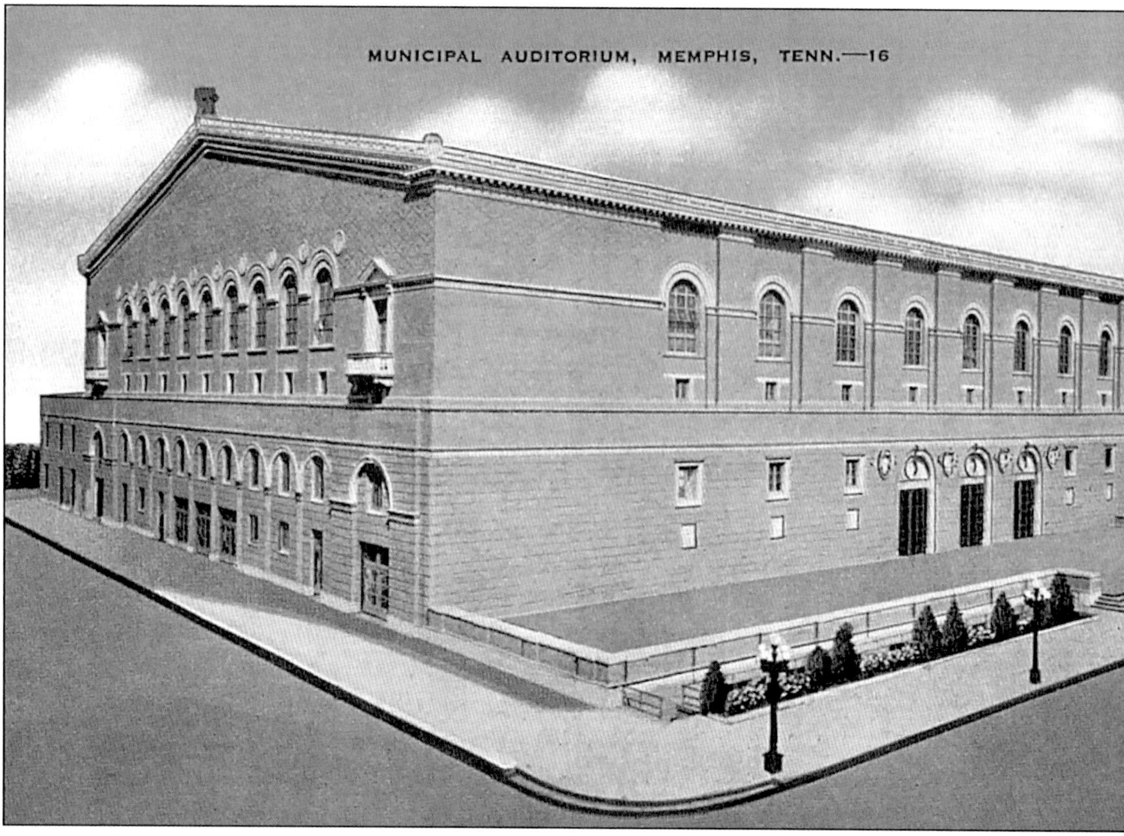

MUNICIPAL AUDITORIUM. By the time this postcard was made, the Ellis Auditorium was referred to simply as the Municipal Auditorium. Its 12,500 seating capacity was considered to be very large at the time. The auditorium can be divided into two halls, for different and simultaneous shows, if necessary.

Eight

TRANSPORTATION

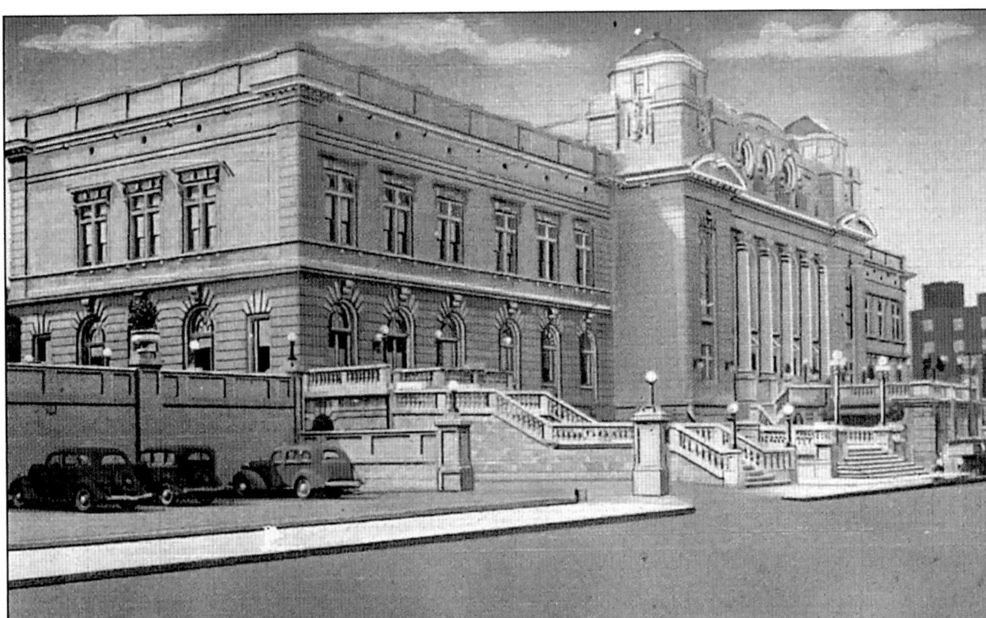

UNION STATION. Like most major cities in the golden age of railroad, Memphis once had an incredible railroad station. The magnificent eight-story Union Station, pictured here, was located at Main and Calhoun and served several major railroads, including the Illinois Central, Rock Island, and Frisco Lines. While many large railroad station terminal buildings survived the end of the railroad era and made the transition to hotels, as in Nashville and Chattanooga, the Memphis station did not. It was torn down in the 1960s.

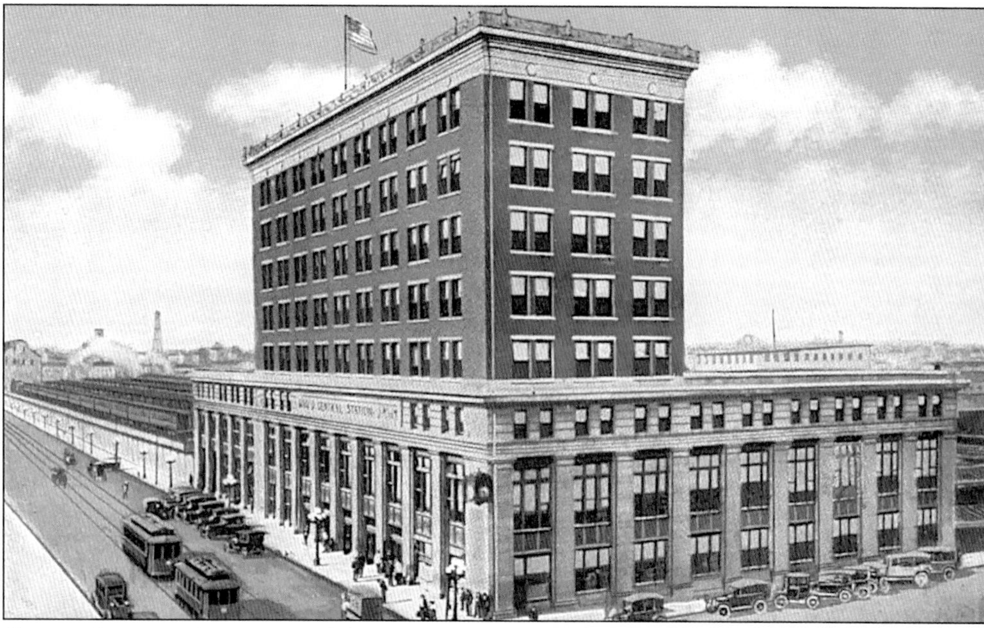

GRAND CENTRAL STATION. While many Memphians think of the Union Station to have been "the Memphis Train Station," there were others. The Yazoo and Mississippi Valley Depot and the Illinois Central Depot were both major commercial railroad terminal buildings which existed downtown during the late 1800s and early 1900s. This postcard shows the train station currently used by Amtrack. (Curt Teich Archives.)

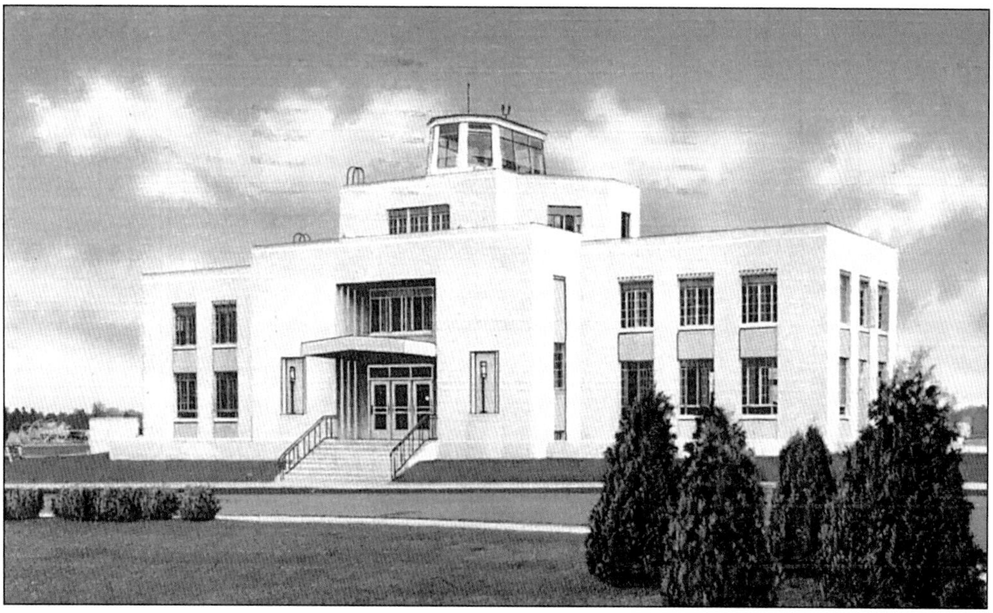

MEMPHIS MUNICIPAL AIRPORT ADMINISTRATION BUILDING. The Memphis Airport Terminal building, pictured here, was constructed in 1929 on a 200-acre site on the outskirts of town. It is indeed a far cry from the new terminal building, which opened nearby in June 1963. Despite the fact that this building was obsolete fairly early in the march of aviation technology, it is still a beautiful example of art deco architecture that is still standing today.

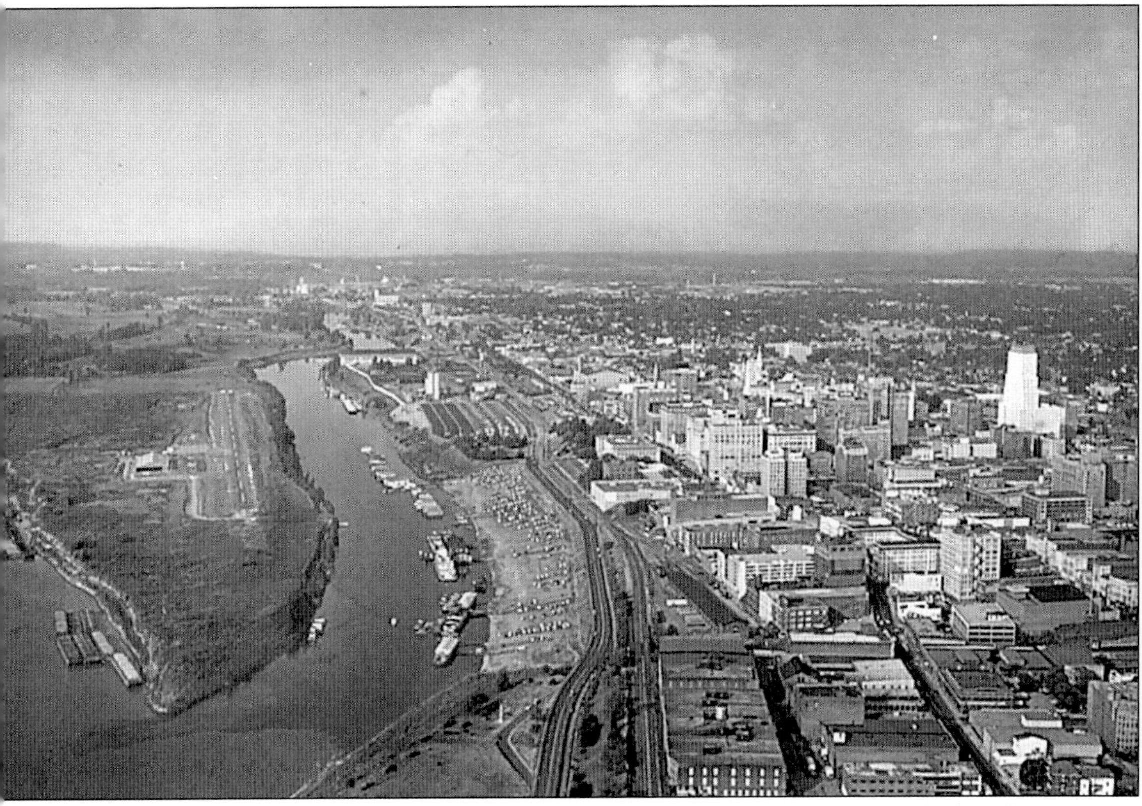

Downtown Airport. This aerial photo shows the Memphis Downtown Airport, which at the time was the closest downtown airport in any metropolitan area in the United States. It had a 3,100-foot "paved" runway. The airport's catchy slogan was "You are strictly uptown when you land downtown." It was closed in the 1970s, and this land became the site of Mud Island and the Interstate Bridge.

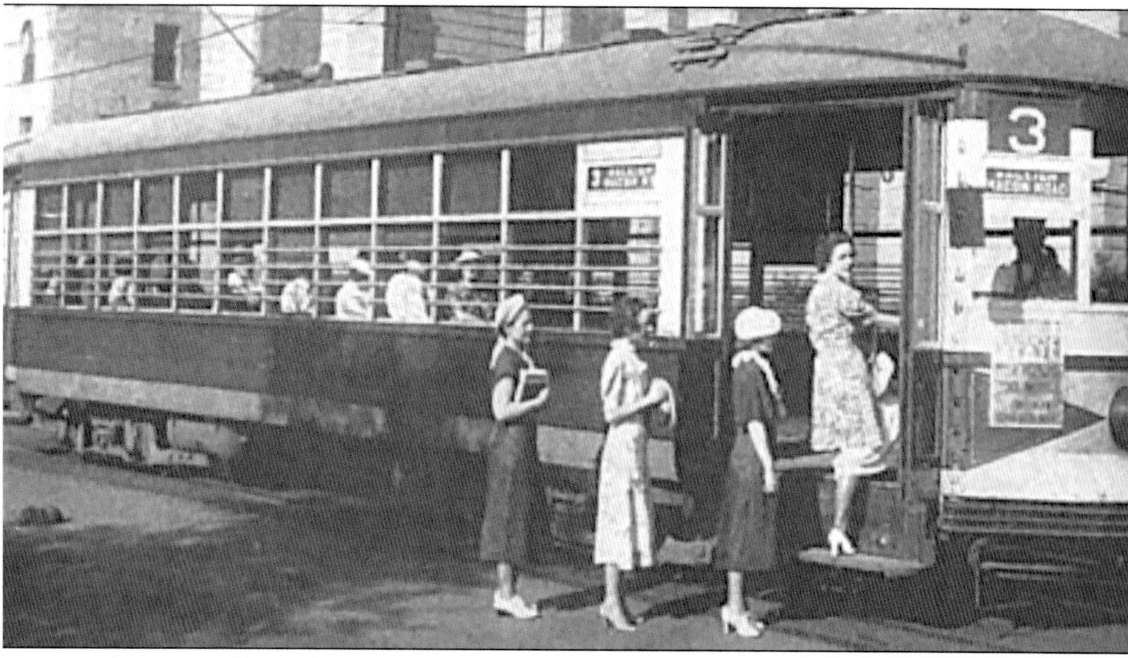

TROLLEY. The trolley was the first modern means of public transportation in many cities, and Memphis was no different. By the 1960s, most major cities had abandoned them in favor of buses. By this time, the majority of Americans had cars, and public transportation was not considered a high priority for most city planners. Soon, however, the sheer numbers of automobiles would create problems never imagined, and many cities are again returning to the trolley as a solution to in-town transportation problems.

Nine

Parks, Education, Churches, Hospitals

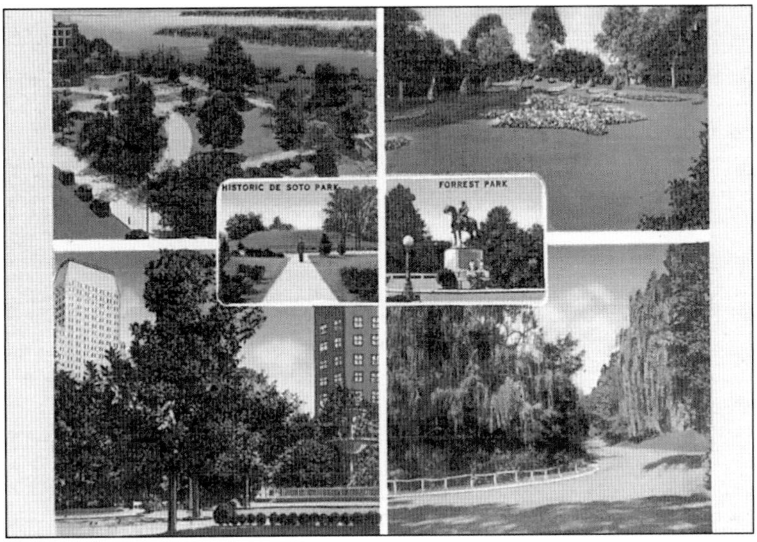

Parks in Memphis. Memphis has been described by many visitors as "a city of parks." This is certainly understandable, considering the large number of parks of all types scattered throughout the city. These areas range from downtown parks, like Court Square, to parks like Riverside and Confederate Park, which overlook the Mississippi River, to Overton Park, with its famous zoo and aquarium. The original founding plan of Memphis, in 1819, included four park squares as well as a river promenade. The Memphis Park Commission held its first meeting in 1900 and, as its first official act, purchased a 335-acre area known as Lea's Woods from Overton Lea, on what was then the outskirts of town. This area subsequently became Overton Park. This collage shows park scenes from Memphis, including views of the Sunken Gardens, Riverside Park, Court Square, Confederate Park, De Soto Park, and Forrest Park.

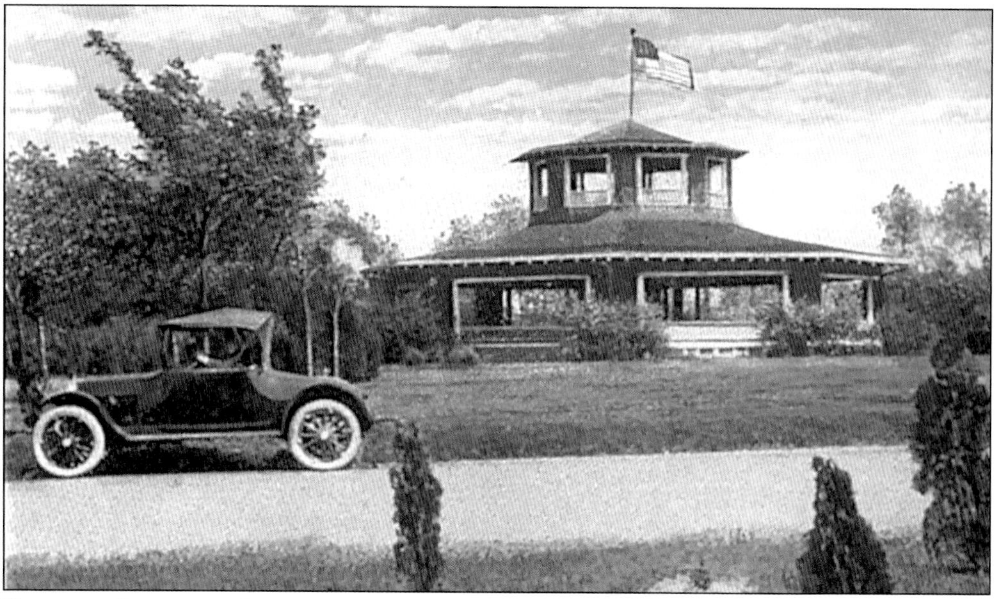

DANCING PAVILLION RIVERSIDE PARK. Riverside Park, now known as Dr. Martin Luther King Jr., Riverside Park, was designed in 1901 by landscape architect George Kessler, who also designed Overton Park. The park was named Riverside because it was designed so that citizens could enjoy a view of the river from a bluff consisting of trees and natural beauty. The land for Riverside Park was acquired in 1902. (Curt Teich Archives.)

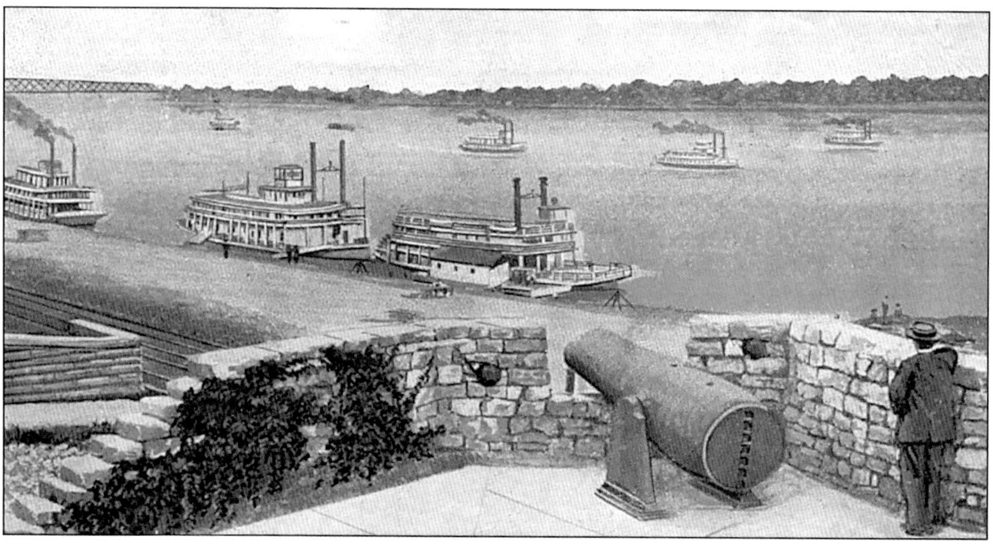

MISSISSIPPI RIVER FROM CONFEDERATE PARK. The lost cause of the Confederacy was of great importance to those Memphians who survived the War between the States. The establishment of many parks and monuments during the period immediately following the Civil War bears testimony to the importance of the effort to the inhabitants of the city during that period. The largest meeting of Confederate veterans ever assembled anywhere took place in Memphis in May 1901. Thousands of Confederate flags draped the city, and a large parade was part of the festivities. This famous Memphis park was established in 1908, in honor of the Confederate cause. (Curt Teich Archives.)

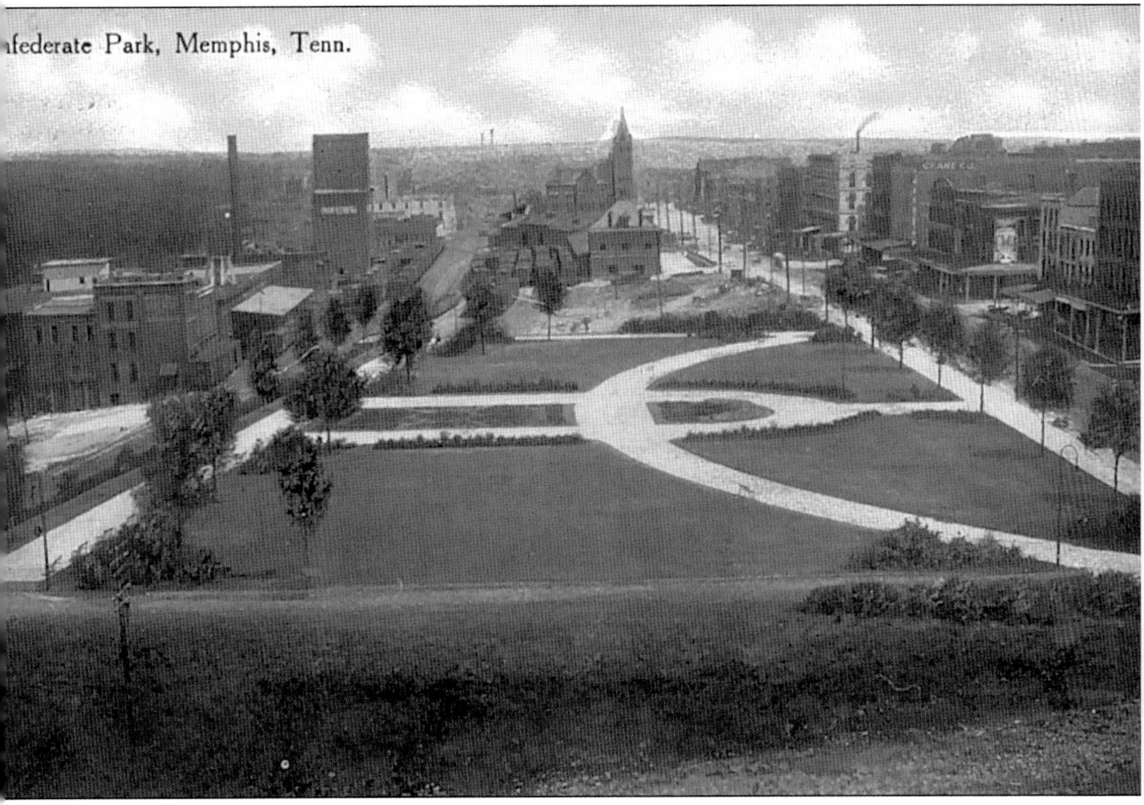

CONFEDERATE PARK. The unusual shape of the paved surface of Confederate Park is seen here as viewed from the U.S. Customs House, Courthouse, Post Office, in this 1911 postcard.

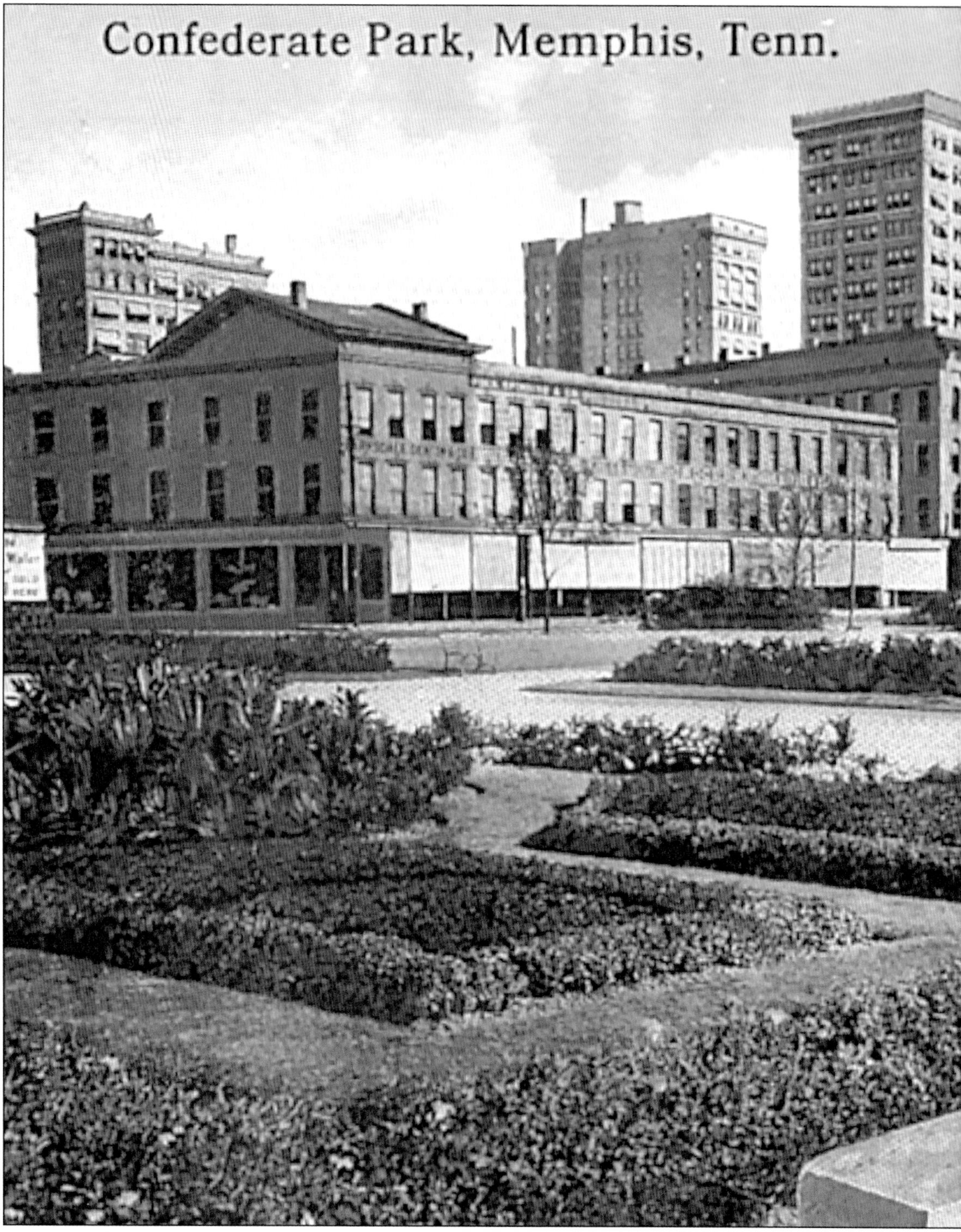

Confederate Park, Memphis, Tennessee. In this early postcard, Memphians sit restfully on benches in Confederate Park overlooking the Mississippi River. In the background, the emerging skyline, with the city's first skyscrapers, is beginning to take shape. Of particular interest is the

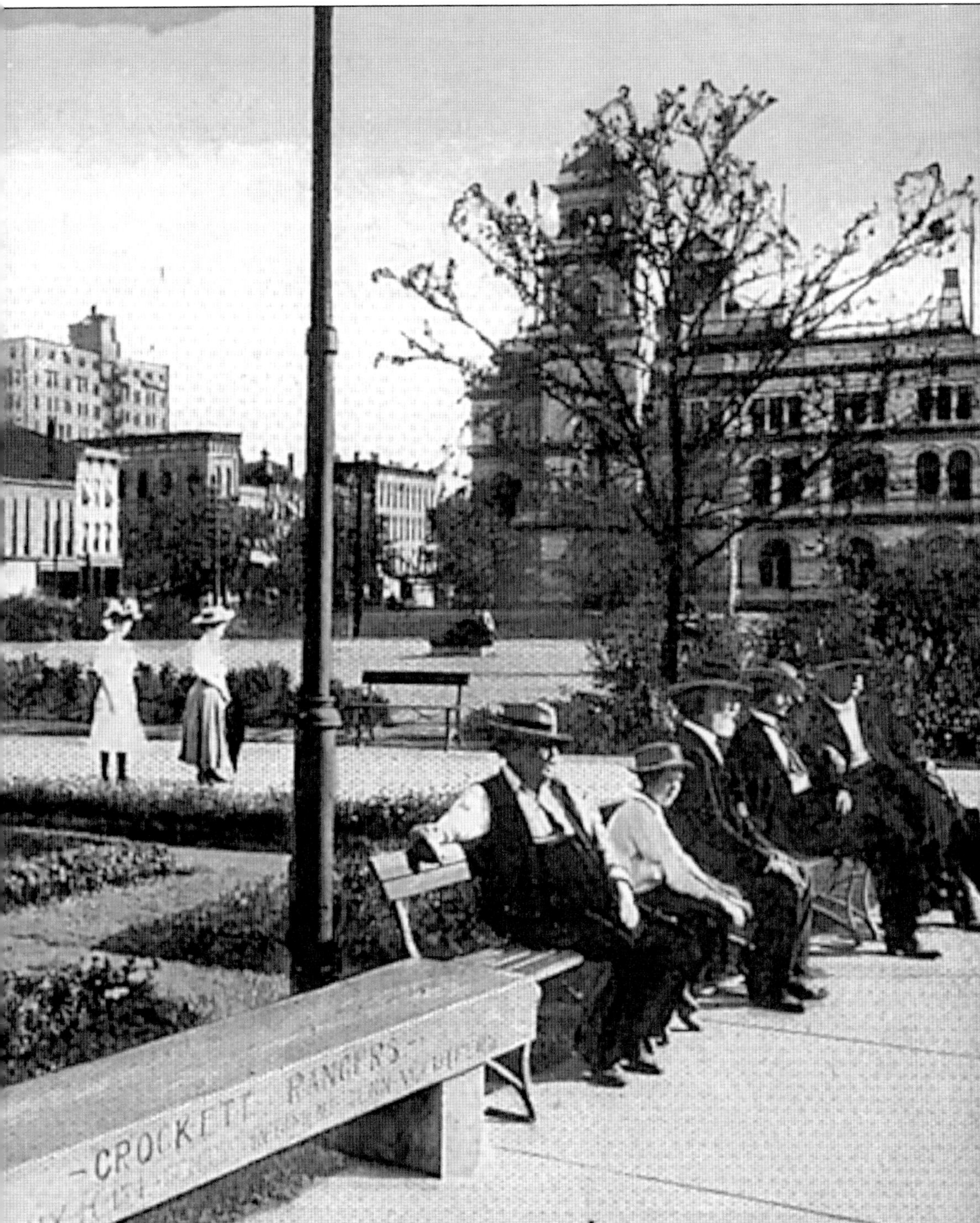

1924 Union and Planters Building. On the far right side of the image is the U.S. Customs House, Post Office, and Courthouse prior to renovation.

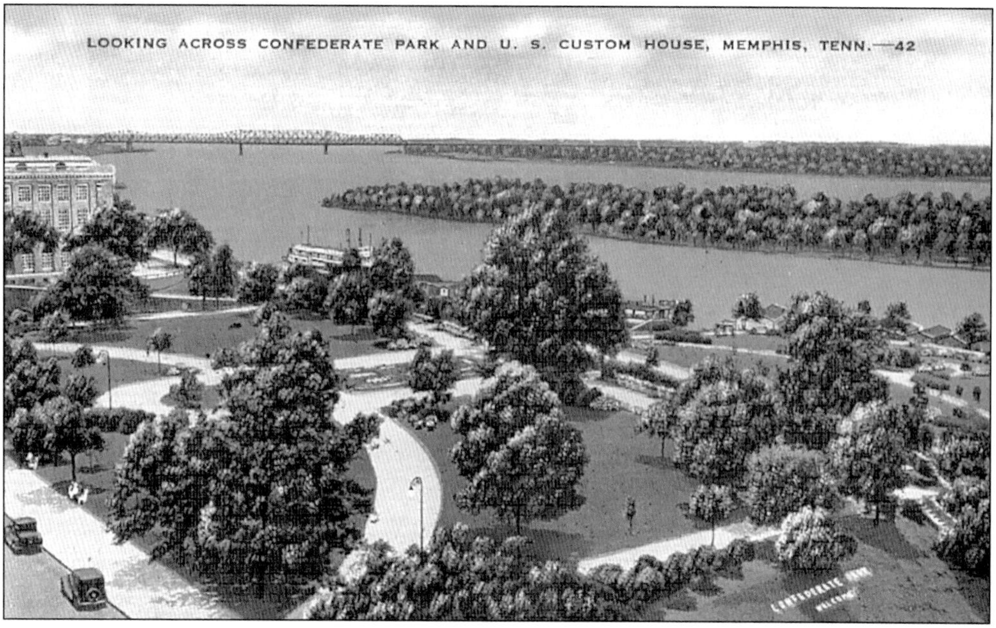

LOOKING ACROSS CONFEDERATE PARK AND U.S. CUSTOMS HOUSE, MEMPHIS, TENNESSEE. This more recent view of Confederate Park shows the presence of mature trees as well as the newer Customs House (at the far left) after 1929 renovations.

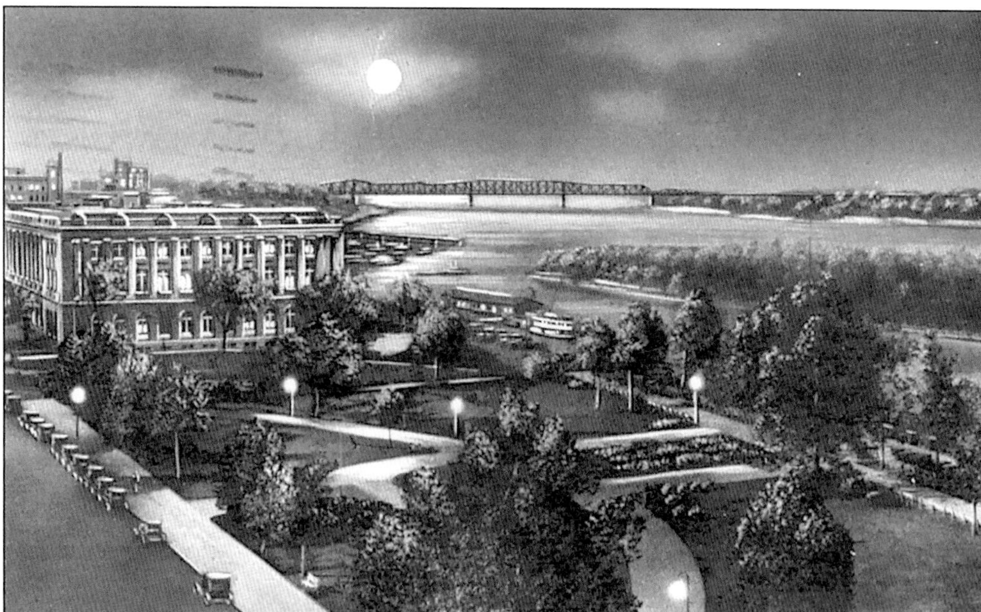

CONFEDERATE PARK, POST OFFICE, AND MISSISSIPPI RIVER BY MOONLIGHT. Moonlight views were a frequent theme of early postcards. This 1940 view of Confederate Park by moonlight shows the Memphis Bridges to the south, the renovated post office, and the park.

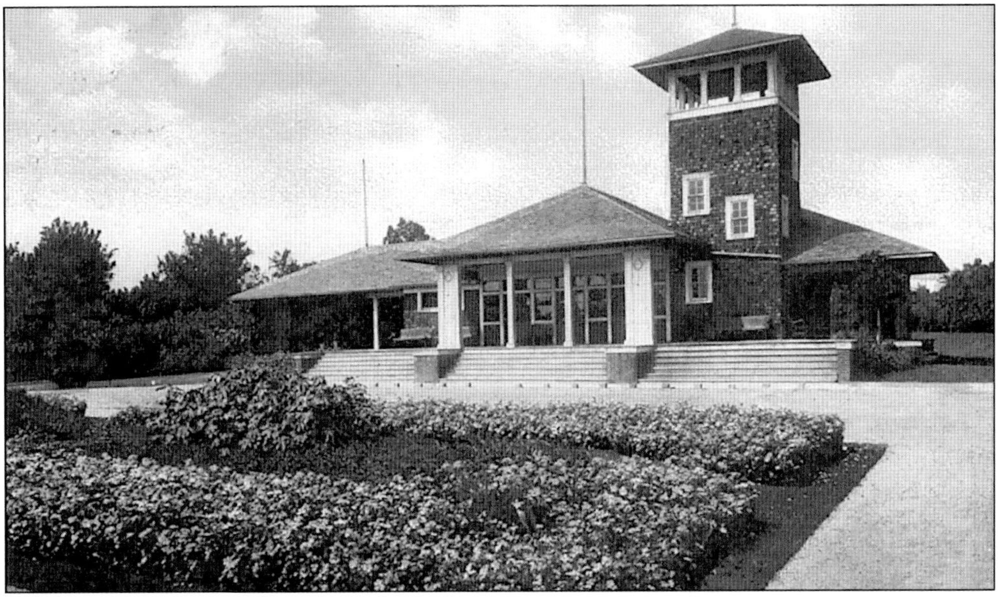

OVERTON PARK, MEMPHIS, TENNESSEE. This Mission-style building at Overton Park was constructed sometime between 1901, when the park opened, and 1910, the postmarked date of this card. Despite the longstanding popularity of the park, there were those who sought to destroy it in the 1960s by running part of Interstate 40 right through the middle, supposedly in an effort to bolster this part of the city commercially. A heated war continued unabated between those who wished to save the park and those who wanted the interstate. The matter was only resolved by a U.S. Supreme Court decision, which ruled in favor of the park.

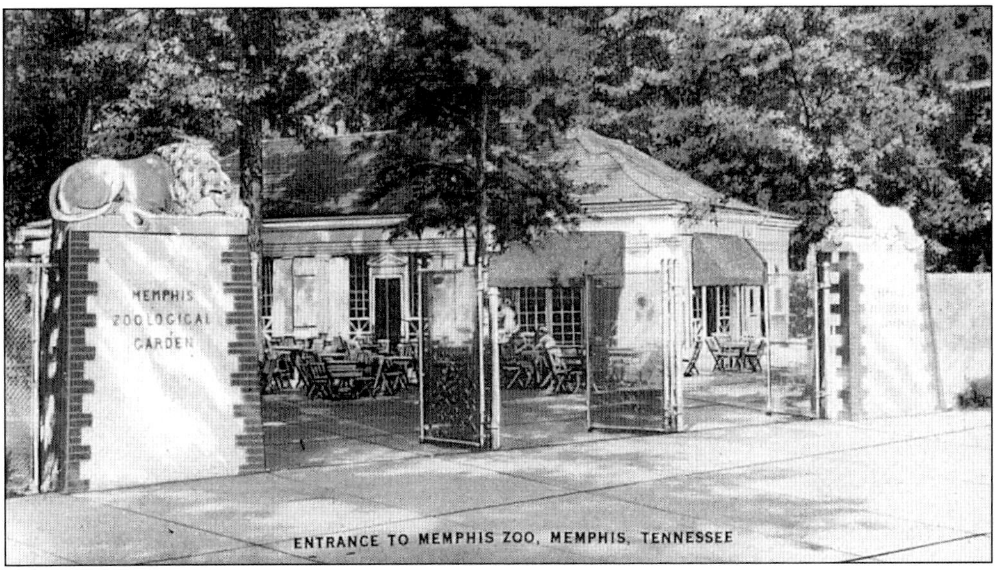

ENTRANCE TO MEMPHIS ZOO. According to history, the Memphis Zoo began when A.B. Carruthers accepted a black bear from Natchez as payment for an order of shoes. His wife tired of the bear, which was tethered to a tree and destroying her backyard, so the bear was subsequently moved to Overton Park. Other animals were donated, and the Memphis Zoo Association was formed, with Mrs. Carruthers being its first president.

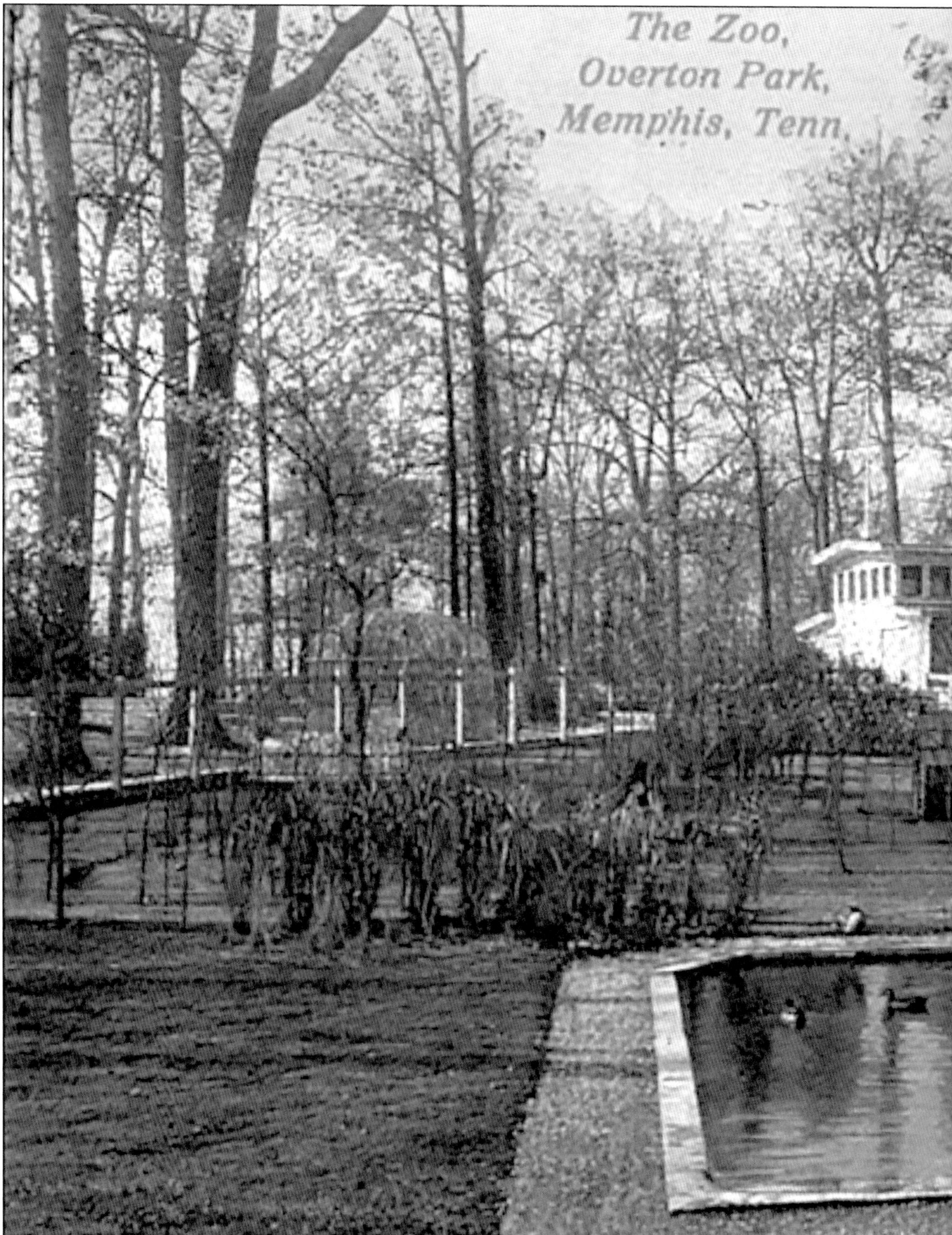

THE ZOO, OVERTON PARK. The Memphis Zoo opened in 1906 but was fully operational by 1914, when this postcard image was made. An aquarium was established as part of the zoo in

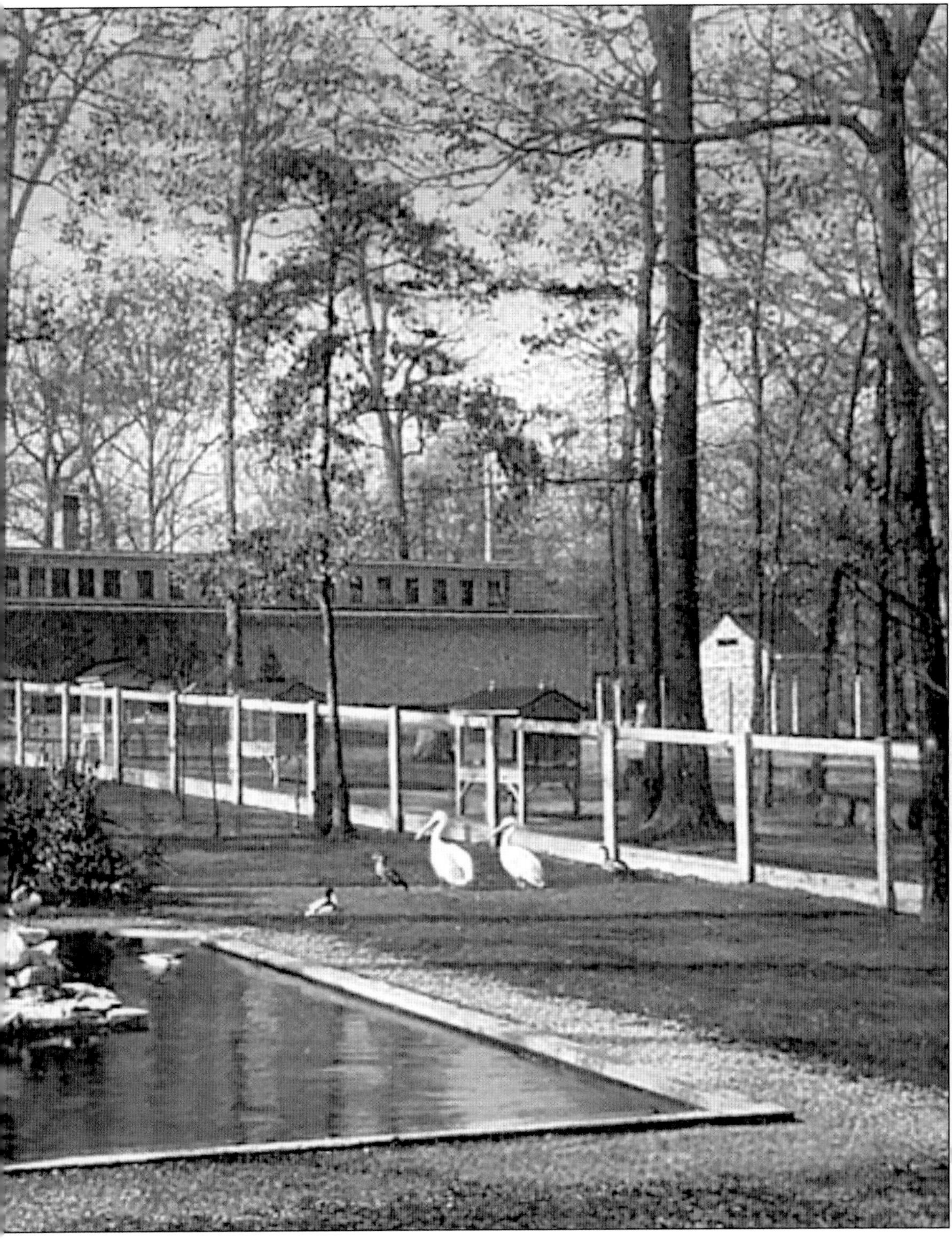

1959, as the result of a gift from a private citizen.

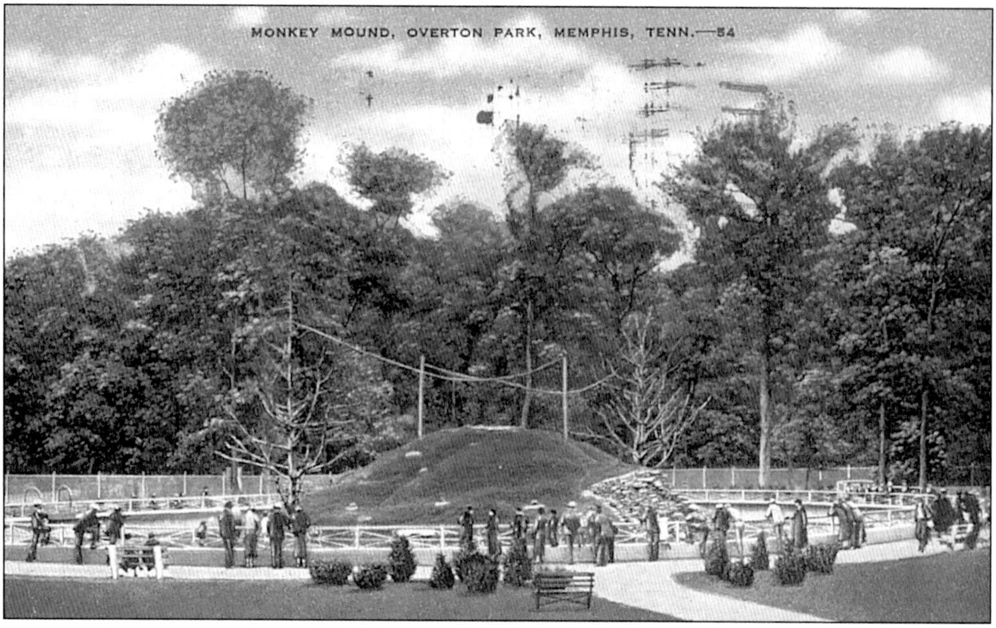

MONKEY MOUND. The Monkey Mound, seen in this postcard dated 1952, has a 27.5-foot moat with a 491-foot circumference that surrounds a sloping island mound. The mound itself, which served as the monkey's residence, consisted of seven 4-by-6-foot rooms, reachable through rustic stone gates located on the side of the mound.

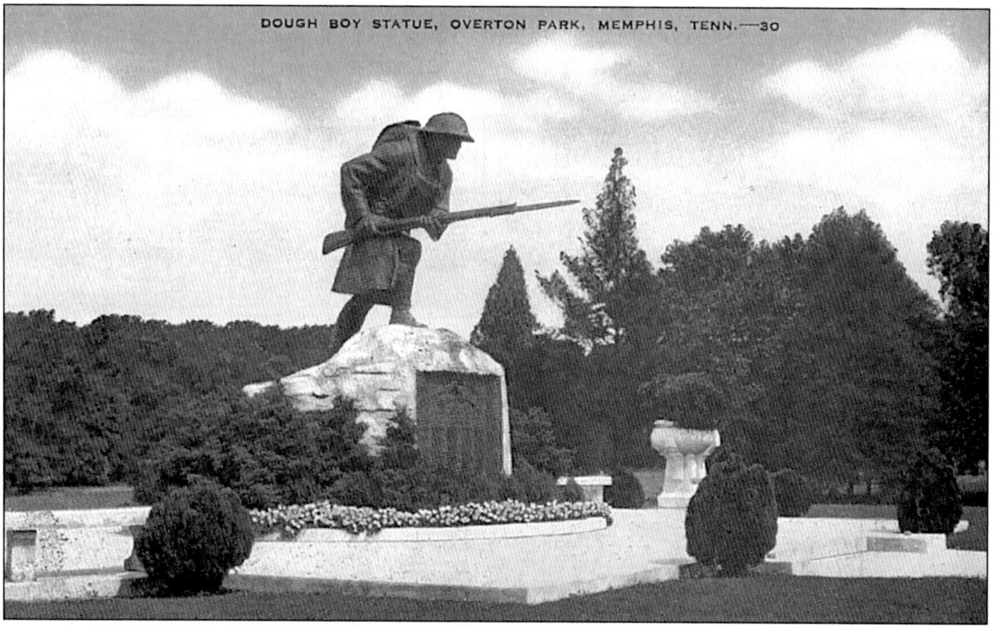

DOUGHBOY STATUE. The Doughboy statue was designed and constructed by sculptor Nancy Hahn. The project was sponsored by local Daughters of the American Revolution and erected in honor of the World War I dead of Memphis and Shelby County. The $15,000 cost of the project was raised by both public subscription and from thousands of pennies collected by school children.

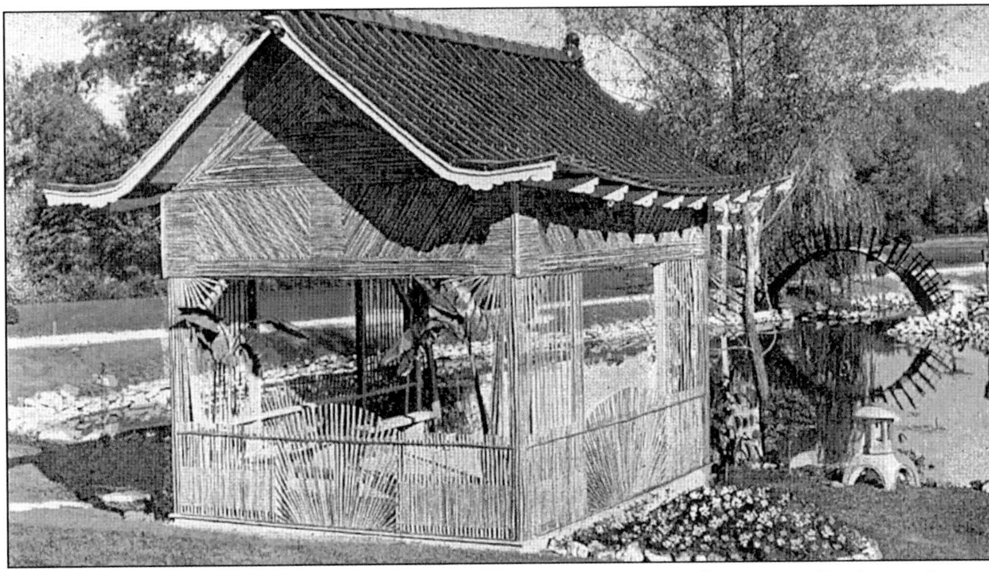

Tea House Japanese Gardens. The fate of the Tea House and Japanese Gardens, pictured here, was determined by the Japanese attack on Pearl Harbor. It was not long thereafter that this entire portion of Overton Park was bulldozed. The city of Memphis had no further interest in promoting Japanese culture. Eventually, the Memphis College of Arts would be built on this spot.

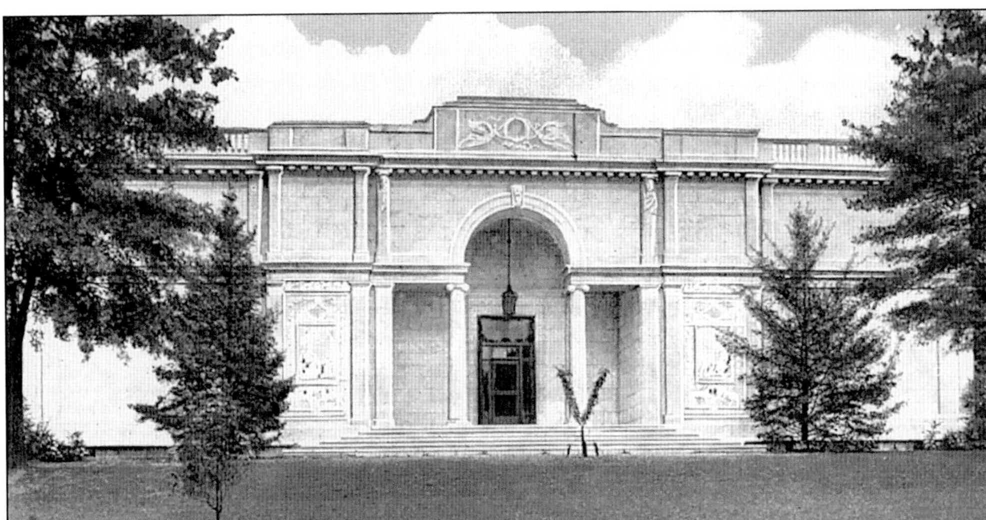

Brooks Memorial Art Gallery. The building now known as Memphis Brooks Museum was designed by New York architect James Gamble Rogers, who also designed the Shelby County Courthouse as well as several significant buildings in New Orleans and other cities. This amazing building was constructed in 1916, with a subsequent addition in 1970. It is easy to tell where the original section ends and the later addition starts. While the building designed by Rogers is exquisite, the newer addition can only be described as "bastardized" at best. Be that as it may, the requirement for additional space has been adequately met, and the museum's permanent collection, as well as temporary exhibits, make a visit to this museum certainly worthwhile. The original building, pictured here, is truly impressive.

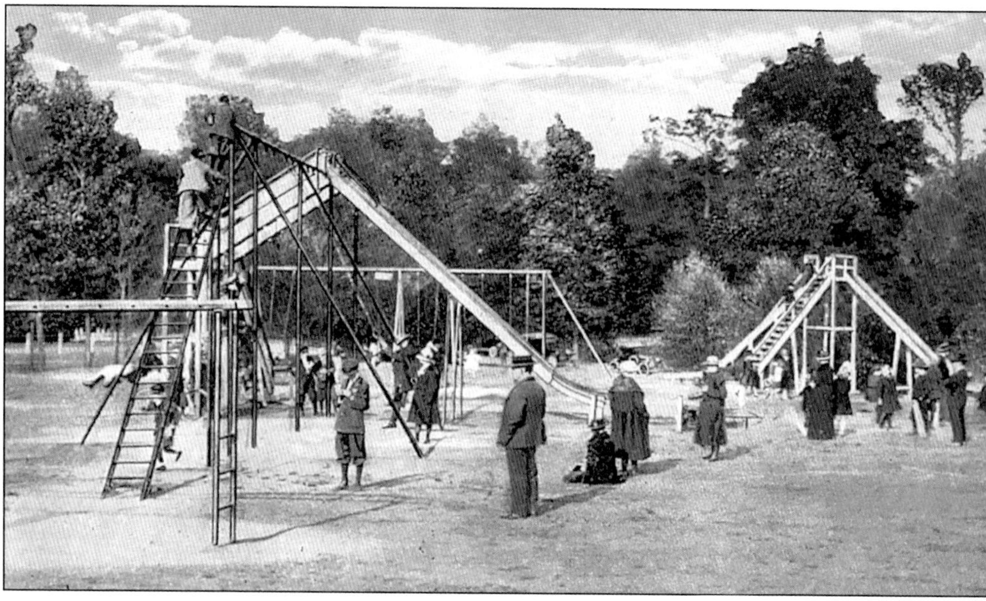

Children's Playground. This 1916 postcard shows the degree to which Overton Park had developed within less than a generation after its opening. This particular playground opened in 1911 and was the first of its kind in Memphis. (Curt Teich Archives.)

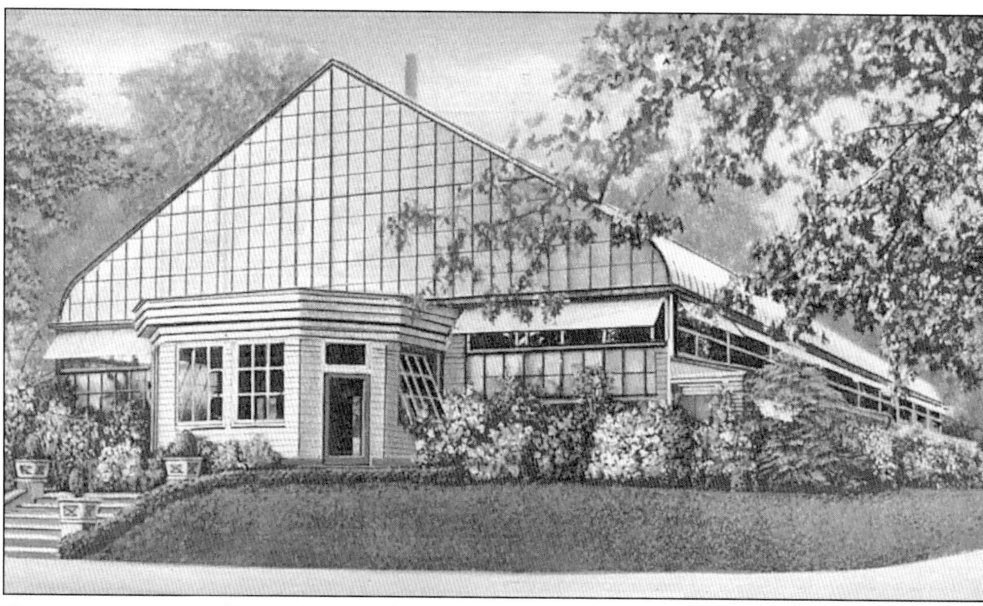

Conservatory and Bird House. The Memphis Zoo was established at Overton Park in 1906. The Conservatory and Bird House are seen in this 1932 postcard. Throughout the history of this park, development has been ongoing, not only throughout the park, but within the zoo itself. Today the zoo complex now houses over 400 species of birds, mammals, reptiles, insects, fish, and amphibians, from all parts of the world. No attention to detail has been spared, not only in the splendid selection of animals, but also in the construction of settings in which the animals are seen. From large jungle cats to the Komodo Dragon to one of the largest snapping turtles ever seen, this zoo is remarkable.

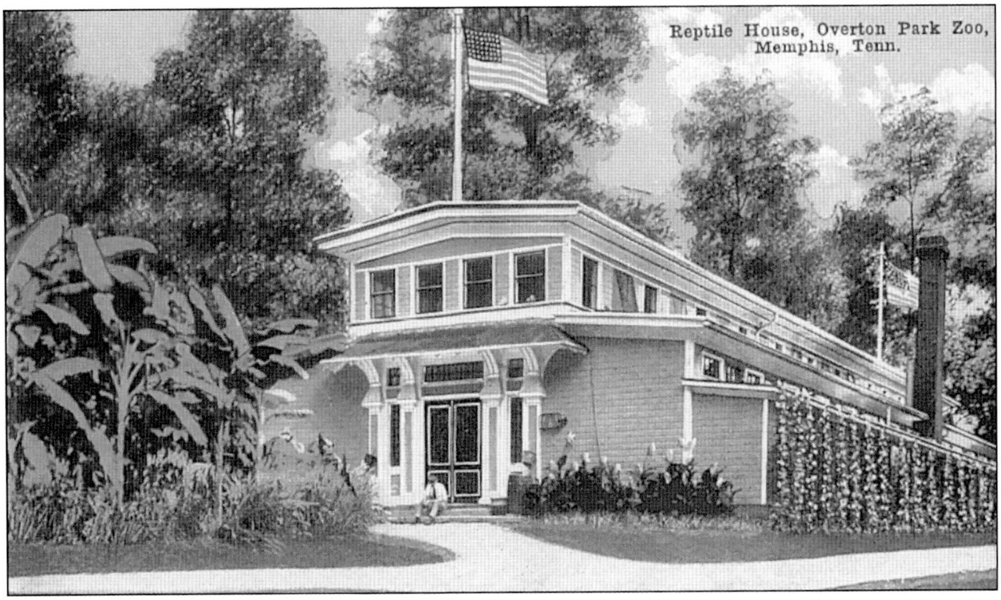

REPTILE HOUSE. The Reptile House is seen in this pleasant summer postcard image. Note the banana trees at the left side of the picture.

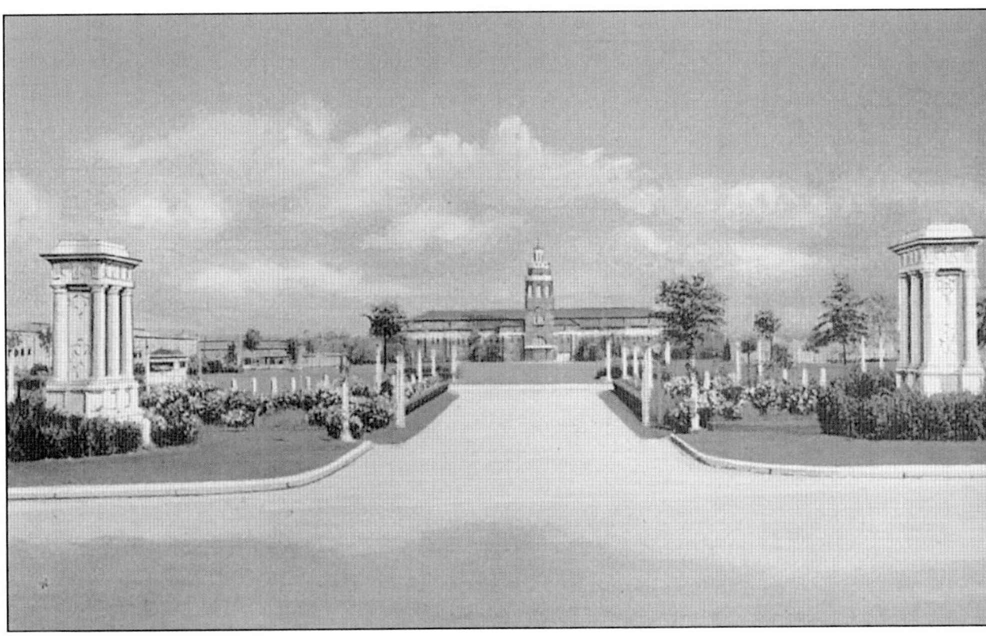

ENTRANCE TRI-STATE FAIRGROUNDS. The Mid-South Fairgrounds is the site of Libertyland Amusement Park, the 50,000-plus-seat Liberty Bowl Stadium, the Memphis Flea Market, and the Mid-South Fair. The entrance, as seen in this 1932 postcard, appears much the same today, including the Shelby County Building seen in the distance. (Curt Teich Archives.)

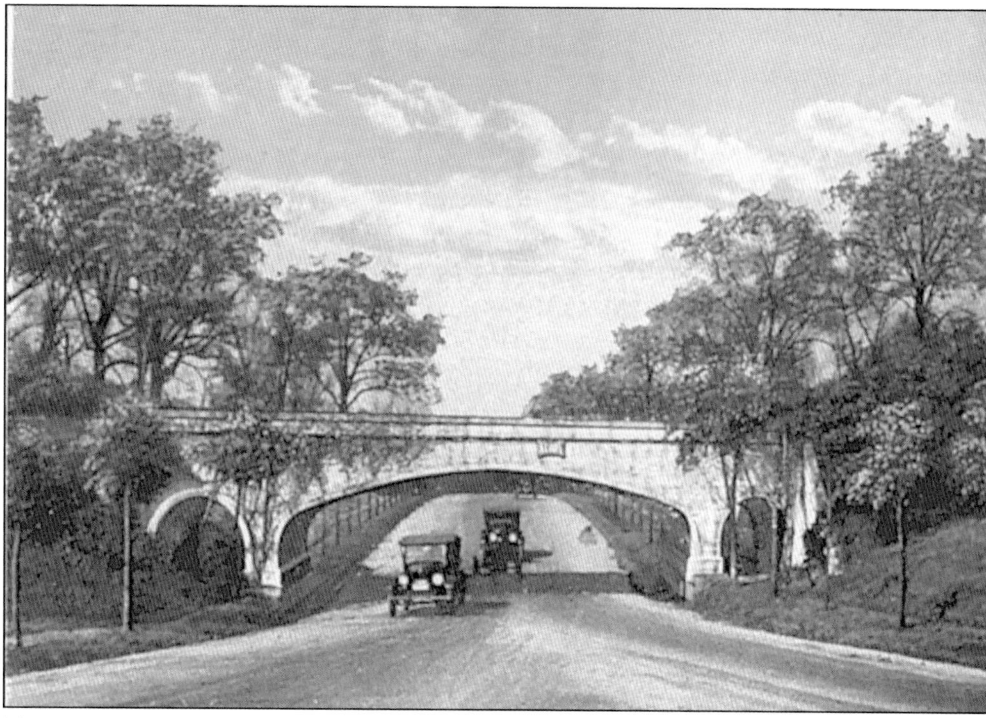

The Speedway. The speedway seen here was not a race track, per se, though there was one located at the fairgrounds at one time. (Curt Teich Archives.)

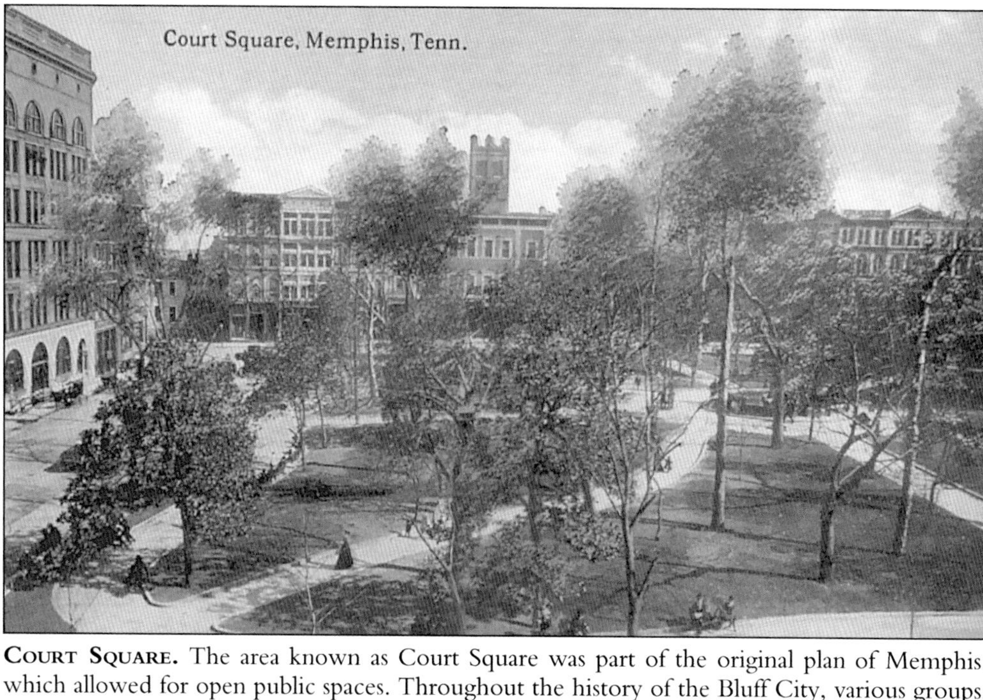

Court Square. The area known as Court Square was part of the original plan of Memphis, which allowed for open public spaces. Throughout the history of the Bluff City, various groups, including both commercial developers and urban planners, have unsuccessfully sought to use this property for parking, building space, or other purposes. (Curt Teich Archives.)

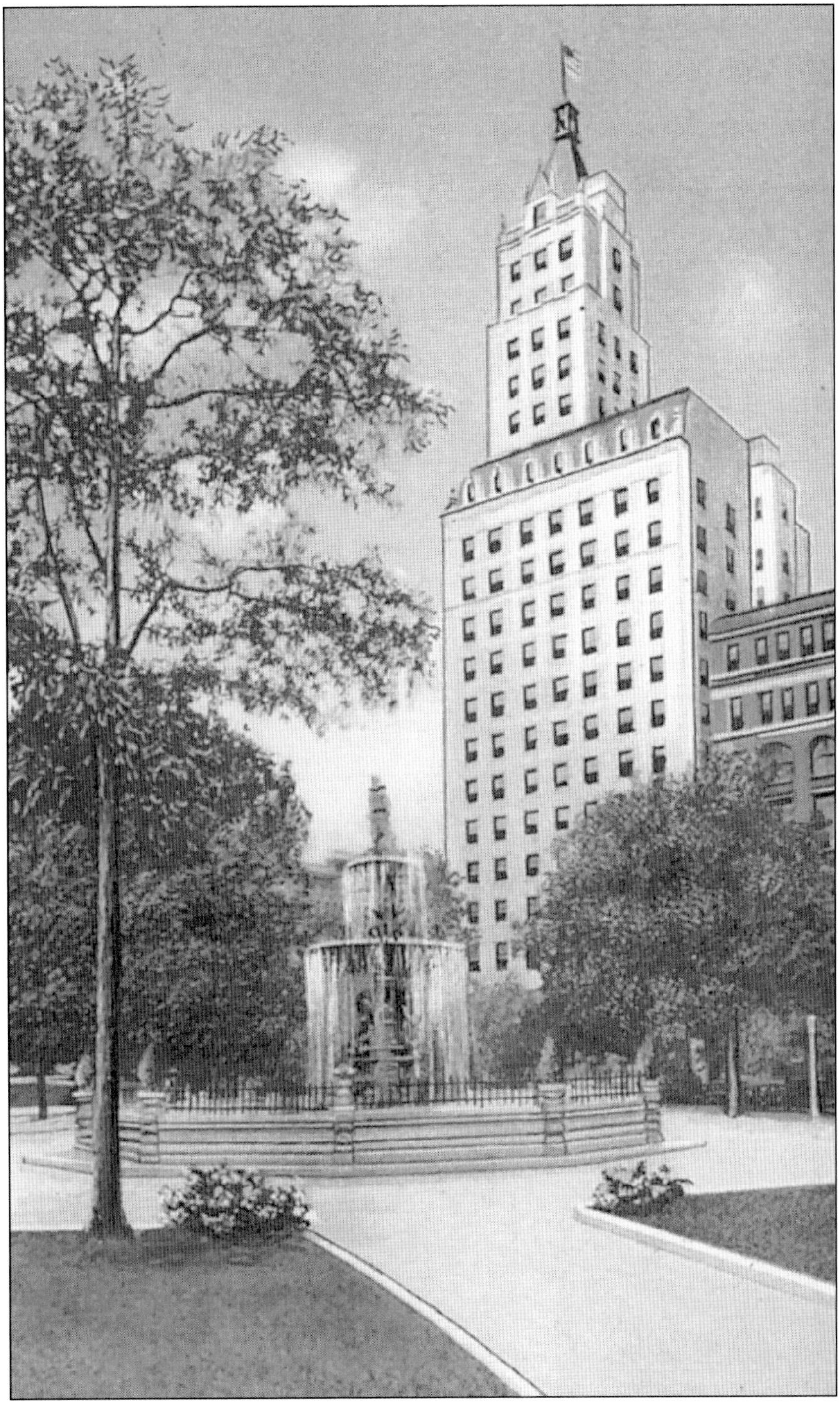

COURT SQUARE FOUNTAIN-COLUMBIAN MUTUAL TOWER. The Court Square Fountain is seen here in this postcard from 1932, with the 21-story Columbian Mutual Tower Building in the distance. The 1924 structure, now known as the Lincoln America Tower, is one of Memphis' first skyscrapers. (Curt Teich Archives.)

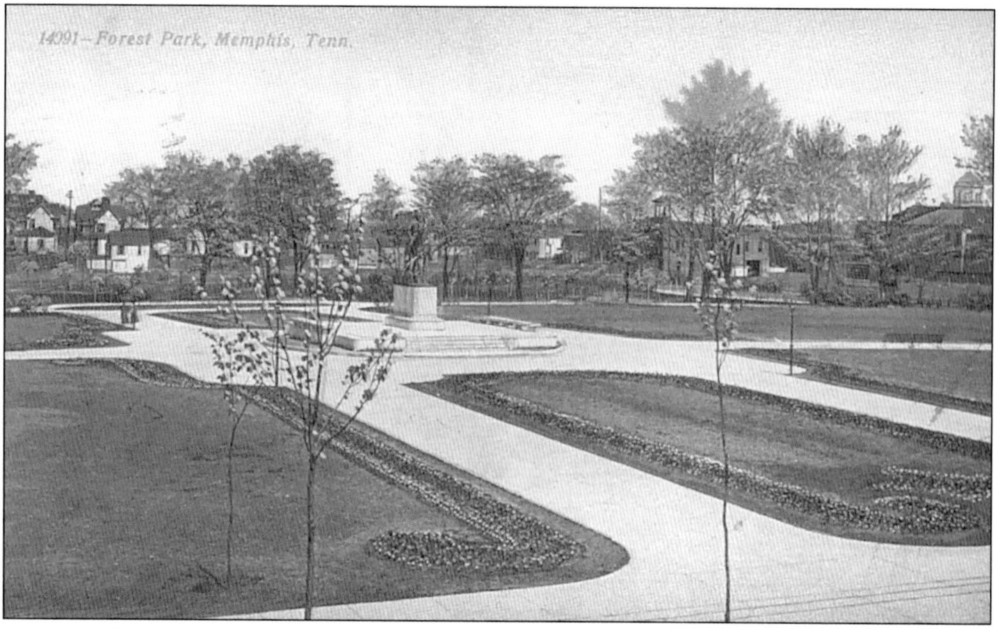

FORREST PARK. Forrest Park was designed by George Kessler, the same man responsible for the layout of Overton Park. The land on which Forrest Park is situated was the former site of the Old City Hospital (see hospital section) and was acquired by the city in 1899, with the park opening in 1915. The park was designed to resemble an English garden, with a pond (see below).

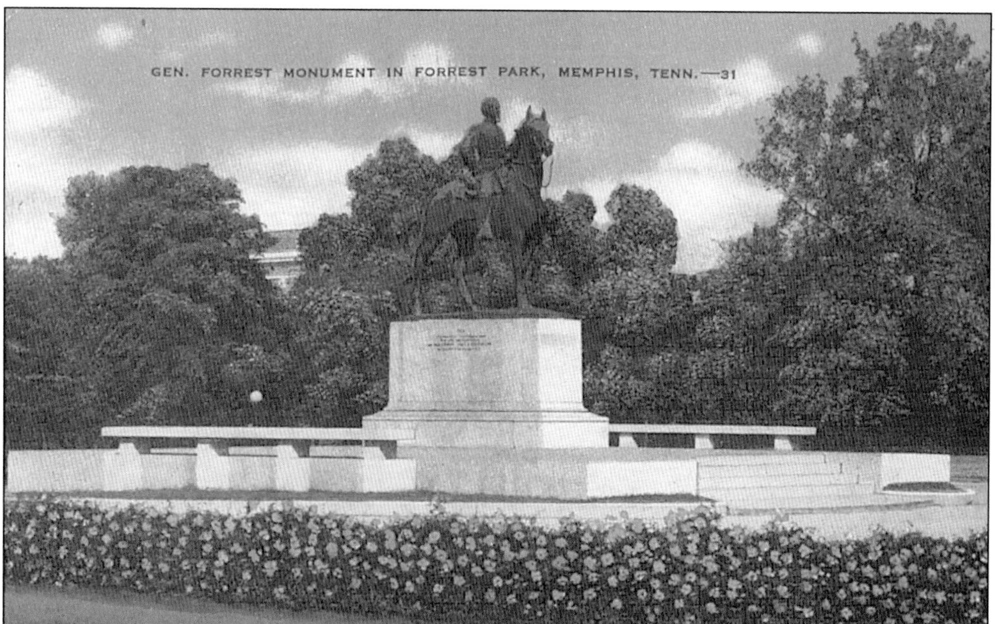

GENERAL FORREST MONUMENT. This 1949 postcard of the Forrest Monument does not begin to capture the incredible workmanship or great detail of this wonderful bronze statue honoring this great military genius.

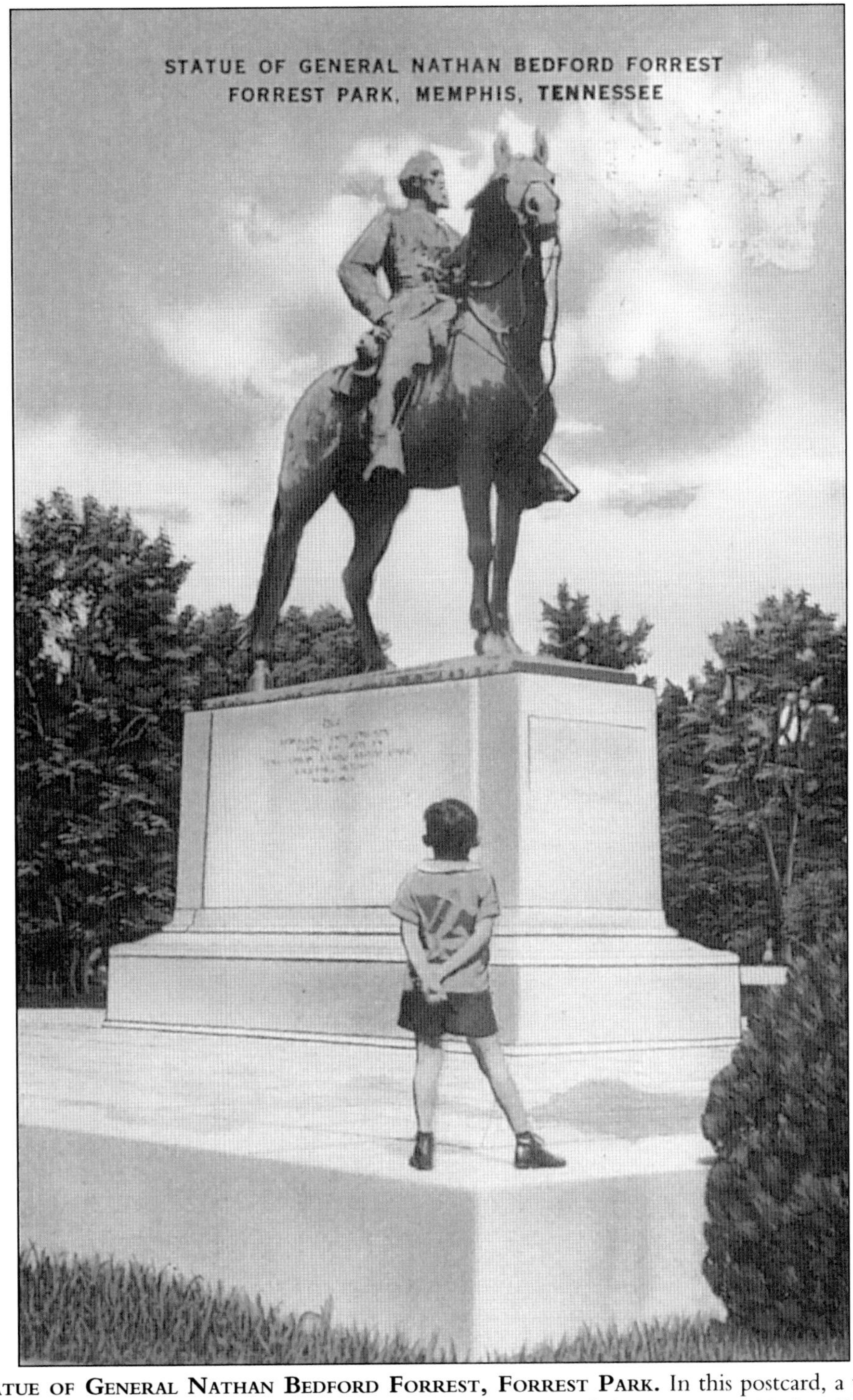

STATUE OF GENERAL NATHAN BEDFORD FORREST, FORREST PARK. In this postcard, a young boy gazes admiringly at the impressive statue of esteemed Confederate General Nathan Bedford Forrest. The remains of General Forrest and his wife were disinterred from Elmwood Cemetery and moved to this park.

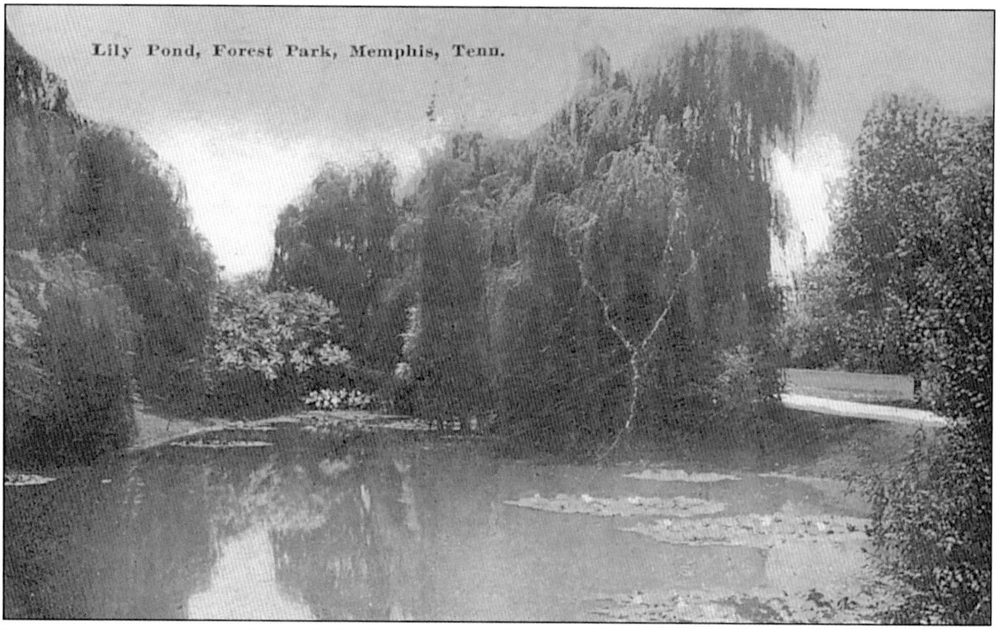

LILY POND-FORREST PARK. This 1916 postcard photo, taken a year after the park's opening, clearly shows the natural beauty of the site. Today, the lily pond is gone, and only a small part of the park surrounding the statue remains.

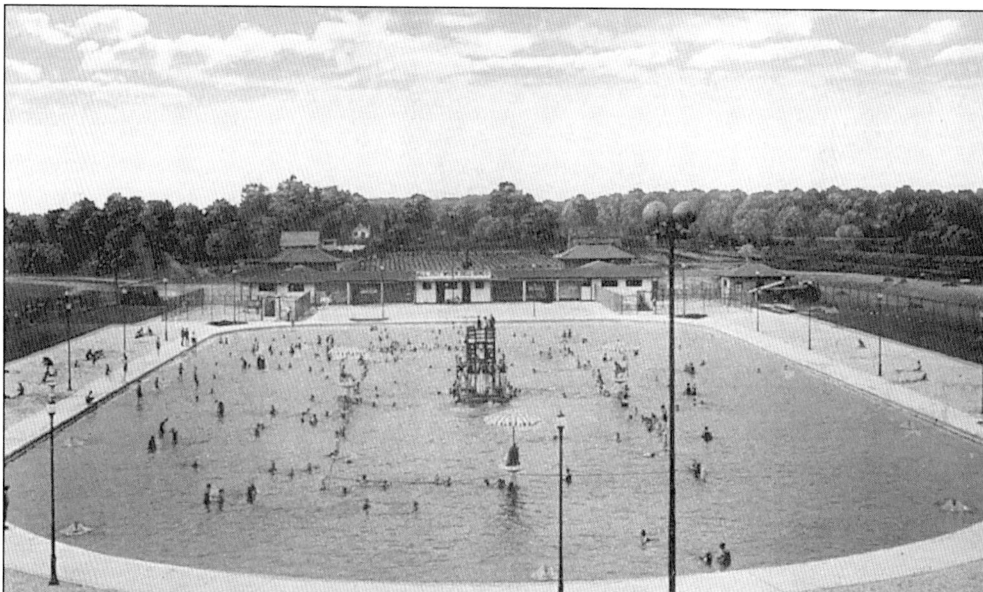

MUNICIPAL SWIMMING POOL. Most larger cities, particularly in the South, had outdoor public swimming pools at one time. This card, showing the public swimming pool in Memphis, was produced sometime between 1908 and 1913, according to the Curt Teich Archives.

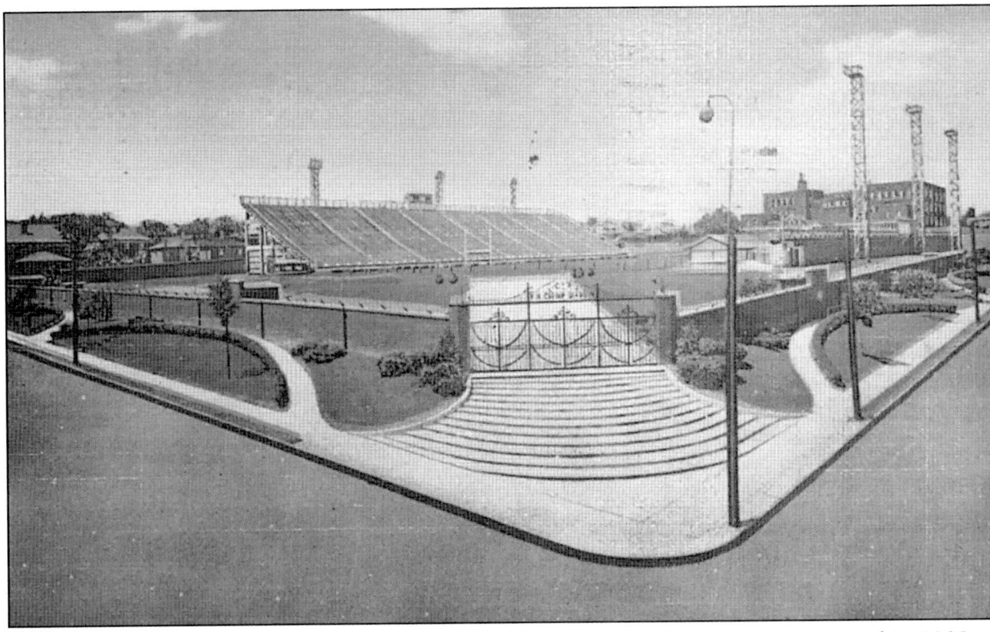

E.H. Crump Stadium. This postcard shows the E.H. Crump Stadium as it appeared in 1939.

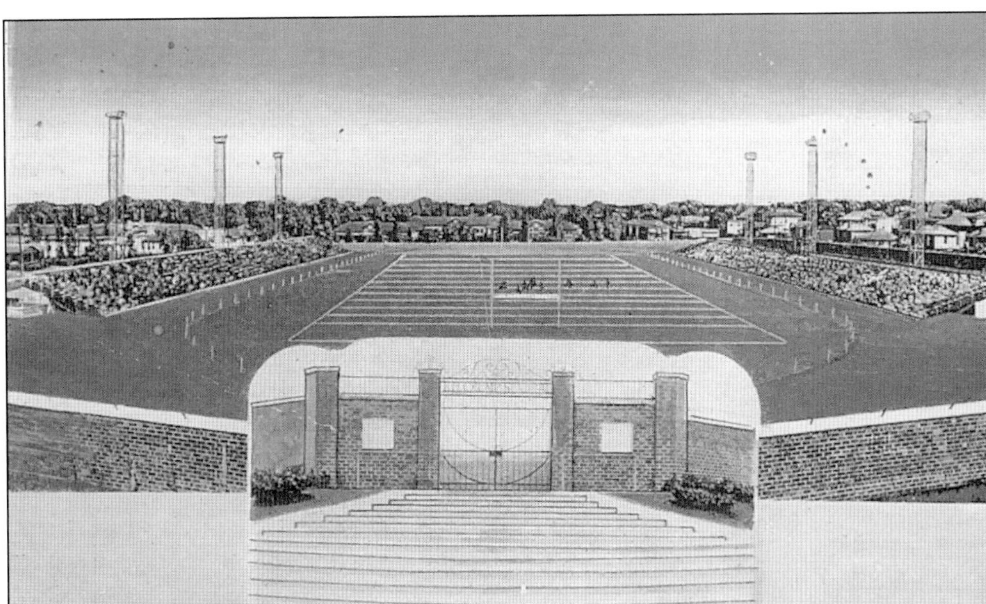

The Athletic Center of Memphis / E.H.Crump Stadium. This postcard, from the same period as the previous one, shows the entrance gates, as well as a more symmetric view of the field.

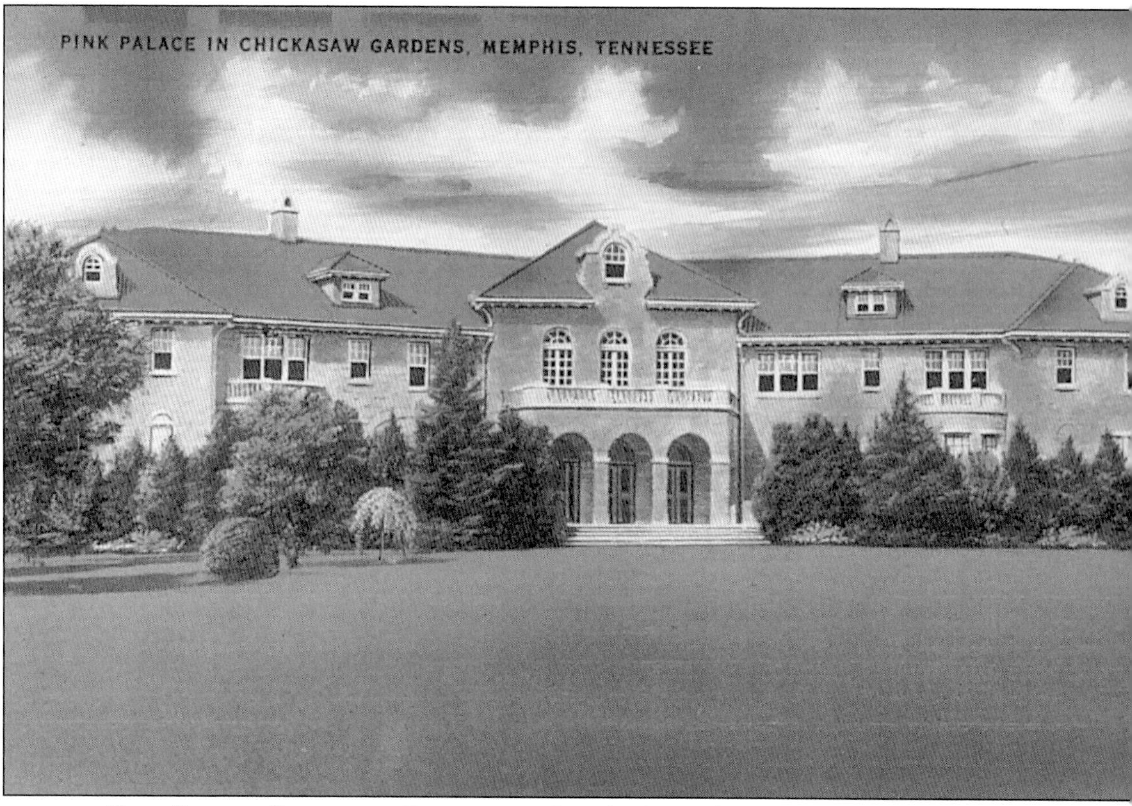

PINK PALACE-CHICKASAW GARDENS. Today, the house known as the Pink Palace is owned by the city and serves as a museum. The house located at 3050 Central Avenue was built as a residence in 1922 by Clarence Saunders, founder of the Piggly Wiggly, the first self-service grocery store chain. There were, at one time, nearly 3,000 Piggly Wiggly stores nationwide, and the chain he founded still exists today. The house itself was named for his three daughters, Cla-Le-Clare, but was dubbed "Pink Palace" by Memphians, due to the pink hue of the marble with which it was constructed. It was situated on 160 acres and had a lake and a planned golf course, as well as many exotic features within the residence itself, including a shooting gallery and bowling alley.

After spending more than a million dollars on the project, Clarence Saunders lost his fortune and, sadly, never occupied the magnificent house at all. The house and land were sold to developers, subdivided, and became the area now known as Chickasaw Gardens, one of Memphis' best residential districts. The house and ten surrounding acres were given to the city, and a museum was opened in 1930. Subsequent development within the house itself in 1977, and later additions, including an IMAX Theatre, have brought the museum to its present status. The museum itself pays homage to regional history as well as to matters of scientific interest. A reproduction of Saunder's first Piggly Wiggly is on permanent display. Other rotating exhibits are housed here as well.

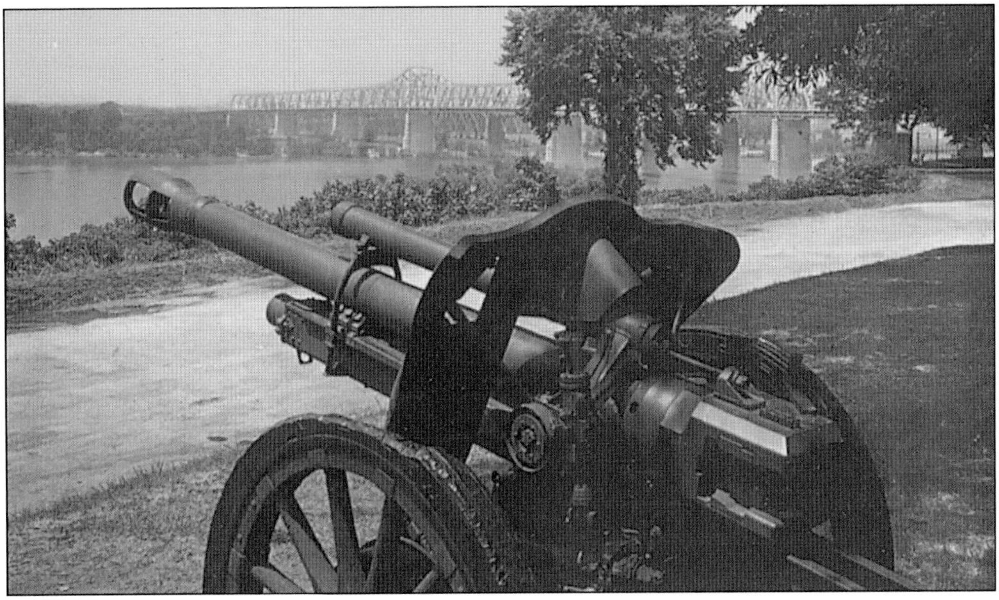

View from DeSoto Park. This 1965 postcard shows DeSoto Park, south of the Memphis Bridges. It was here that Spanish explorer Hernando de Soto first looked across the Mississippi River.

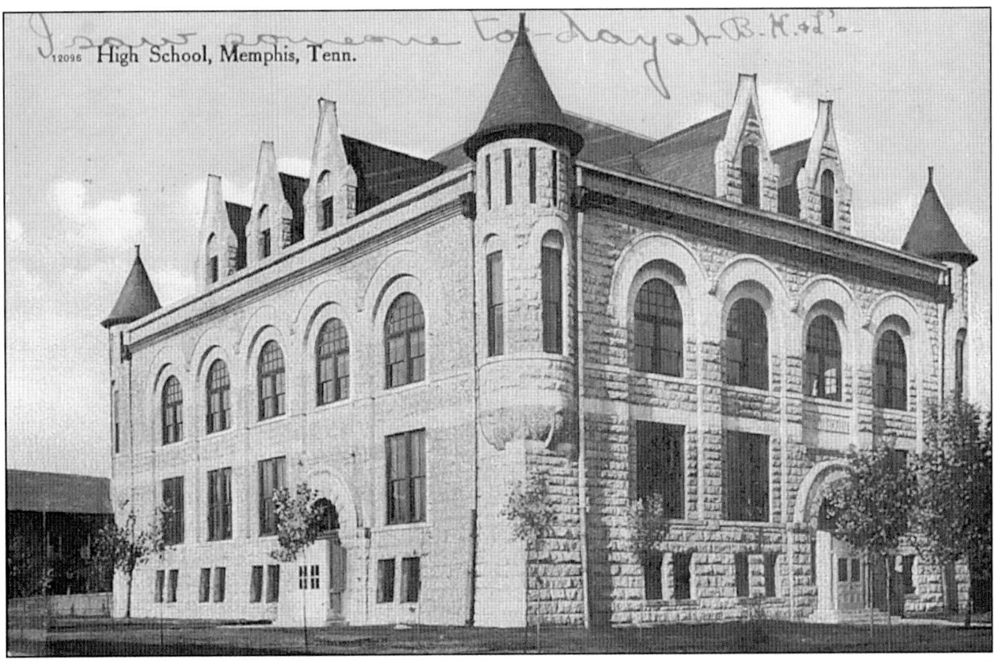

High School, Memphis, Tennessee. The Memphis High School pictured in this 1909 postcard resembles a great stone castle more than anything else. It was located on Poplar Avenue and was the first public high school in the city.

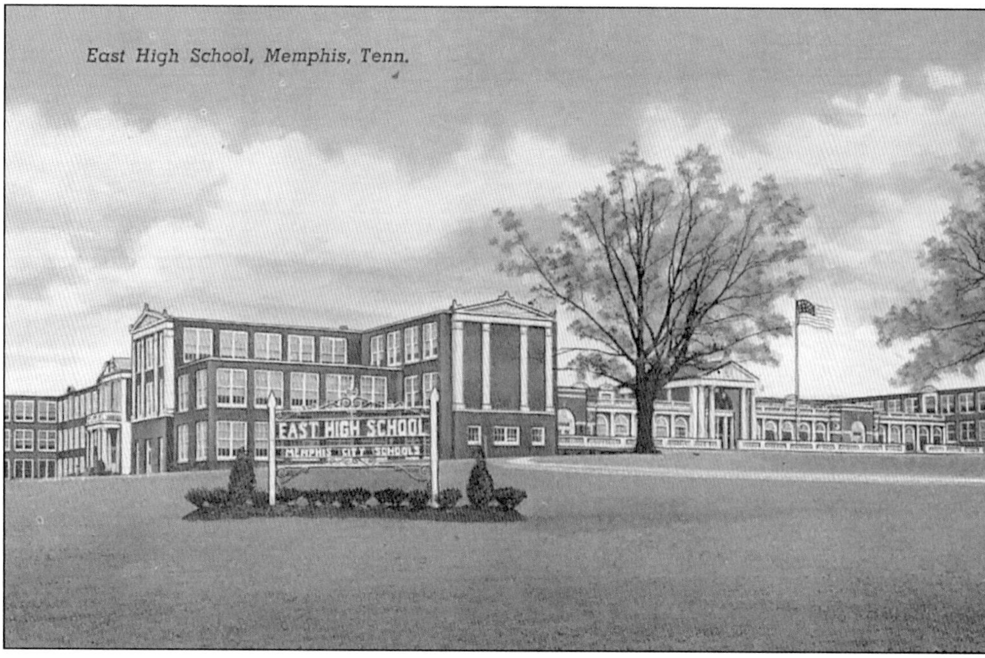

EAST HIGH SCHOOL. This postcard shows East High School on Poplar Avenue looking much the same in 1958 as it does now. At the time the high school was built, it was considered to be in east Memphis. Today, Memphis continues east on Poplar for miles. (Curt Teich Archives.)

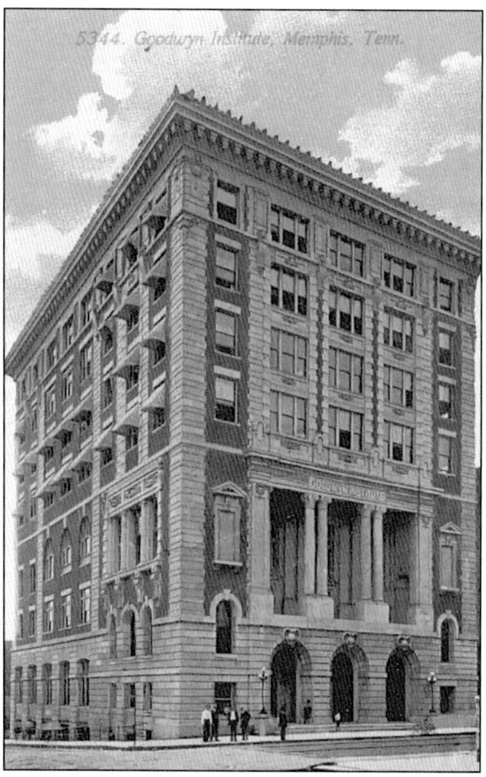

GOODWYN INSTITUTE. The Goodwyn Institute was built at Second and Madison in 1907 after the death of William Goodwyn, whose will provided for this educational gift to the city. A large library and 900-seat auditorium were available for public use. The auditorium was used for free public lectures by prominent figures of the day and featured a raked main floor and a circular balcony supported by massive square columns topped with elaborate Corinthian capitals. Unfortunately, the building was razed in the 1950s and replaced with a bank building.

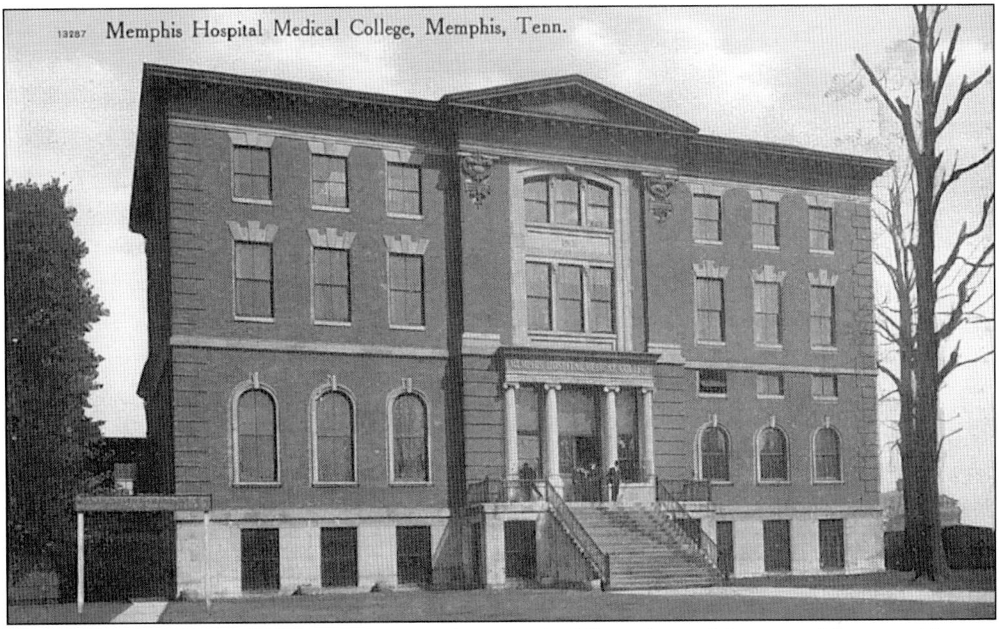

MEMPHIS HOSPITAL MEDICAL COLLEGE. The 1902 building pictured here was known as Rogers Hall at this time and was part of the Memphis Medical College. It would, along with several other medical facilities of the day, end up as part of the University of Tennessee medical system.

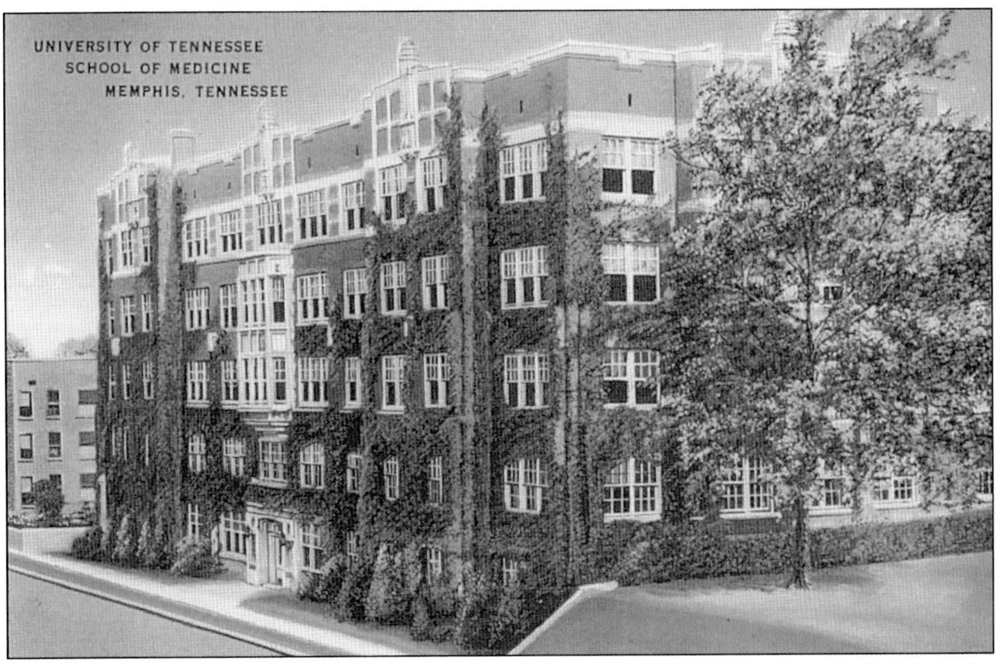

UNIVERSITY OF TENNESSEE SCHOOL OF MEDICINE. What would ultimately become the University of Tennessee School of Medicine came into being in 1911 when the University of Tennessee opened in Memphis and merged with the existing Memphis College of Physicians and Surgeons. Development of the Medical Center continued over the ensuing years, and today, the Medical Center is one of the largest in any urban area in the nation.

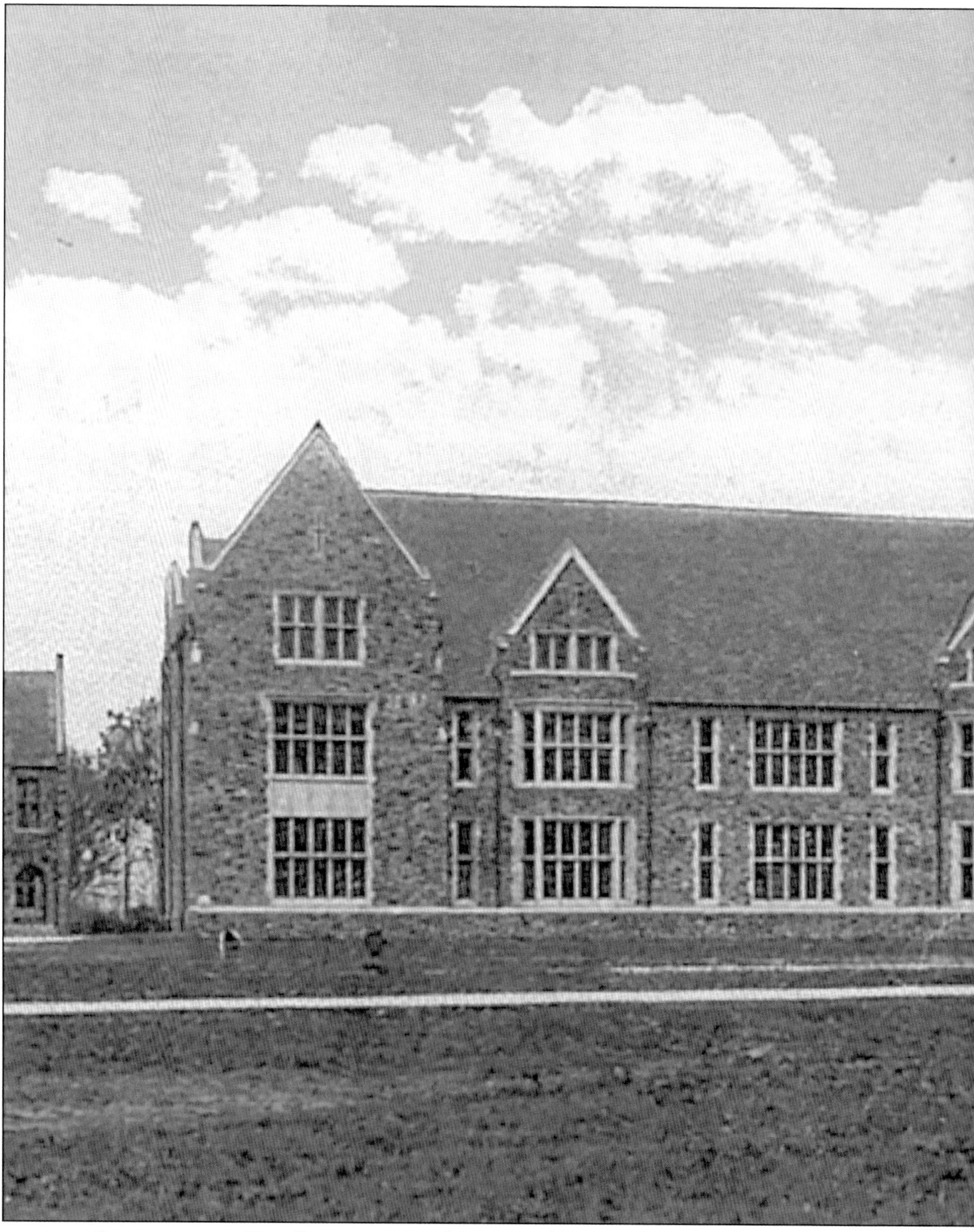

SOUTHWESTERN–THE COLLEGE OF THE MISSISSIPPI VALLEY. The roots of Rhodes College extend to Clarksville, Tennessee, to what was known at one time as Southwestern Presbyterian University. The institution moved to Memphis in 1924, and the name was changed to Southwestern at Memphis.

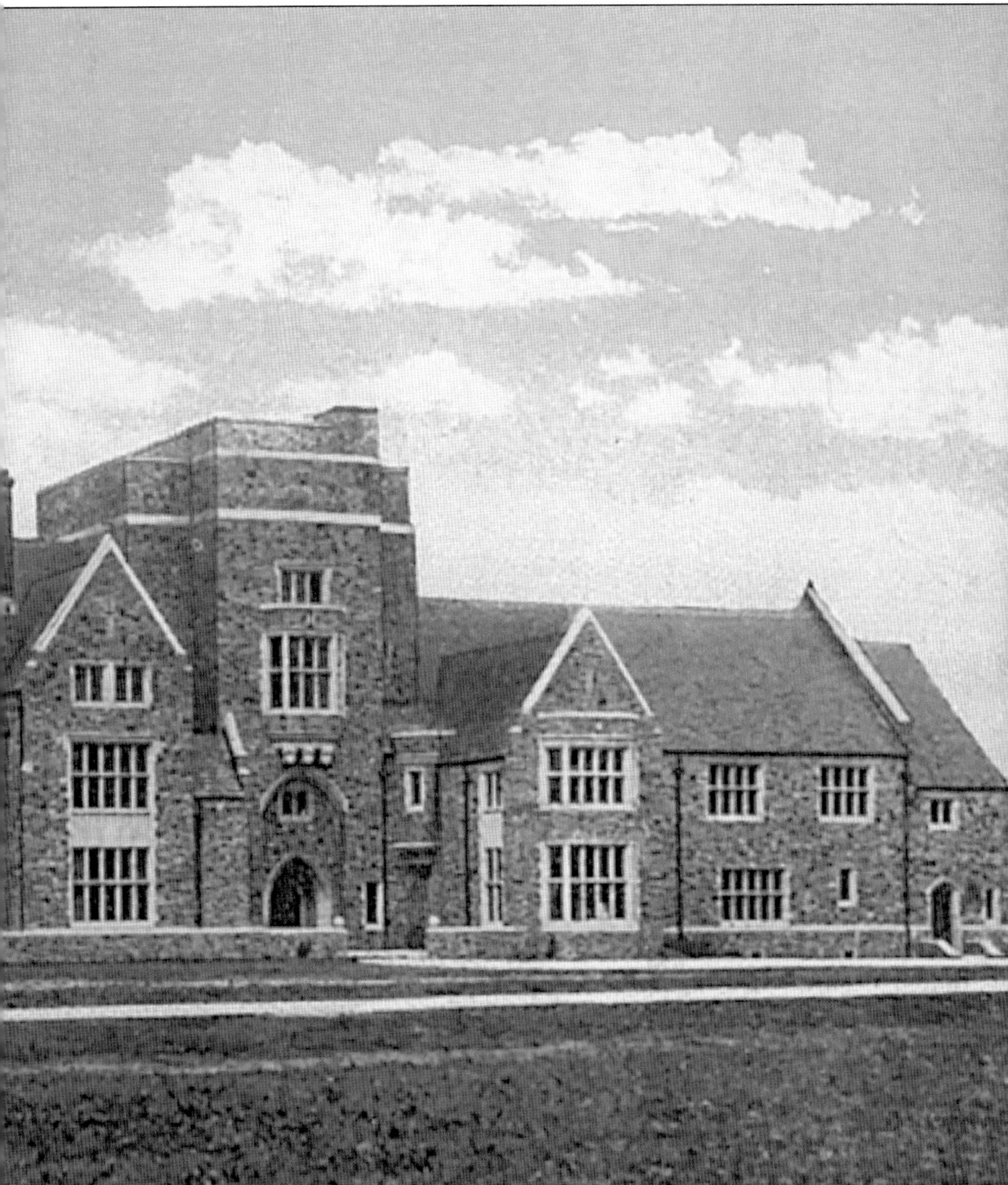

The administration building, seen in this postcard, is the most recognizable building on campus, and the most photographed. The caption here reads "Southwestern, The College of the Mississippi Valley." In time, the school was known simply as Southwestern. (Curt Teich Archives.)

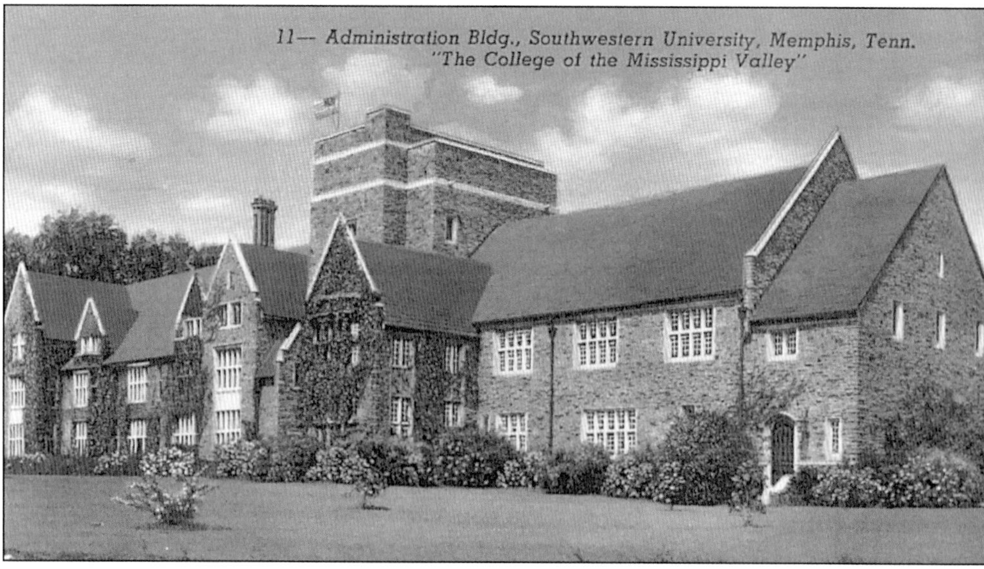

ADMINISTRATION BUILDING, SOUTHWESTERN UNIVERSITY. What was well known and respected as Southwestern College regrettably changed its name to Rhodes College in 1984, in a move viewed by many as pretentious. Be that as it may, the college grounds and buildings are beautiful, with the majority of buildings constructed of cut stone and Gothic in design. Except for the presence of shrubbery and ivy, this 1942 postcard shows little difference from the previous, much earlier postcard. (Curt Teich Archives.)

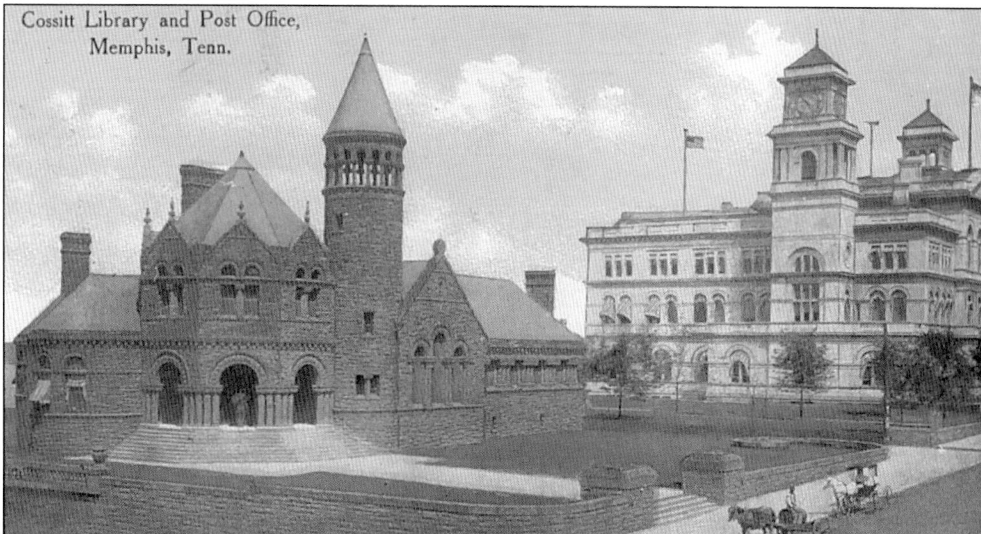

COSSITT LIBRARY AND POST OFFICE. This massive 1893 Romanesque stone building was the city's first public library. It was, as may be seen in this 1910 postcard, an imposing structure from any angle and was an impressive landmark, clearly visible from the river. It was named in honor of Frederick Cossitt and was given to the city by his daughters. The magnificent building seen to the right was the 1876 Post Office, Courthouse, and Customs House. The building underwent several significant architectural additions and changes before reaching its present configuration, the most significant of which was the 1929 removal of the two towers seen here.

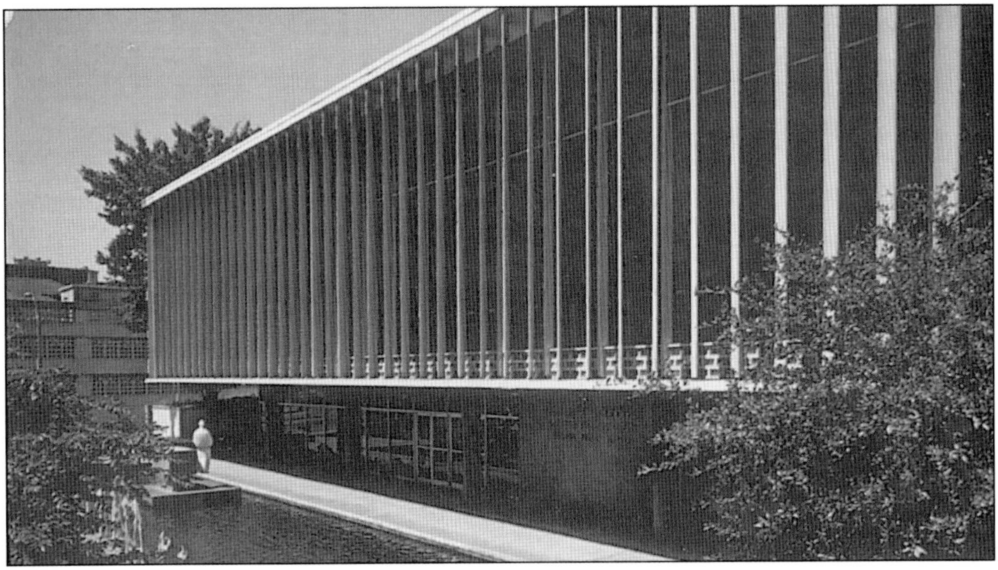

Cossitt Library. The new Cossitt Library, located at 33 South Front Street, replaced the original (see above) library, which was razed in 1958. As may be seen from comparison, the original building was a beautiful, if ponderous, work of art. The newer building was built at a time in American architecture when the older, heavy-looking buildings were considered by most city planners to be obsolete vestiges of another, less progressive era. America, as a nation, seemed to be totally concentrating on the future.

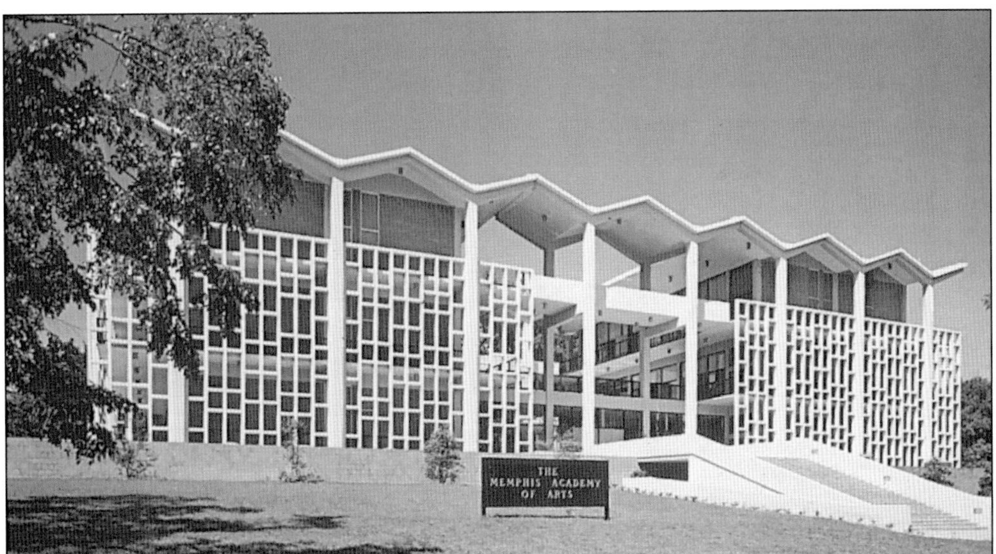

Memphis Academy of Arts. The Memphis Academy of Arts, now known locally as MCA, was founded in 1936 and was originally housed at the Board of Education Building on Adams, in the area currently known as Victorian Village. It eventually moved to a new building at Overton Park in 1955, after the Japanese Gardens and Tea House were bulldozed following the attack on Pearl Harbor. The tranquil Midtown setting offers an excellent location for this fully accredited independent art college. Today, the school is called the Memphis College of Art, after a name change in 1985.

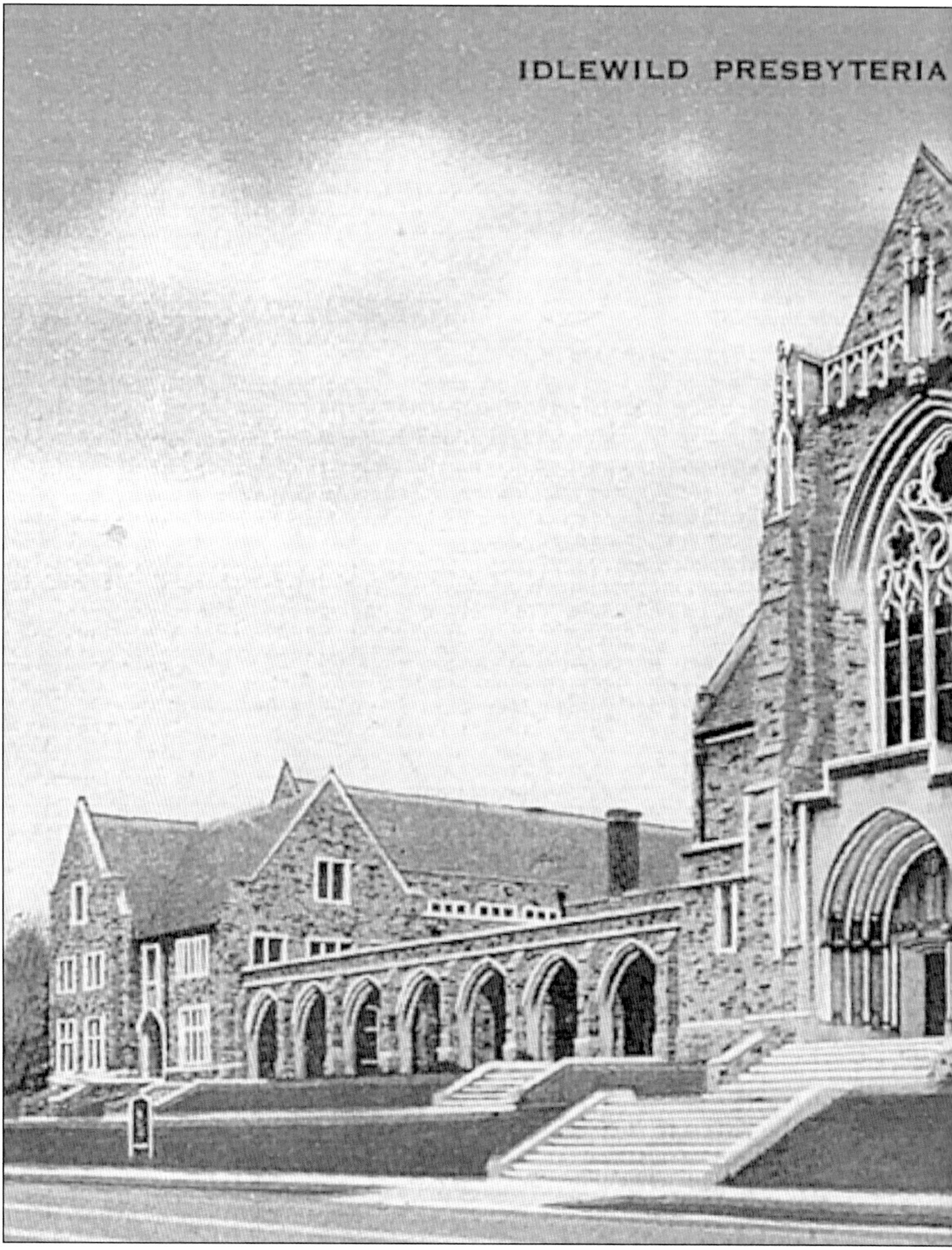

IDLEWILD PRESBYTERIAN CHURCH. The church, built in 1927 and located on Union Avenue, is a splendid example of Gothic Revival architecture and is reminiscent of the great cathedrals of

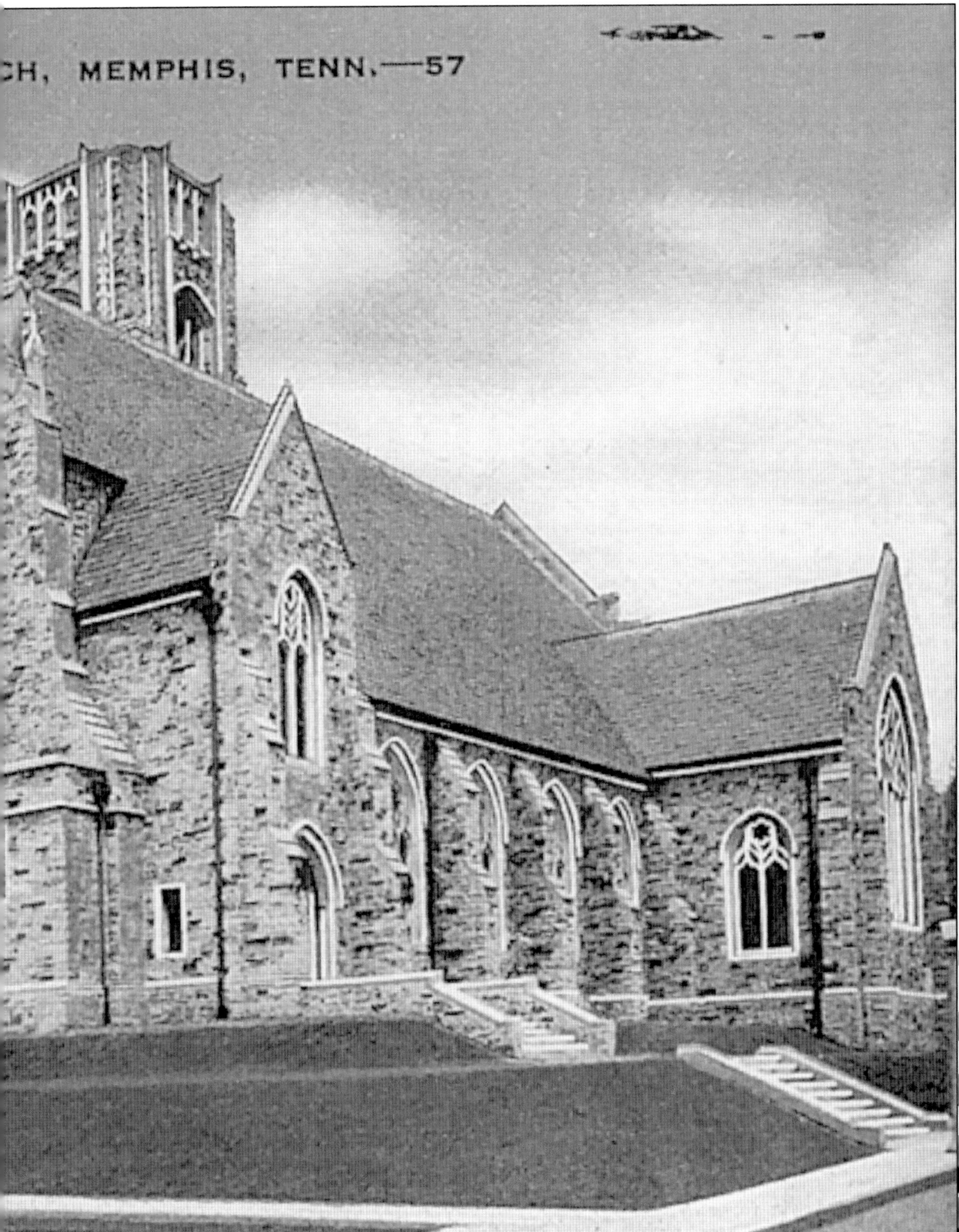

Europe. This heavy-looking style was employed extensively in the construction of churches in America during the 1920s.

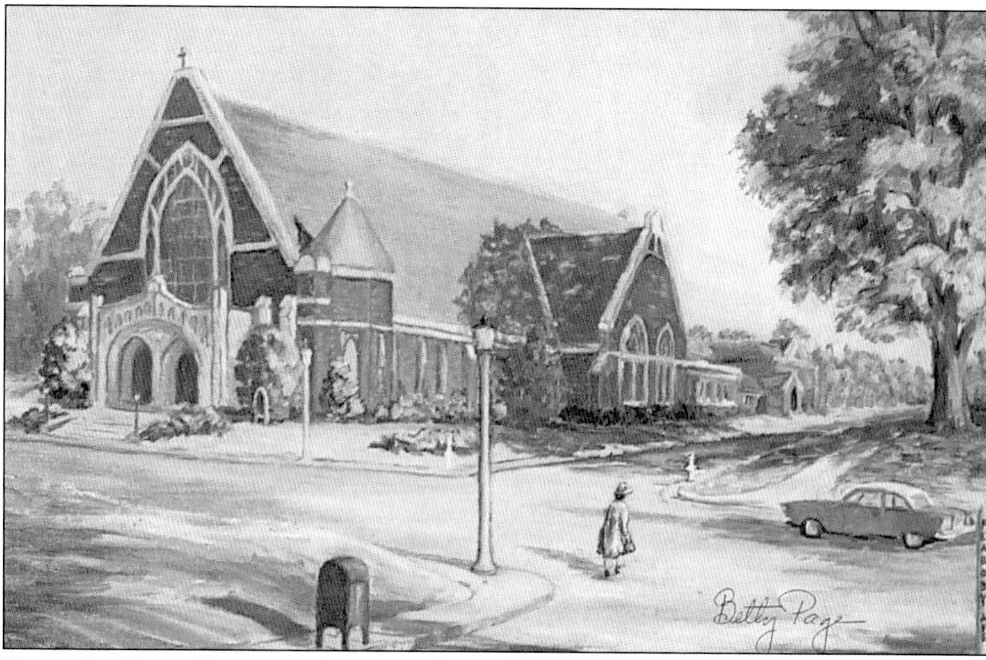

GRACE ST. LUKES EPISCOPAL CHURCH. This painting, of the church located at 1720 Peabody, is signed Betty Page. Although the famous 1950s pinup queen (a Nashville native) abandoned her photo modeling career and took up Christian ministry in the 1950s, it is doubtful that she painted the postcard image seen here. Nonetheless, one cannot help but wonder.

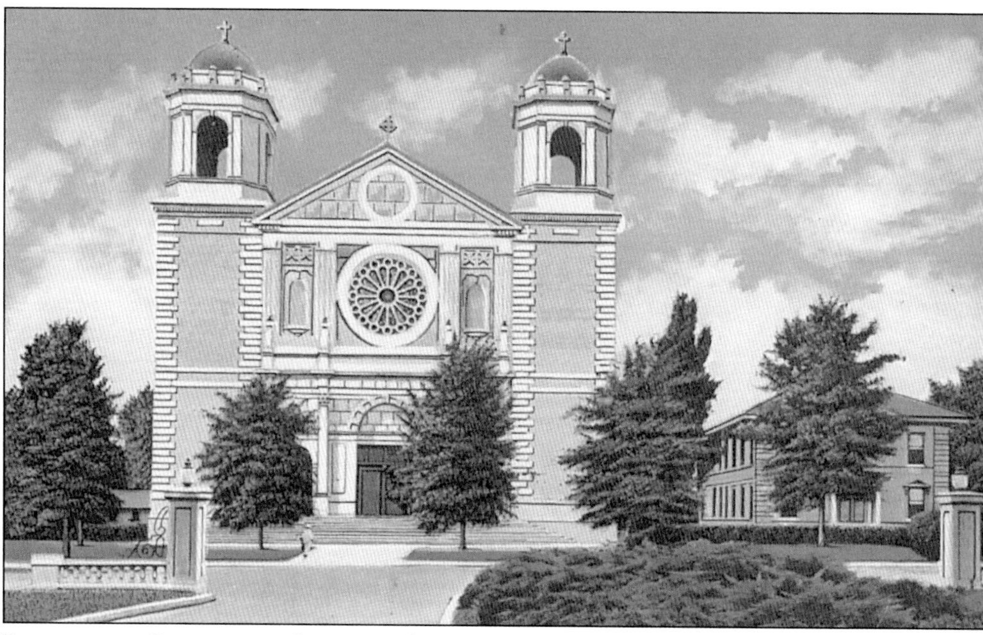

IMMACULATE CONCEPTION CHURCH. The Immaculate Conception Church, located on Central, was completed in 1938 and was, at the time, the largest Catholic church in Memphis. In some ways, this structure is reminiscent of a modernized southwestern mission similar to those found in New Mexico and Arizona. (Curt Teich Archives.)

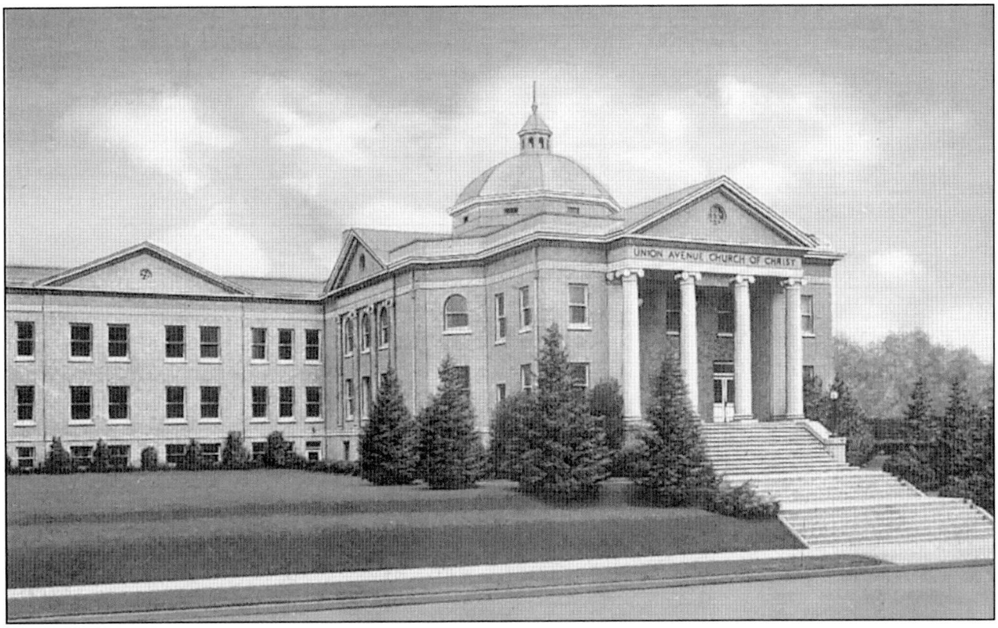

Union Avenue Church of Christ. The Union Avenue Church of Christ is located at 1930 Union at Tucker Street, and at the time of its construction, it had a 1200-seat auditorium, a smaller 400-seat chapel, and 38 other rooms. At the time of this postcard in 1943, there were 27 separate Sunday bible classes and eight regular services weekly. Total membership was 1,400, a fairly large membership for any Southern church at the time. (Curt Teich Archives.)

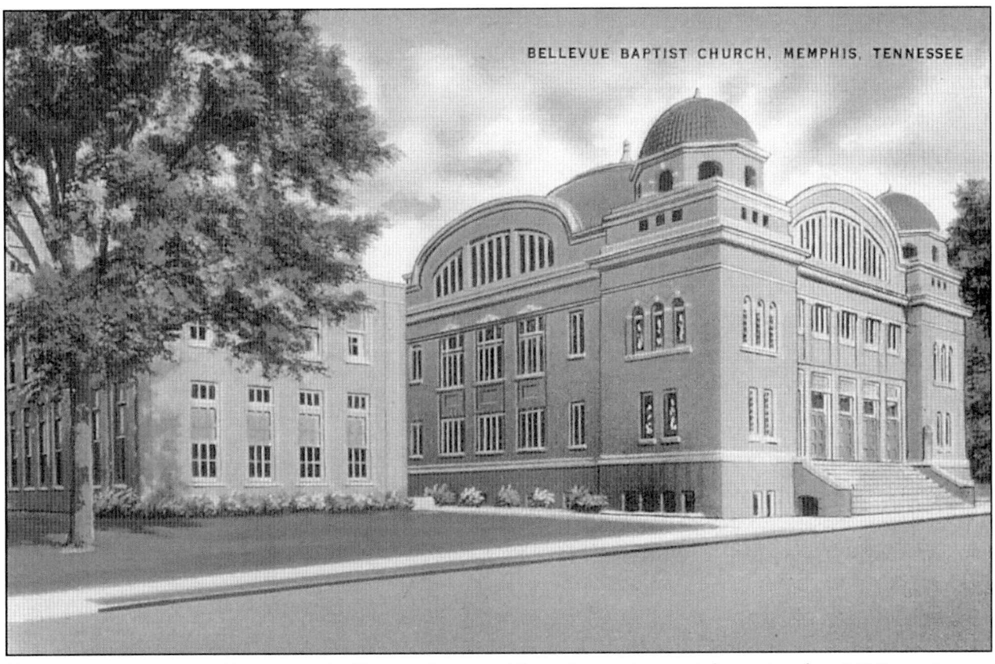

Bellevue Baptist Church. Bellevue Baptist Church is pictured here in the 1930s, prior to the congregation's move to East Memphis. The building seen here began as a small chapel but underwent many additions as the congregation continued to grow in size.

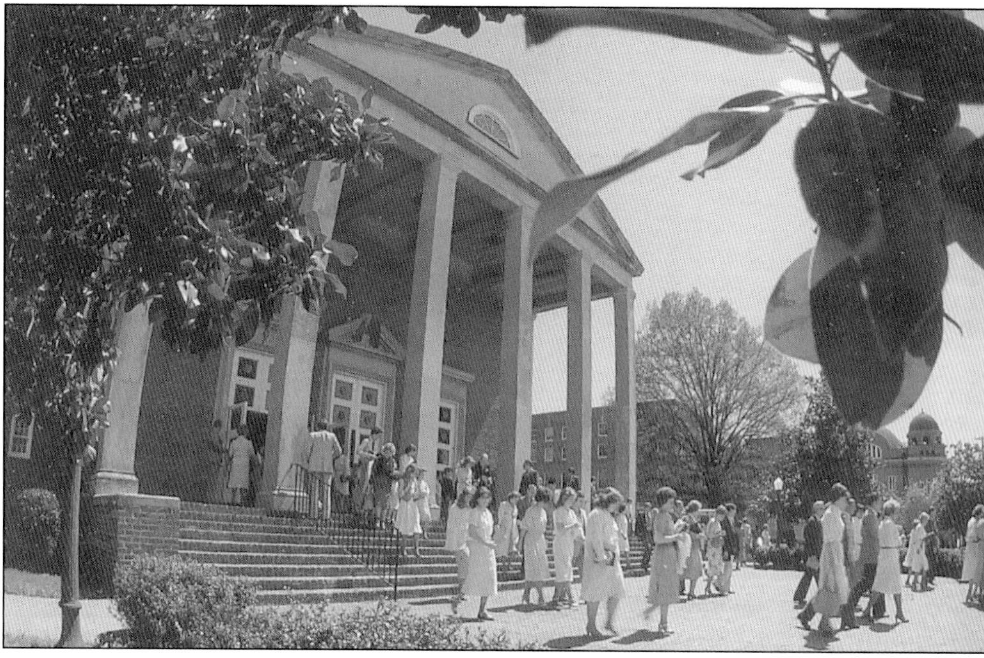

Bellevue Baptist Church. Here, parishioners emerge from the newer (1952) main sanctuary after a Sunday service. The older building, pictured above, is visible to the far right of this image.

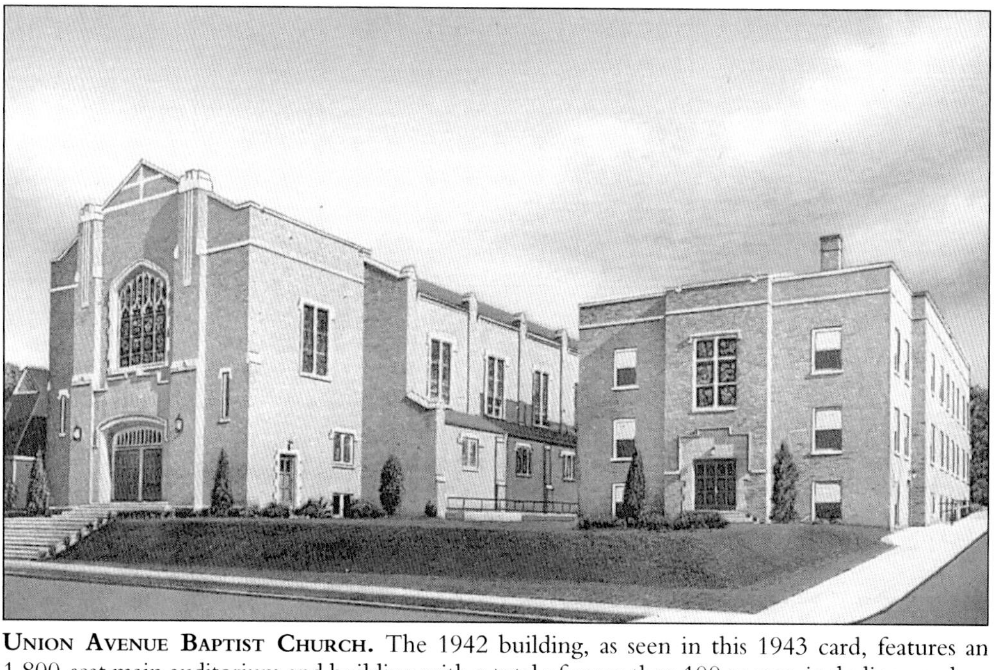

Union Avenue Baptist Church. The 1942 building, as seen in this 1943 card, features an 1,800-seat main auditorium and building with a total of more than 100 rooms, including modern offices, a kitchen, and dining facilities. (Curt Teich Archives.)

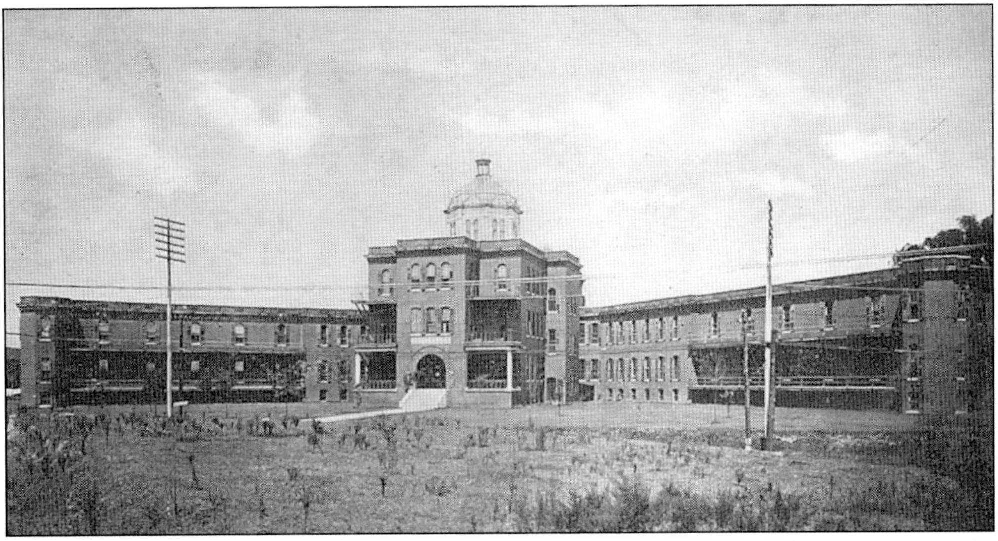

City Hospital. Memphis has been a major medical center since the early 1900s. From the massive Baptist Memorial Hospital to the Medical Center, St. Jude's Childrens Hospital, and University of Tennessee Medical School, the city offers a wide array of medical services. The old City Hospital, as seen in this 1908 postcard, was the city's first municipal hospital.

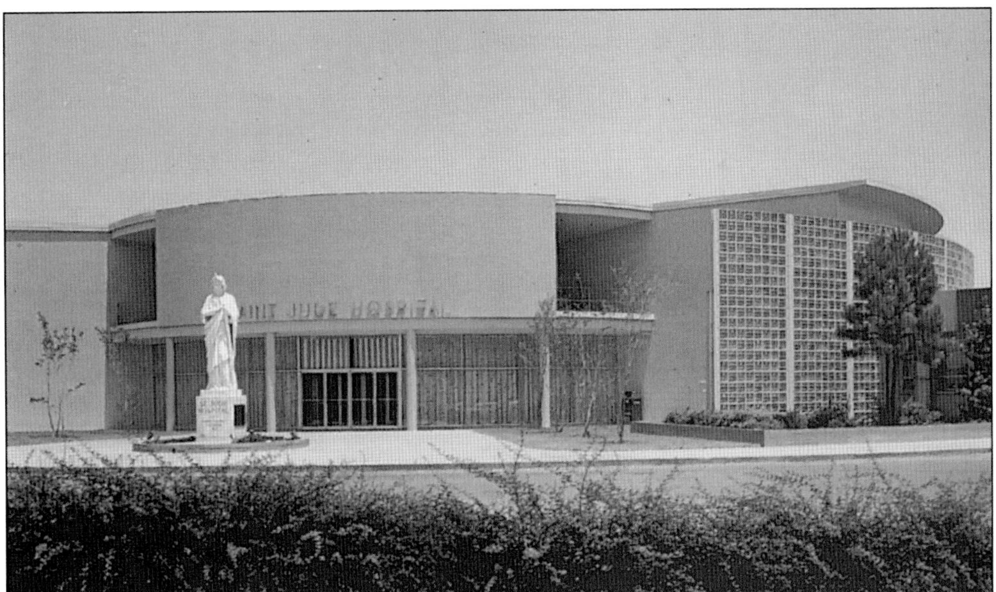

St. Jude Hospital. This early picture is of St. Jude Children's Research Hospital. The story of this children's hospital is well known. Actor and comedian Danny Thomas was down on his luck and struggling to become successful. He prayed to St. Jude and promised that if he became successful, he would build a children's hospital. He became very successful and kept his word. Today, this hospital is a living tribute to his philanthropy.

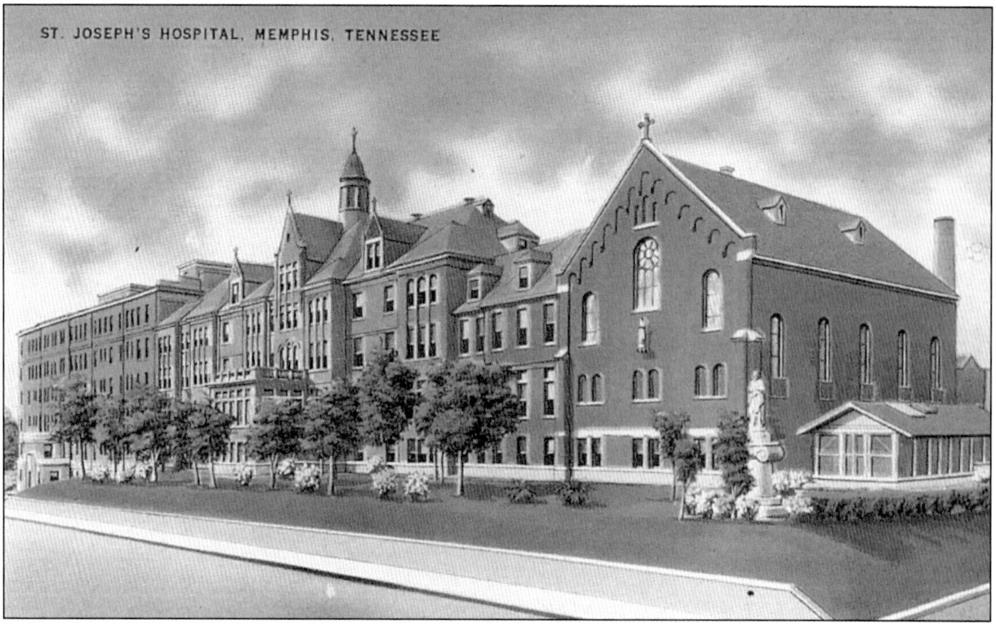

ST. JOSEPH'S HOSPITAL. St. Joseph's Hospital, as seen in this postcard from the 1930s, shows little change from earlier images. It was founded in 1889 by Franciscan Sisters, with the large brick structure seen here built in 1885. In 1969, this hospital was the target of a 12-week strike by the American Federation of State, County, and Municipal Employees.

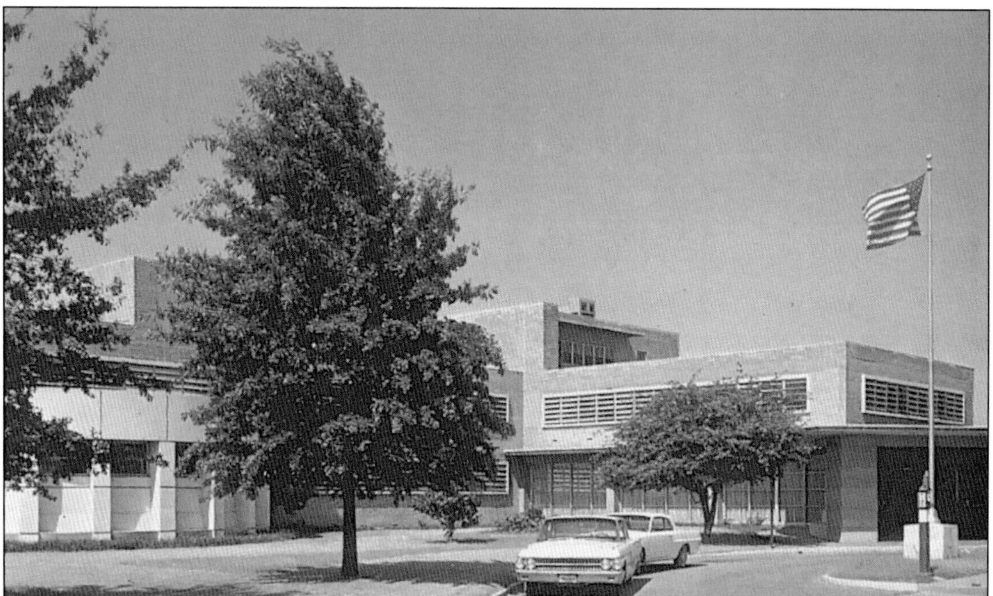

LE BONHEUR CHILDREN'S HOSPITAL. The Le Bonheur Children's Hospital is seen here in this mid-1960s postcard photo. Le Bonheur became a part of Methodist Healthcare in the mid-1990s.

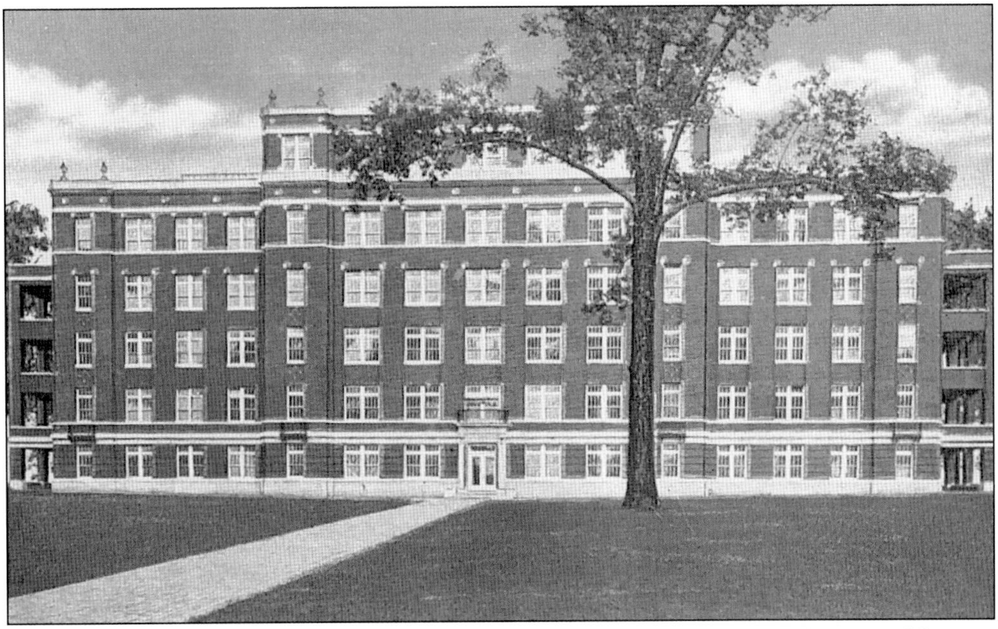

U.S. War Veterans Hospital. The massive U.S. War Veterans Hospital, pictured here, is located at 1025 Lamar and at the time of this photo, during World War II, "is caring for the World War veterans who paid, with their health and strength the price of victory."

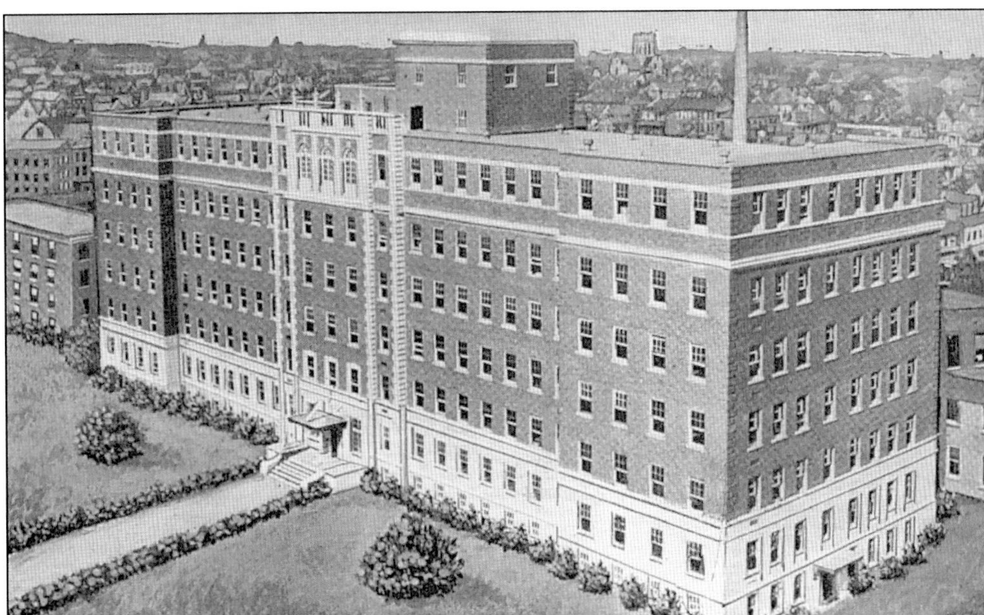

John Gaston Hospital. At the time this postcard was sent, the city-owned John Gaston Hospital, located on Madison Avenue, was one year old. It was started with a $300,000 endowment replacing the Memphis General Hospital in 1936 and eventually came to be known as the Regional Medical Center at Memphis. It served along with other hospitals as a teaching hospital in conjunction with the University of Tennessee Medical School.

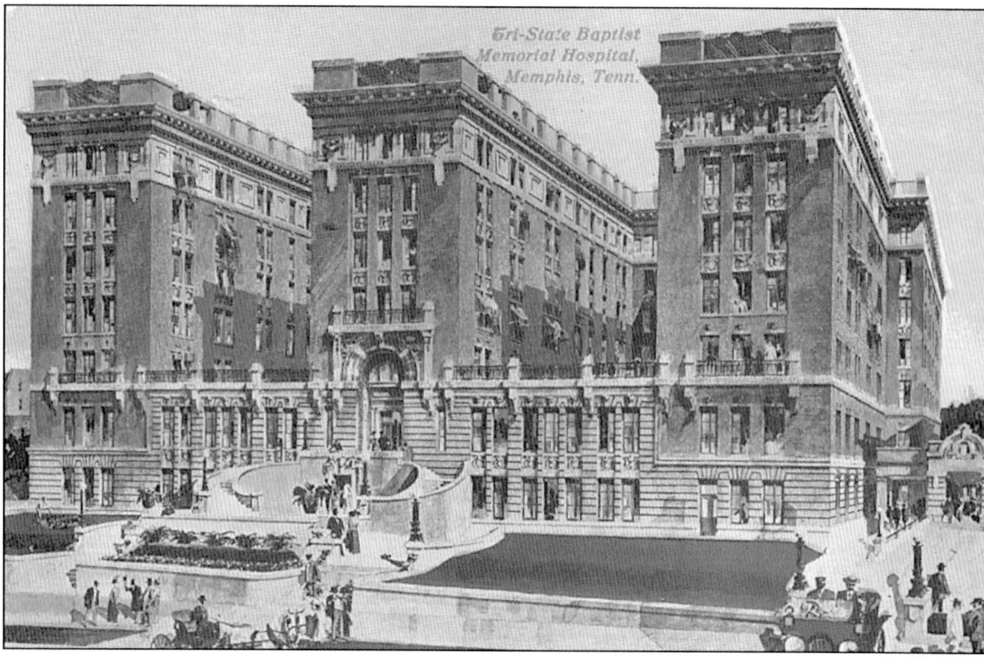

Tri State Baptist Memorial Hospital. This old postcard photo shows the 150-bed Baptist Hospital, which opened in 1912.

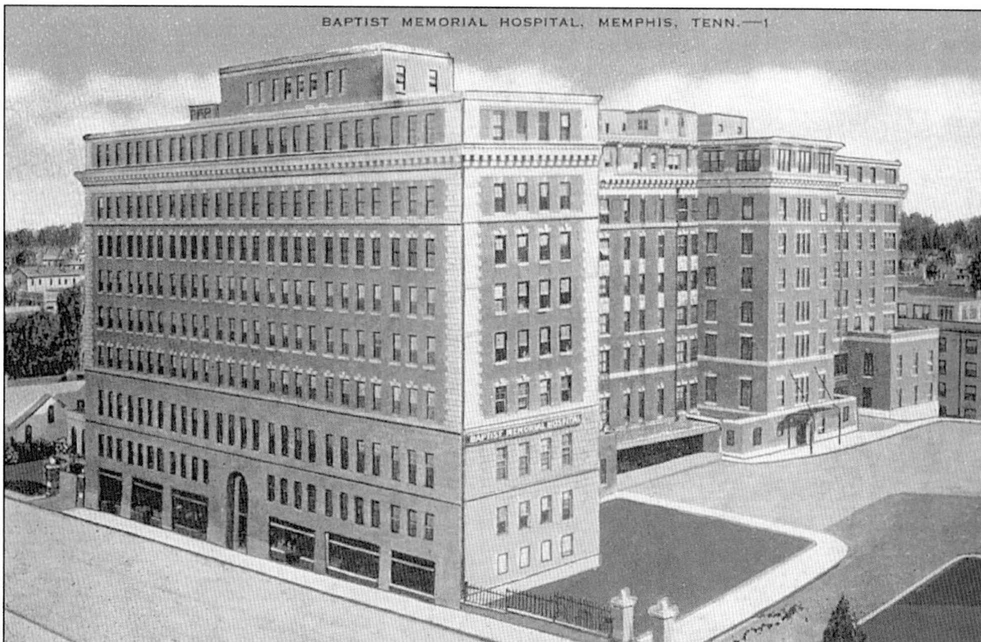

Baptist Memorial Hospital. The 550-bed Baptist Memorial Hospital, seen here, was the largest non-government owned hospital in the South at the time of this photo in the 1930s.

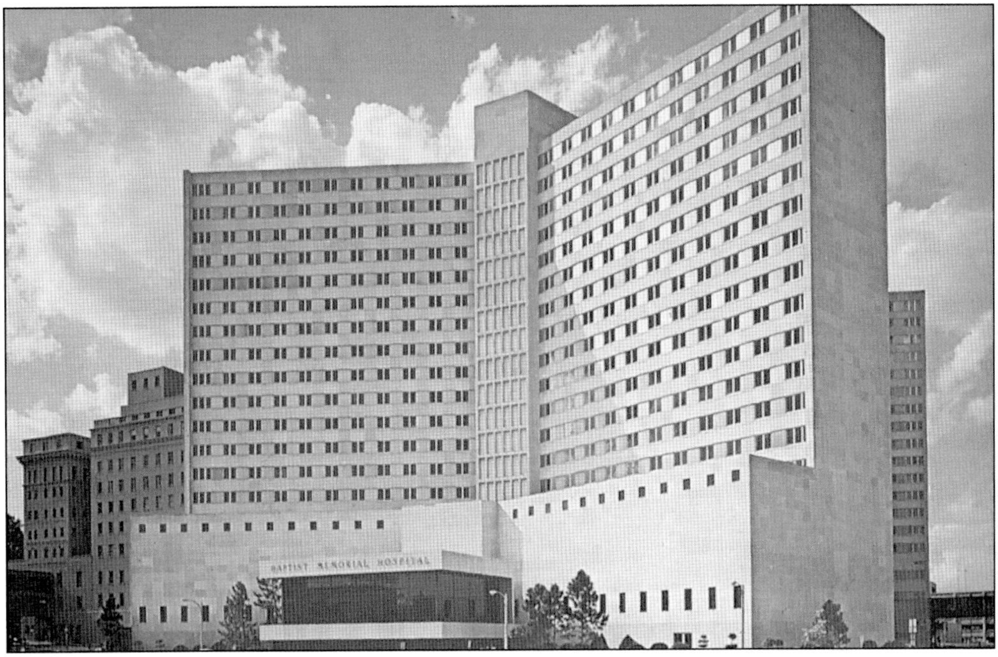

Baptist Memorial Hospital. At the time of this postcard, in the 1970s, this was the world's largest private hospital. It is located in the Medical Center site of the University of Tennessee Medical School.

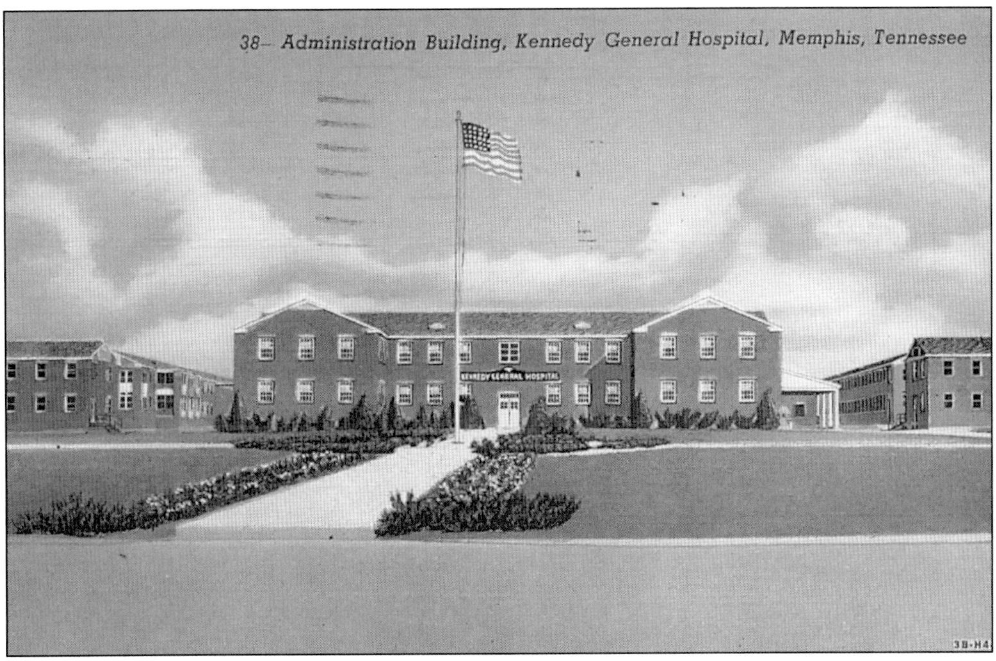

Administration Building, Kennedy General Hospital. This postcard from 1945 shows the main building of the Kennedy General Hospital, a large complex that served wounded soldiers during World War II. The approximately 150-acre site on which this hospital once stood is now part of Memphis State University's South Campus. (Curt Teich Archives.)

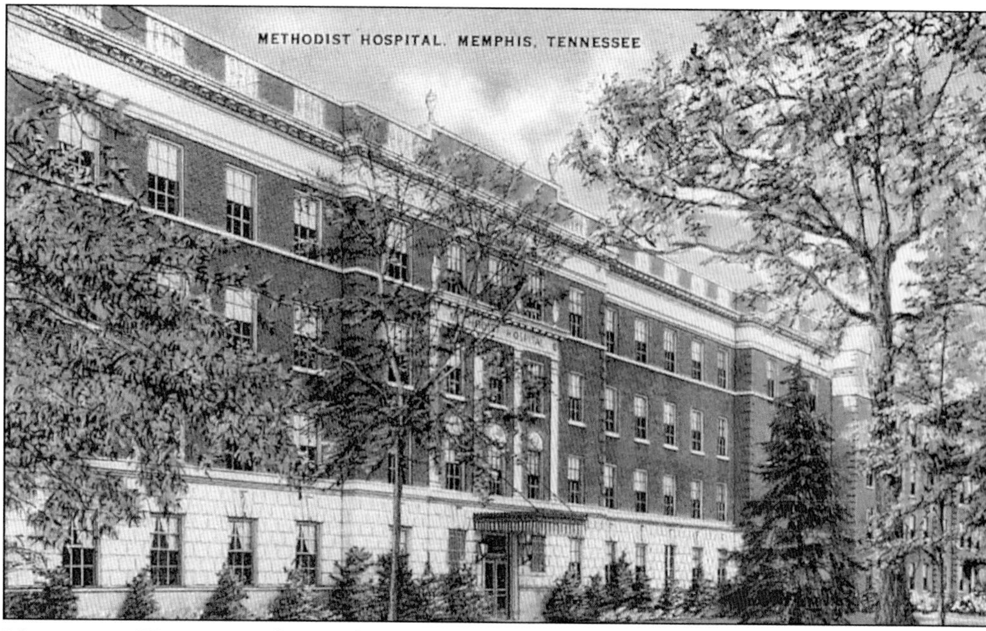

Methodist Hospital. The Methodist Hospital, seen here, was completed in 1921. Today, Methodist Healthcare is the largest hospital system in the mid-South, with 12,000 employees, 5 hospitals in Memphis, and another 8 hospitals in other west Tennessee cities.

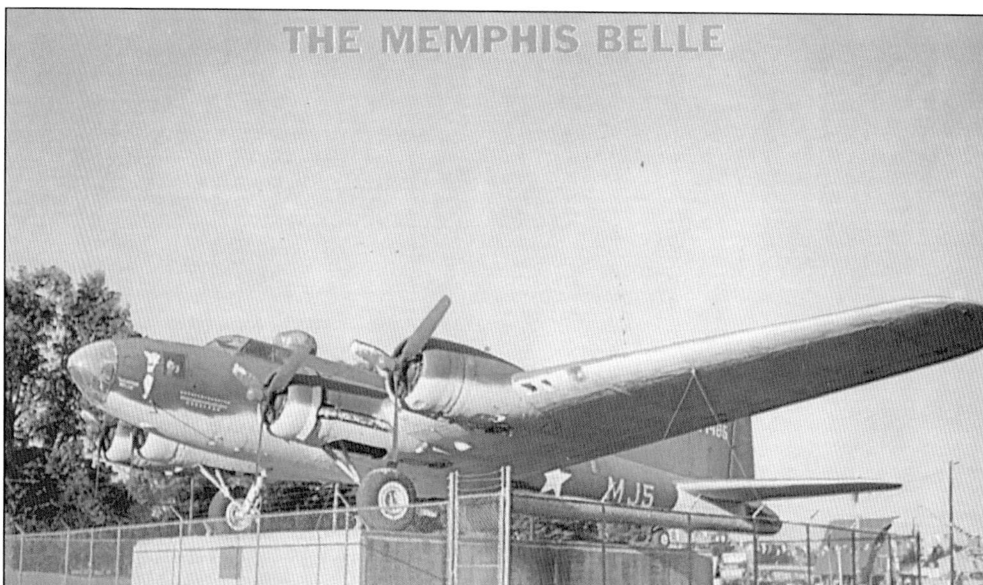

Memphis Belle. The *Memphis Belle* is undoubtedly the most famous Boeing B-17 bomber in history. After surviving many successful European missions, the plane, named for Memphian Margaret Polk, returned with its crew to the United States, and went on an extended publicity tour in support of the war effort and the sale of war bonds. It eventually returned to Memphis and was on display for years as pictured here, on fairgrounds property. When the area on the banks of the Mississippi River known as Mud Island was completed, the *Memphis Belle* was moved to an indoor display area on the site.

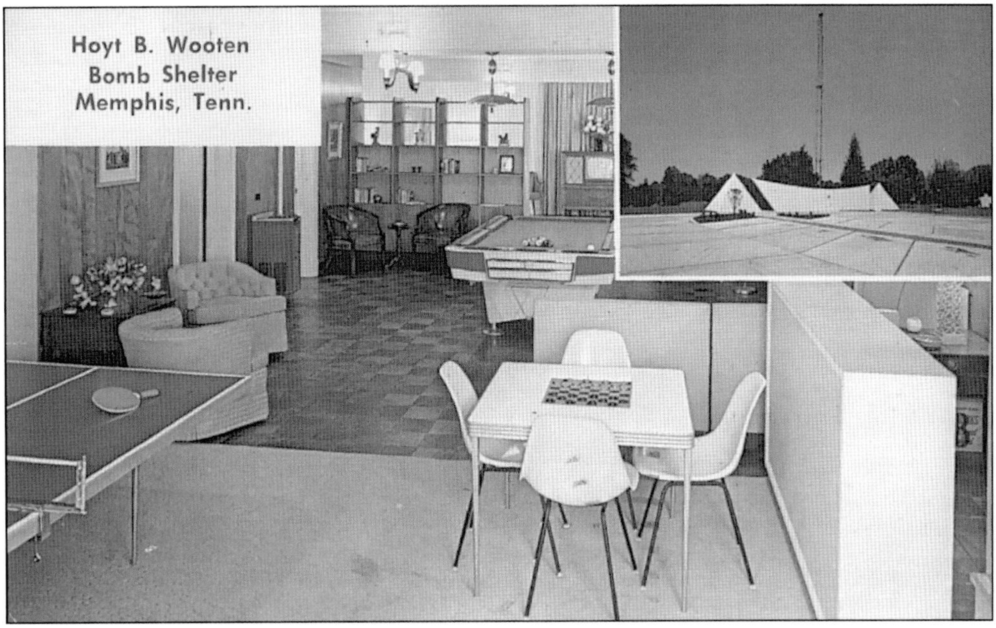

BOMB SHELTER. This underground bomb shelter, which cost more than $200,000, provided the absurd illusion that things would be pretty much the same as usual after a nuclear attack. The ping pong table and checkers, as well as the interior decor, left little doubt to the observer that a missile attack need not be overly inconvenient provided one's surroundings were fairly comfortable.

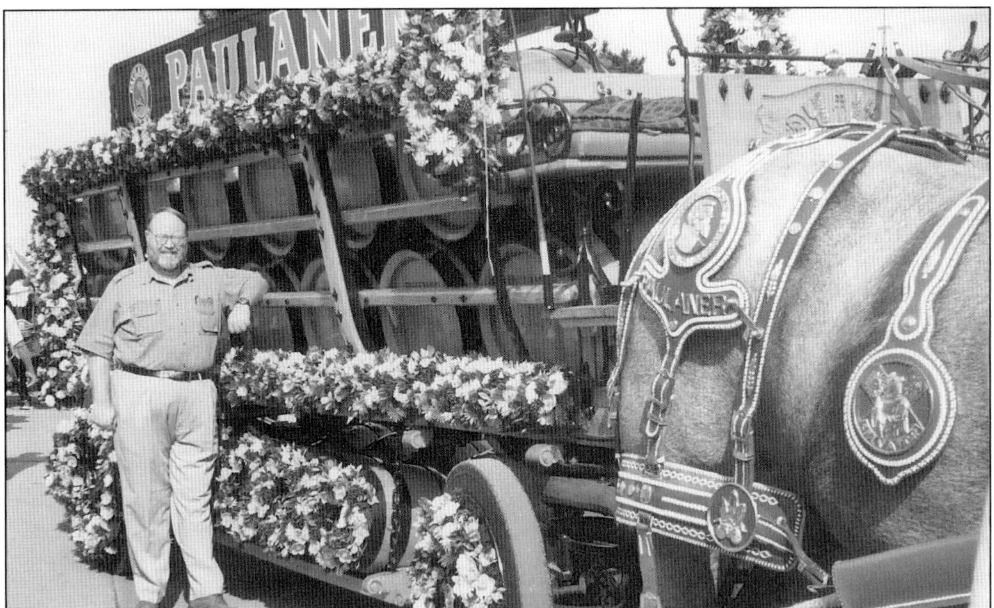

OKTOBERFEST. This is a rare photograph of reclusive Memphis financier Bard Selden at Oktoberfest. His efforts revived the once popular festival, which was discontinued during the First World War and again during the Second World War, as the result of anti-German sentiment. (Photo: Oswald Banks Lobrecue-Mid-South Cultural Archives.)

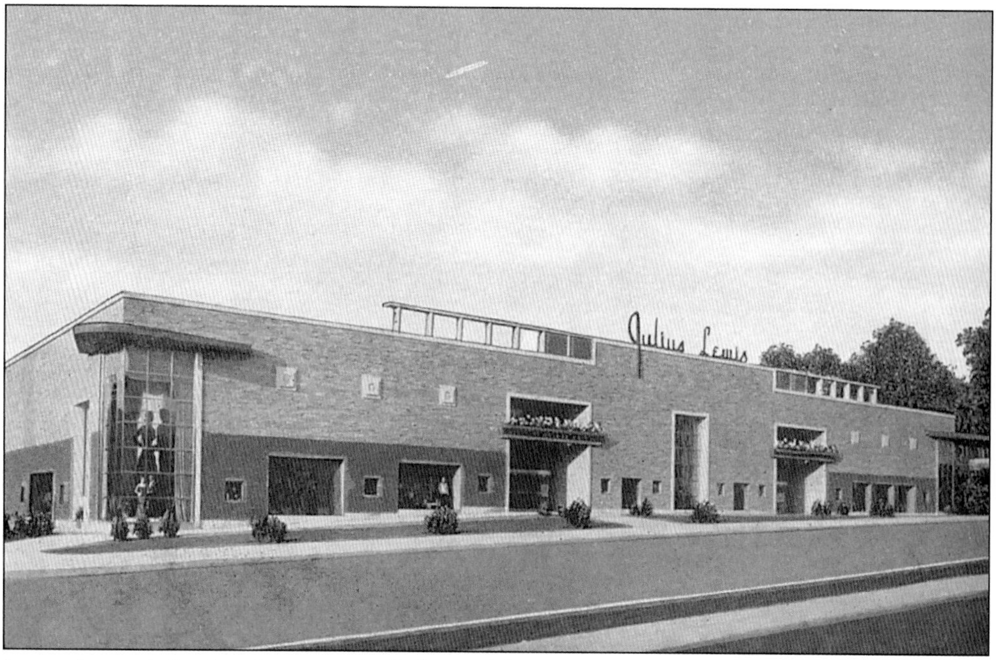

JULIUS LEWIS. Julius Lewis was originally located downtown at 145 South Main Street along with the majority of Memphis retail stores. As the city expanded into outlying areas, a second store was opened at 1460 Union. By the end of the century, this clothing store, a Memphis tradition, had closed for good.

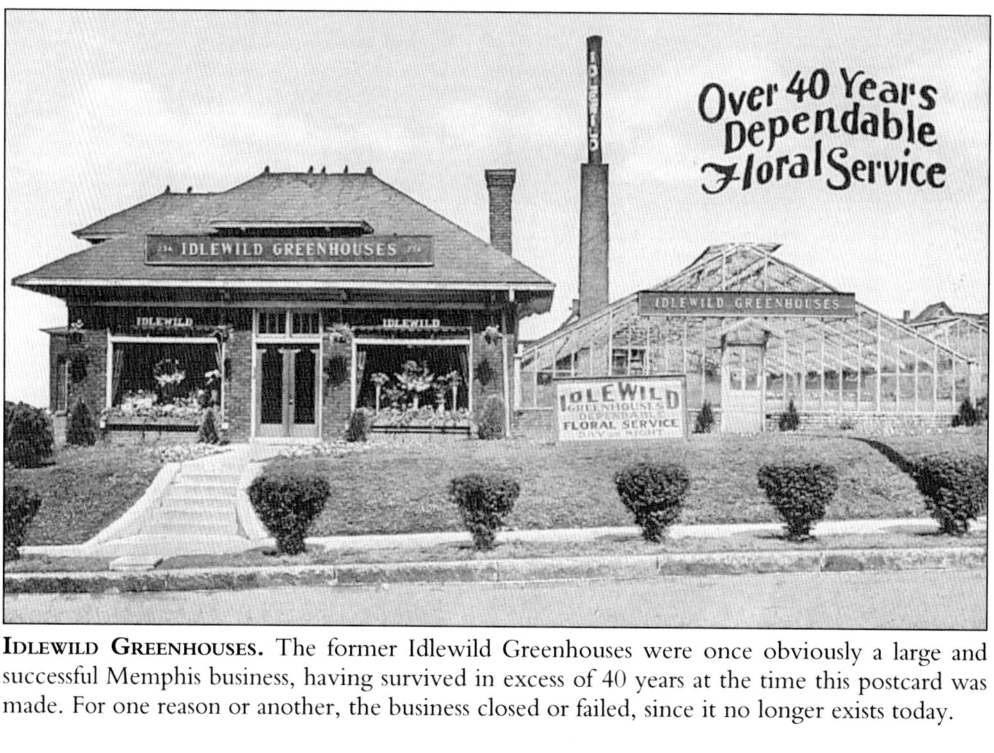

IDLEWILD GREENHOUSES. The former Idlewild Greenhouses were once obviously a large and successful Memphis business, having survived in excess of 40 years at the time this postcard was made. For one reason or another, the business closed or failed, since it no longer exists today.

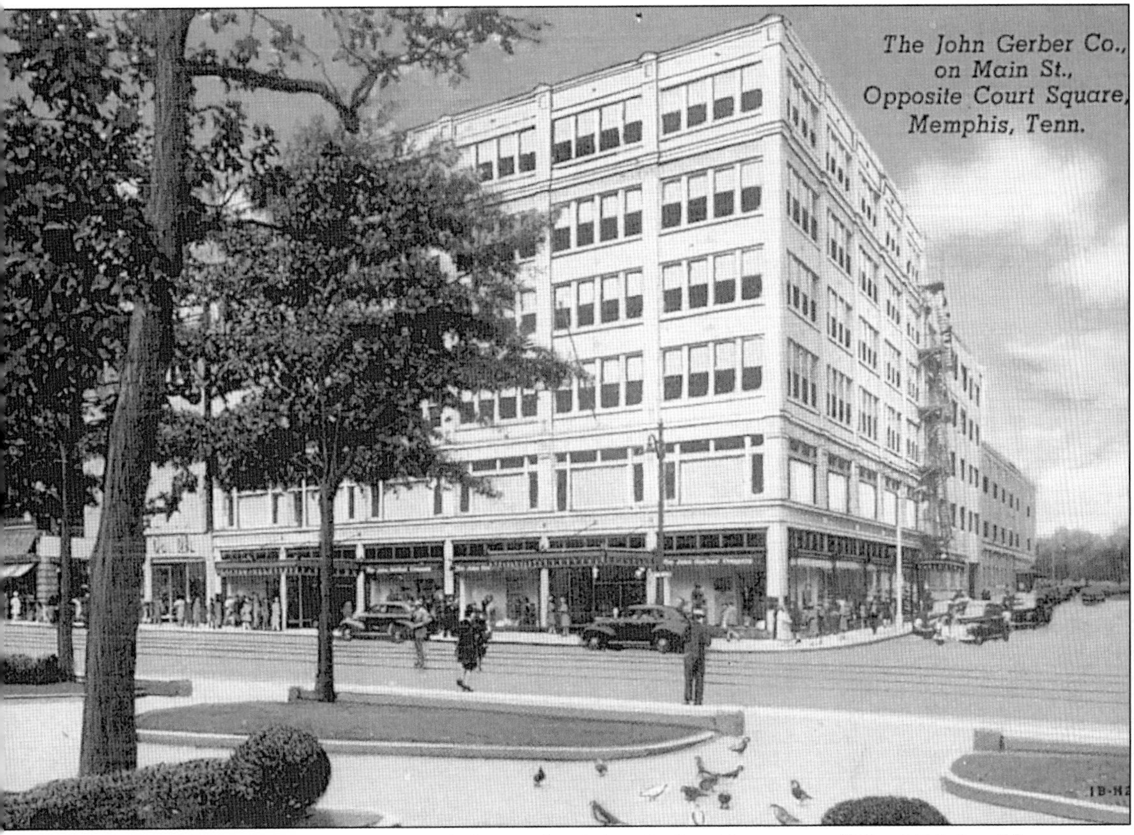

JOHN GERBER CO. This 1941 postcard shows the John Gerber Company, "The Mid-South's Finest Store," located opposite Court Square, with 1960 parking places within two blocks. The business opened in 1880 at Main and Court but closed for good in 1975.

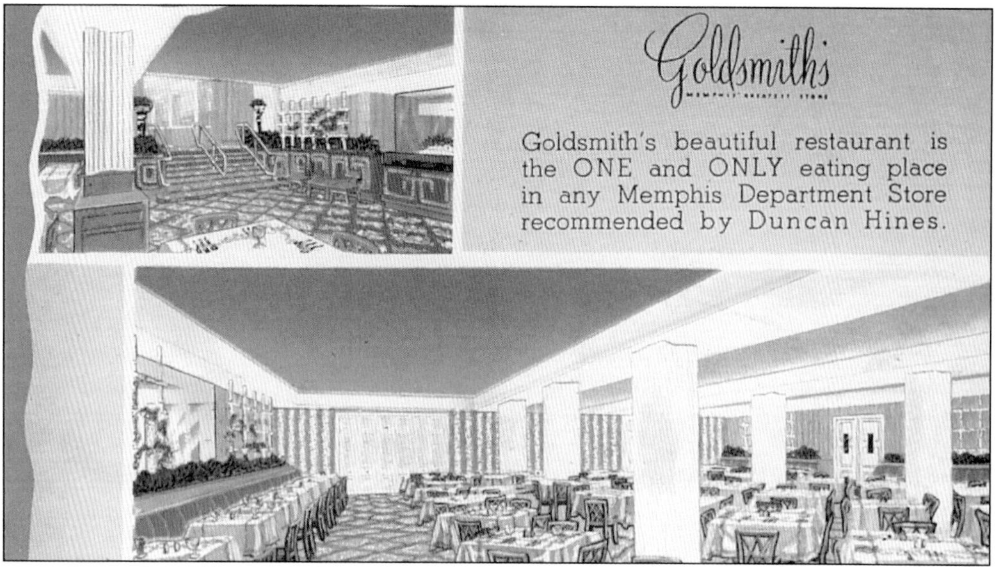

GOLDSMITH'S. Goldsmith's has long been Memphis' premier department store. It is doubtful that the private "Men's Grill reserved for gentlemen only" would be as appreciated today as it was in the days prior to the misguided notion of "political correctness." At the time this postcard of the downtown store was made, a recommendation by Duncan Hines carried considerable influence nationwide. The store originally opened on Beale Street in 1870 as I. Goldsmith and Brothers but moved to a larger building in 1895 or 1896. Today, there are several stores in the Memphis area.

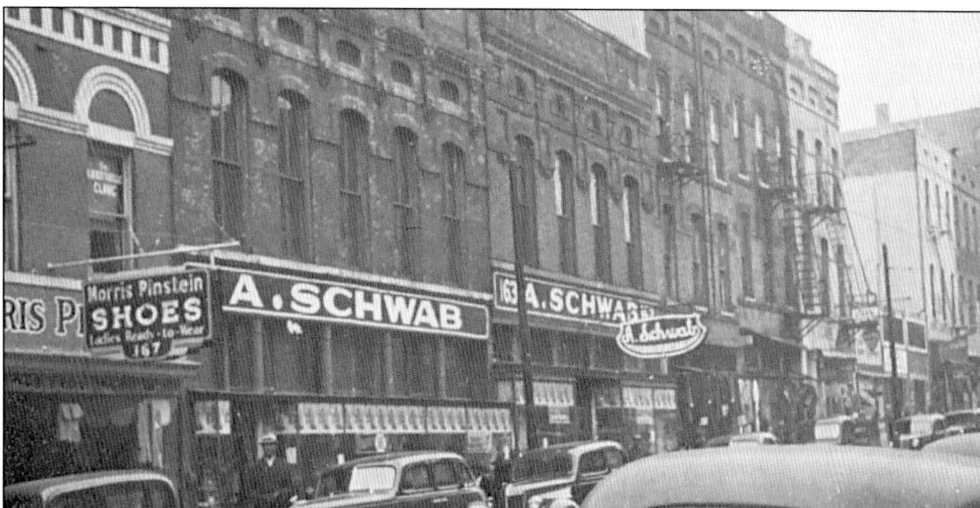

SCHWAB'S-EXTERIOR 1930S. Schwab's Department Store on Beale Street is a Memphis tradition. The store, seen here in 1939, opened in 1876 and is the oldest business on Beale Street. The merchandise carried by this store runs from the useful to the bizarre. Out-of-town visitors never failed to be astonished at the wide assortment of folk remedies that grace the shelves. John the Conqueror roots, Essence of Bend Over, and Uncrossing Oil are all necessary staples for any well-stocked gentleman's cabinet, and Jickey Jockey and Lodestone perfumes rival those found in the great perfume shops of Paris.